# The Second Life

*Collection of novellas and short-stories*

Carmen Firan



EAST EUROPEAN MONOGRAPHS, BOULDER, COLORADO
DISTRIBUTED BY COLUMBIA UNIVERSITY PRESS, NEW YORK, NEW YORK
2005

EAST EUROPEAN MONOGRAPHS, NO. DCLXXIII



ISBN: 0-88033-571-8

Library of Congress Control Number: 2005933561

Printed in the United States of America

# Contents

# The Boiler Man

In buildings like this boiler men are indispensable. Especially during winter when the radiators clog, filters need to be changed and pipes crack just when you need them most, on a frosty weekend. The residents at 89-13 were lucky. The super of the building was also a boiler man, a profession learnt and practiced diligently in Eastern Europe where everything's out of order, or out of place.

Maybe the term "plumber" is more precise, but in his native country his specialty had been radiators. Back during communism, the boiler man had an ace up his sleeve because rumors had it the secret police kept track of suspects by planting microphones in the radiators of questionable buildings. He had to be trusted – not just skilled – in case he didn't even work for the police.

Dick, who had won the green-card lottery, took his wife and daughter by the hand and didn't stop until they reached Sunnyside, Queens. There, in only two weeks, he found this job as a "super" – the guy who does everything.

"I don't believe in lotteries and all that stuff about luck. I played on a whim to prove to myself that I couldn't win. Everything I ever got in my life was through hard work. Nothing ever fell into my lap. This time, God knows, the devil stuck his noose into it. I didn't really want to move to America, but since I got the visa, I figured, why not go and see how they live over there." That's what he confessed on every occasion, as he caressed a bushy moustache he thought boosted his sex appeal. "But I don't like it here. I miss my little house and the vines and fruit trees in the courtyard, I miss my drinking friends and life over there, poor, sure, but happy. I worked, I didn't work, something came up and I lived well, whatever. If it wasn't for my wife, who kept bugging me about my daughter's future and stuff, I would've never left everything behind."

Dick looked like he could lift three buildings at once. He wore large denim overalls without a shirt, an outfit that showed off his toned arms and hairy chest. His "super's" office was in the building's basement, surrounded by boilers, air conditioners, tool sheds, old furniture, torn mattresses, all kinds of useless items, and garbage bags. Basically, Dick ruled over an underground empire.

At night, when the garbage was taken out in the well-to-do neighborhoods of Queens, Dick hit the streets in his vintage car, packed it with whatever could be reused and unloaded his loot in the basement. He managed to stack up a serious collection of TV sets, microwave ovens, tape recorders, chairs, vacuum cleaners, rugs, outdated computers, and whatever else one might need to outfit a brand-new home. Some were in great shape; others he fixed and then sold for nothing to newly arrived immigrants who'd ended up in Sunnyside. "I'm doing a good deed," he'd explain defensively, "this is what I learned at home. Take from the rich, and give to the poor. What I get out of it isn't important. It's more of a communal gesture, since everybody here is so into the collective spirit."

Dick had won over all the residents in the building he administered with competence. He carried old ladies' grocery bags to the elevator, walked dogs, babysat for young families, tended the lawn outside the building, and, of course, replaced pipes and filters, unclogged toilets, and, since this was the country of technology, fixed computers. He couldn't really be called industrious, but, he was smart, skilled. He never refused a tip, but didn't rip anyone off, either. This new world didn't scare him anymore, he'd found out he could get by alright even here without speaking the language, because Sunnyside was populated by his countrymen. The stores, restaurants, pastry shops, medical offices, churches, and newspapers in his native tongue tempered his longing for the mother country. Occasionally the ghetto bothered him and he'd snap with superiority: "You immigrate to get rid of these folks and end up living with them. It's the same ethnic soup, only thicker."

Despite his rebuffs, he was capable of shedding tears for a native folk song, heard in bodegas where people smoked a lot; and he argued for the democratization of the old country, which some denigrated, some regretted, though none of them would ever admit that they felt like foreigners in both places. It was an unspoken dilemma they would be buried with.

"Well, they have everything here, except tomatoes like the ones back home," Dick would sigh over a glass of vodka, which got emptied more and more often and earlier and earlier in the day.

Dick was a romantic. A giant with delicate features, he was sensitive to miniatures. He loved small animals; maybe that's why the mice and bugs that haunted his "super's" office in the basement didn't faze him.

He didn't protest the rabbit his daughter brought home, which they kept in the bathroom; he loved the flashy fish swimming in an improvised bowl, the jar for pickles that they took out in the balcony in summer. He loved etchings and had even tried to find work as a house painter. With or without his clients' consent, at the end of a job he painted thin stripes and floral motifs that set off the walls from the ceiling, a delicate water lily around the chandelier or colorful birds above the kitchen window.

"We have to embellish our life," was his motto, which he practiced how he knew best.

His large hands, accustomed to pipes and hardware, could be gentle and soothing. He caressed animals, tended flowers, and cried during love scenes. Despite the dirt under his nails, and his T-shirts soaked with sweat at the chest and underarms, he wasn't a repulsive boiler man. You noticed his virility and not his smell, his vigor and not the clothes worn out from crawling underneath sinks and toilets. He loved his wife and adored his daughter, whose every whim he accepted. Provided she was good in school and behaved.

"Life is a simple thing. I don't believe in chance. Everything fits together and, as long as you act with common sense, there are no great surprises. If you can avoid abuse and excess, life is decent, the way it's supposed to be. I'm not an intellectual but I feel certain things, I don't know how. My grandfather was illiterate but he knew everything. He died in peace one afternoon, after he'd washed and shaved, called grandmother to his side, held her hand, and told her that his time had come. He closed his eyes and a few minutes later he was gone. Light, beautiful, serene. Now people die with violence, death isn't liberation any more, but a condemnation, a humiliation."

He hadn't read one book since he graduated from professional school, a two-year program where he learned all about heating profession. He only watched movies and sometimes leafed through newspapers. Still, nature had gifted him with poise that could pass as wisdom, maybe inherited from his grandfather. The boiler man had some odd habits too, which could make him an interesting drinking partner. In the evening, a few friends he'd made in the building descended to the basement, where Dick had improvised a warm, bar-like atmosphere that resembled their home back home. He'd brought in a plastic garden table from the street and a few odd chairs, even a sun umbrella that they stuck proudly through the hole in the center. Next to it he kept a cooler filled with beer and vodka. They played folk music and debated the state of the world. One neighbor came from his hometown, they'd been neighbors even back then, left the country just a few months' apart. It's a small world, but even smaller in Queens.

"Guys, I don't know why, but since I left the old country, I've been plagued by memories. I remember everything, you know, everything! Early childhood, my birth, even before it."

The boiler man amazed them with his stories, which included some disturbing details, like remembering his own birth.

"No kidding," Dick would tell them, his eyes blurred by the power of memory, "I witnessed my own birth."

At first they didn't take him too seriously, but in time Dick won them over and then they listened with baited breath. Each time, they asked him to tell them more stories about being born. They emptied one glass after another not fully believing what they heard, but moved by such an odd experience.

"Actually I remember details from before I was even born, from the time I swam fettered in my mother's belly. You don't have much space to move around in there and your movements are restricted. The last stages of the pregnancy are the worst. Moving gets more and more difficult, you want to turn but can't, you kick with your feet and hands but nothing happens. I remember that during the last weeks I wanted more than anything to do a somersault. A few times I rebelled, I'd grown too much, and I think I kicked my mother too hard because I immediately felt her hands grabbing my heels to calm me down. I recognized her palms instinctively. They caressed me even when I hit her with rage. I wasn't nervous or restless, I had no reason to be, it's warm in there and you don't lack for anything."

"Didn't you choke?" Dick heard a puzzled voice.

"How could you choke?! I never breathed more at ease in my life. Everything's natural and clean, you wish you breathed air like that all the time! The temperature is constant, same with the humidity, everything's constant, know what I mean? Just the way it has to be, just as much as it should be. Nothing unpredictable or uncomfortable. You're always satisfied. You're never hungry or thirsty, and if you need food all you have to do is think about it and you're immediately fed with delicacies. You want fish, you can be sure that soon your mother will crave just that, and, because a pregnant woman is always granted her wish, she'll get fish, and you'll extract its very essence, the reason why you want to eat fish in the first place. And even if she doesn't eat fish when you crave it, you end up eating the essence of fish, because you extract from her whatever the fish contains. Get it? I'm trying to make everything simple but I'd like you to understand how it works. You suck in everything you need from her and the poor mother knows it. She loses iron, even calcium. Some even lose their hair or teeth, their nails turn white, their faces have spots and they're always worn out. Whoever says that a pregnancy invigorates a woman doesn't know what they're talking about. It drains her but you couldn't live better anywhere else. In there I was happy. After I got out, I never felt as protected, intangible. It's a divine harmony that's hard to define because we never experience it in real life. My friends, we are born happy. Whatever happens afterwards, God knows!"

Sometimes he'd be paged for an emergency. A flood, a pipe, an anxious old woman whose vacuum cleaner wasn't working. Dick would run to it right away, fix whatever needed to be fixed, and come back to the basement where his friends waited for him enveloped in cigar smoke. He came back with even dirtier hands, sweat dripping down his forehead. He'd curse, gulp a glass of vodka that would ruffle his moustache, knock his fist against the table, and continue with his stories.

"What bothered me there though was that I had to keep my eyes closed. Strangely enough, I could still see. I don't know what it feels like to be in other women's bellies, but in my mother's womb I saw an extraordinary world. But I never felt any smell or saw any color. Unfortunately I don't know anybody who can confirm my impressions, exchange an opinion, I haven't met anybody who was aware of his fetal life or who witnessed his birth. I have a memory, some say, ancient, abnormally large and old. It's possible. And since I moved to Queens it expands every day. Although I believe that memory, like everything infernal, is infinite. But people don't try to remember that far back, or maybe they can't imagine that it's possible to remember the time before your birth, not to mention their birth itself, which seems so natural, since everyone was present at their birth, right? If you remember yourself when you were five, why not remember the five seconds after you came into this world? Isn't it the same time? The same life?"

His drinking friends would nod in approval. For a moment, the boiler man's point of view made perfect sense.

"I saw many things in my life, but nothing can top the world in my mother's belly. Entire cities, archipelagoes made of jelly tubes, galleries of pipes stretching like nerves along fluid walls, a complicated architecture of channels, mazes, tunnels and grottos, abysses, a sky of stars, perfect shapes swimming through a delicate spider web, everything colorless, like a dim drawing, like a miniature map of the universe. I could hear my heart beating in the middle of the universe, and I kept floating like a spaceman caught in those transparent laces that enveloped me, and rocked me gently like a light summer breeze. Even more stranger, I recognized all these as if I'd seen them before, I behaved as if I had been in my mother's belly before, as if I had memories from another pregnancy. I wonder if I was born more than once."

At this point his audience usually lost patience. Some mumbled in protest that they were being dragged into surreal territory, others looked at Dick with pity, a grown up man, a giant, raving and ranting, but they were all curious to find out the conclusion. Then Dick swallowed another glass of vodka, wiped his moustache with the back of a hand covered with brownish creases, lowered his voice, and his eyes sparkled conspiratorially.

"There's no pleasure in being born. First of all, because it's a painful, long, dangerous process. You pass from that perfect harmony to an unimaginable convulsion, you struggle, you push with your head first, you kick with your legs, desperate to get out, nobody knows why, because it was so cozy in there! But at some point you're not allowed to be inside any more, you have to leave! The worst is that you feel your own mother straining against you, as if she wanted to get rid of you. At first you lose your balance, you slip, and no matter how much you wrestle, the head drags you down, it suddenly becomes very heavy, as if it was filled with lead, your ears pop and your stress increases. Your head enters a dark tunnel. This is the most difficult and frightening part of the process. The tunnel of darkness."

"I've heard that story about the tunnel before," one of the neighbors told Dick, "but it happens when you die, not when…" He didn't dare say more. The word *birth* had already sent shivers down his spine.

"When you die it's a tunnel of light," another interfered, "and in this one it's dark."

"Pitch dark," Dick confirmed. "The first sensation is terrible. You choke, you drown, your hair gets caught in all kinds of roots, I heard something rumbling like a volcano ready to erupt, I pushed as hard as I could, my neck was stiff and I thought I'd be trapped inside forever, one of my shoulders was stiff from all the effort. I suffered from pains in my left shoulder until I was 5 because of my passage through that thin, black, cold, a damp tunnel. Then I felt the first smells, just as unpleasant as the sounds that were waiting for me once I was pulled outside. Because the truth is that you can't make it by yourself, eventually you are pulled outside by others. I coughed and I began to sob. They grabbed me, wiped me dry of the lava, and undid the roots wrapped around me, irritating my skin. I was dying of cold and I'd turned green from all the effort and shouting. I opened my eyes but saw nothing. I heard strange, metallic, piercing screams around me. Suddenly I felt hungry but this time no essence satiated me. I'd be administered hundreds of gallons of milk until I was fed up with it. They wrapped me, covered me, and laid me in a bed. I was alone. In my mother's belly I'd also been alone, but here, outside, it was a different kind of solitude. Dry. Cold. Deafening. I had only known happy loneliness until then. Now desperate loneliness began, and I think that's when I was scared for the first time. I understood what it means to be alone. To waver between happiness and despair. To be expelled from the world. To see, to hear, to feel and to not be understood."

The neighbors were already sad; they drank to spite themselves and experienced everything as if they'd just been born.

"Look, I remember the first night of loneliness as if it were now. They put me in a bed face up. From there, through the dark window, I saw the moon for the first time. You will ask me how I knew it was the moon. I knew. I'd seen it before. Here, how? Hell knows! And, all of a sudden…."

Dick's phone rang violently. Mrs. Simpson from the 9th floor had an emergency. Her toilet was clogged and she had guests in half an hour. The boiler man got up at once, duty came before everything else. He left his audience with the story unfinished, grabbed his toolbox and a few minutes later knocked on Mrs. Simpson's door. She was waiting eagerly for him.

"Dick, you're a miracle. What would I do without you?! God sent you to us!"

*Translation by Doris Sangeorzan*

# Light In The Attic

Lya wasn't a woman to be easily fazed. Still, that sweltering afternoon it all seemed more than she could handle. It was unacceptable. Unbearable. Like the melting asphalt into which the heels of her shoes – these days not as narrow as they once were – that sank into the asphalt with a muffled squish. Like the stench wafting from the open doors of the stores. Spoiled delicatessen, rotten fish. Sweaty bodies streaming along the street and bug-eyed girls on the look-out for the swallow of the nearest subway entrance. Stalls blanketed with watches, belts, sunglasses, postcards with aerial views of Manhattan, overcrowding the already crowded sidewalks teeming with insane passers-by.

She gripped the book tighter under her arm, gritted her teeth, and fingered her handbag, where she had carefully placed the money. The book was merely a cover. She hadn't taken it along to read it but to distract people's attention from the handbag crammed with one-hundred dollar bills. No one would dream of attacking a dear old lady, walking peacefully with a book under her arm. No one would discern what the respectful and distracted lady was hiding in her scuffed handbag, deliberately chosen. Only her expensive sunglasses might, perhaps, give her away. But in a sea of imitations, they might easily pass for an ordinary five-dollar pair, such as the ones that could be found on every street vendor's stand.

The entire street reeked of tobacco, a clear indication it was already time for the work force to go home. Lya shielded herself the best she could, waving a hand in front of her nose to fan it, grimacing with a barely suppressed disgust. She was choking. In the clammy humidity and the oppressive heat smoke seemed to coagulate in the air, floating like murderous tar clouds. Disgusting. Detestable. As she was scanning the street for a cab, she reached the entrance to the subway. As a rule she avoided the subway-primarily out of consideration for her former lifestyle when she had had the use of a chauffeured limousine.

What she was doing on that particular day, in that area of downtown was another story. Silently she cursed the moment she had decided to take the New York train into Manhattan, to once more bail out Ricardo and his damn talent. What a loser! A millstone around her neck! And how long was she going to be able to drag it along?

In the more than twenty years they'd been married, he hadn't amounted to anything. Made not one penny, not one show to display his paintings. What's more, he hadn't even been learned English properly. Well, she had wanted an artist for a husband, now she's got one. And now she had to keep him as if he were a disobedient child, with his head full of non-sense, spouting stuff like, "the closer you get to the horizon, the farther away it gets from you" or "the rarified yellow light, like a morning of honey" or "the underneath of things, inner states, sensations, representations." Baloney like that. A painting, either you sell or you don't. But for a long time now he hasn't been painting anything anyone would want to buy. At least when she met him he was painting flowers, still lives with fish, women – a bit abstract, but women nonetheless. His work was promising. He had shows, he sold a lot. Now he's gone off. Definitely off. He experiments with all sorts of who knows what, tears it if he doesn't like it. And he doesn't like almost all of it. He reads like a fanatic, paints like a madman and can't wait to be alone. What the devil he is doing when he is by himself? Collages, stupid modern stuff no one understands anything thing about! Half of what he produces he destroys, the rest he stores up in his attic, wherever he can fit it, hardly any room left now to drop a needle, in this attic big as a church. No doubt he's lost his marbles.

In the past, she was the one who brought home some customers, now and then, who would sometimes buy a painting or two. Once a gallery owner bought the entire set of wild flower paintings. This was right after they had moved from Italy to West Orange, New Jersey, full of hope, imagining Ricardo becoming famous in New York, and rich, too! Yet another stupid mistake. Why leave Bologna, where, at least, Ricardo was somebody? What stupidity, to sell their old home, with high ceilings, classic columns and frescoes, surrounded by oleanders, fig-trees and grape vines, to an American, for a mere one hundred thousand dollars and a cheap, plywood shack of a house in New Jersey?

They had met in Florence, at the opening of one of his exhibits of oil paintings. He had been married twice before. Lya's first husband – much older than she – had died, leaving her a tidy sum. She and Ricardo could have been a happy couple. He the talented one, she the rich one. He the artist, she the shrewd one, with her feet firmly planted on the ground. She had learned quite a few things from her late husband, an antique collector from an old Italian family, with a nose for business. "A duo, with her on the drums and me on the violin. You can imagine the sound," Ricardo imparts whenever the subject of their marriage comes up. Why doesn't he just keep his mouth shut, what would he be without her? He wouldn't have survived one day without her in America. "She's too tied down to the real world," he wails. "She sees nothing but what's in front of her eyes; never the light beyond the horizon, never the North Star."

That damn horizon, with its shining line! And now what? Who in his right mind would have gone out on such a scorching day, ride the train into the Penn Station; then from there board the subway, get off and start walking along those slimy, stinking little streets all the way to Chinatown, to get to that old jeweler's store? In the past ten years Lya had been gradually selling off all the diamond broaches, the ruby earrings, and the pearl or emerald pendants. And today she parted with her engagement ring, which her first husband had custom-ordered from Paris. These few thousand dollars would cover their needs for another three or four months. So many sacrifices for a man! While Ricardo, he couldn't give a damn.

She found him in the neglected, weed-overgrown garden, behind the house. He was stretched out on the chaise lounge, on the shore of the artificial lake, reading, his wide-brimmed hat low on his forehead.

"Ricardo! Ricardo!" Lya called out to him, impatient and nervous.

Her damp clothes had stuck to her body. Her shoes widened by sweat were slipping off her feet. She was out of breath and panting, her face was congested and her lips purple from the effort, she looked like someone struggling with life itself. And with Ricardo too, who was always fond of tricks and ironic pranks, flaunting a sense of humor that aging, illnesses and failures had not been able to blunt.

"Ricardo! You deaf fossil!"

The straw hat did not budge. Maybe he fell asleep with the book on his chest. Still, he is definitely deaf – had been so from about the age of fourteen. In those days he was swimming in competitions and was jumping from the trampoline. "I once jumped so high, my eardrums popped and I lost my hearing completely in the left ear. When they drafted me into the army, they assigned me to telephone duty. In communications, can you believe it? We were once conducting war games. I was sitting in the trenches, with the headphones over my ears. Whenever I heard, *Target number so and so*, I was supposed to pull a lever, after which a soldier was ejected outside, who would then fire the canon, the machine gun or whatever weapon was called for. The trenches were just a bunch of large holes filled with mud. I was just waiting there, numb with cold, to hear *Target number 3!*, at which I was supposed to pull the lever, and so on. And suddenly I saw in the trench a thin little green lizard, with delicate features, like a piece of jewelry. And on that green fell – I don't know why or where from – a stunningly beautiful ray of sunshine. I was watched her, entranced. Apparently, in my headphones, call after call had come and gone, unanswered – *Target number four, Target number five, Target number six!* and so on. Well, not only was I deaf, but now also completely under the spell of this enchanting little creature. So, naturally, I heard nothing, and gave no response. I merely stood there rooted, watching the delicate being for a long time, thus compromising their war games, sowing confusion among the armies and their enemies."

"Ricardo! You deaf idiot!"

Lya heard herself say as the stood right next to the chaise lounge lying in the shade.

"What *are* you doing? Sleeping? Aren't you ever going to wake up? You are really driving me crazy, you know! I could be assaulted!"

Ricardo opened one eye and looked her up and down, with barely suppressed amusement.

"Assaulted? But who's the fool to try to rape you?"

"I'm not talking about rape! I could be attacked. Did you forget I had nine thousand dollars with me?"

"Why in the world are you carrying so much money with you?"

"Because you are not able to make any yourself! I sold the diamond ring, that's why!"

"That's a good girl."

"Is that all you have to say? After all I've done for you! Perhaps I deserve a different lot in life – have you ever stopped to think about this?"

"You're doing the thinking for the both of us!"

"Stop it! Oh, I' m wasting my breath on you. I might have died of fright, for all you care. Or of heat! This city has become unbearable."

"OK, OK, calm down. Why don't you go and make some lemonade! And bring me a glass too."

"How about if *you* go and make the lemonade and bring *me* a glass."

"I don't like that lemonade. Brian is not feeling well. He hasn't stepped outside all day."

"I don't know about that, but for a week now he hasn't taken out the garbage, hasn't done any repair around the house. And look at this mess of a lawn! As for the fence, it's in such bad need of repair it won't be long before it falls on us. I seem to have a special knack for surrounding myself with loafers and free loaders. I'm going to take a shower and then lie down for a while. I'm exhausted, and depressed. I feel used and ridiculously generous. It seems I can't expect even as much as a kind word, let alone a bit of genuine gratitude or tenderness from anyone around here. I am a fool. If you want to eat tonight, you had better cook yourselves. Brian can do his usual potatoes with dill, provided he cleans up after himself."

Ricardo had stopped listening. He pulled his hat back over his forehead and was now thinking of how much time he had wasted in his life talking on and on for hours with all kinds of poets, artists and other assorted alcohol or drug addicts, reeking of talent and decadence. They would write their poetry on napkins, did their drawings on table-cloths, were vomiting and urinating wherever they could. Some died of cirrhosis, others overdosed, a few had heart attacks. They left behind a very thin, but brilliant volume of work. Or perhaps he had not wasted his time. That's how things were meant to be. Great things sprang from those meetings of theirs! Sparkling ideas, O, what a lot of ideas!

He heard Brian bustling about in that garden cabin in which he had been living for over ten years. It wall started when Lya had a brilliant idea: to give a party. Not so much to celebrate Ricardo's fiftieth birthday, as to mark the purchase of ten paintings by a Soho gallery, a unique event in Ricardo's artistic biography. They had invited several New York friends, Italian artists from New Jersey, art critics and journalists from the local papers. Things had begun to sour between the two of them. They had no relatives in America, no children. And this violin-drums duo sounded progressively discordant, jagged. Lya impatient, Ricardo passive. Lya thorough, pragmatic, possessed of social and earthly goals. Ricardo airy, absent-minded, dreamy, with his ethereal joys, happy with the light's elasticity, with the vapor of his breath rising each morning when he awoke, thinking only of his easel.

Brian had been brought to that party by a New York photographer – himself an Italian. He might have been Ricardo's age, perhaps a bit over fifty. In the general melee, Brian remained unnoticed, even to the hosts at first. Lya was trying to look busy, conversing gracefully with anyone whose interest she could arouse, in an attempt to convince them of the saleable nature of Ricardo's work. Ricardo, of course, was patently absent! She hoped to enlarge her circle of friends and identify potential buyers for his strange-looking, large-size canvases, which somehow escaped destruction at the hands of their author, who was always unhappy with the way light came through in them or with the apparent lack of the ineffable. Conceits, thought Lya; silly whims, betraying an obvious immaturity. An irresponsible man, grating her nerves under the guise of the unsung, odd artist in search of devil knows what.

That evening Ricardo was rather sad. He was bored and irritated with all that bustle and din the guests were making, with his wife's affected smiles and contrived laughs, with the polite conversation and insincere admiration of the guests, who, once they were in your house, and gobbled up all the food, drank all your alcohol, certainly were not going to tell you they didn't like your artwork! He was sitting in a corner, rather secluded, muttering something unintelligible, in a polite but careless tone, whenever someone approached to congratulate him. And all along he was getting more and more intoxicated, just looking vacuously at Lya, who was milling about busy and agitated, solemnly overwhelmed by her role as a matron, public relations manager and impresario.

Brian was sitting in another corner, just as lonely and bored, wondering what he was doing there, why his friend the photographer had insisted that he come with him. He neither knew, nor wished to know anybody. Later in the evening everyone walked out into the garden. Most of them were already quite inebriated. Lya had planned a barbecue near the artificial lake, on the far side of the garden – a place of spectacular beauty that greatly enhanced the market value of the house. She was hauling all by herself wine and beer bottles from the garden house, platefuls of hamburgers and assorted meats.

"Get off your butt and do something," she hissed through her teeth to Ricardo, while keeping her pasted-on smile for the benefit of the party-goers.

"I'm sore from hauling all this stuff, I'm practically falling off my legs. After all, this party is for you!"

"For me? All this circus? Have you even asked me whether I wanted it? I can't wait for them all to leave!"

"Why don't you at least try to make some conversation with them?"

"What should I tell them? I can't speak English. Besides, I'm deaf."

"You're drunk and, as usual, a pig! In fact you deserve nothing."

"OK, then I'm not going to lift a finger. Did I ask you for anything? All I want is to be left alone, so I can mix me some paints. Have you seen the trees reflected in the lake?"

"The hell I've seen!"

"May I be of some help, madam?" Brian was heard speaking. Lya started pleasantly and quickly changed the tone of her voice. Turning her back on Ricardo, she spoke tenderly to Brian, flattered by his gesture.

"O, you are so very kind, sir! If you wish, you can take these bottles out of here. And could you look after the grill? A man is badly needed in this house!" she added, ostentatiously, looking furtively, out of the corner of her eyes, to Ricardo, who couldn't hear her anyway.

Brian took over the husband's role in the household. For one evening it was fun. He had no inclination for mundane things, so he took care of everything, from the drinks to the grill, serving the guests and satisfying their every wish. He had just finished collecting the empty bottles, and had dumped the used paper plates in the large plastic bag. Moreover, he had taken the garbage out and placed it at the curb, to be picked up the next day. Then he sat down in a chaise lounge, looking out over the lake. He stood transfixed, watching the trees, listening to the buzz of the insects in the darkness imbued with the odor of burned leaves that had descended over the property of this dysfunctional but otherwise decent couple.

Ricardo came over and sat down next to him. He had brought a bottle of wine, which he held tightly to his chest, and two glasses. Neither spoke a word, their silence standing out against the distant background of croaking frogs and women laughing elatedly in the early stages of inebriation.

"Looks like a storm is brewing."

"What's that?" Ricardo said, turning his head in Brian's direction.

"We're going to have a storm. The birds are flying in circles, with frequent divings, as if someone was shaking them loose out of a desk drawer."

"Very well. I hope all those people will leave soon, so we can be by ourselves and drink a glass of wine in peace."

Brian looked at him silently, for a moment.

"I like what you are doing."

"What are you saying?"

"I saw some of your paintings. They are good."

Ricardo was pouring wine into the two glasses. He put the bottle down, on the grass and handed a glass to Brian.

"Are you a photographer too?"

"No. I'm not an artist. Actually I quit my job. There comes a time when you just have to stop."

"I see, nodded Ricardo in acknowledgement. I know what you mean, although I've never had a job in my entire life. I am not disciplined. But I do paint, and sometimes even as much as ten hours a day. Then I tear up everything, laughed Ricardo. There's very little I like of what I create. I'm just playing. Now I'm toying with some pastel pictures. Rafters and haystacks. Do you know what a haystack is?"

"I do," smiled Brian for the first time after many weeks.

"What kind of job did you have?"

"I worked in a biology lab."

"And what does a biologist do?"

"He researches structures. Tissues. Systems. What is called the inner nature of things."

"I think all crafts and all arts deal with the same issue. The inner structure of things, whatever the devil that might be. I imagine we are made up of an infinity of micro-organisms, which fit together into a perfectly functioning whole. A living puzzle. Diversity and coherence. And should one of them take off on a tangent, error occurs. Some call it a virus, others just a disease. All have been in us from the beginning. Health is just a matter of balance. To keep your inner self in harmony, lest you stir one of those organisms. But how can we possibly know what we are doing? Do we have in us the necessary control over our inner structure? Are we aware of what's going on in there?"

Ricardo refilled their glasses with wine.

"Let's see, now. What methods do we have to get beyond what is seen? Science? Good. She is always doing her job. Studying, searching, decoding, and, especially conquering. Yes, conquering! As a matter of fact, science is warfare. She wants to dominate, to control everything. On the other hand, we have faith. Goood! Something more intricate. Illusory states of spiritual uplifting. We seem to understand, only to sink into the unfathomable. Naturally the Creator was not so careless to leave the mystery unprotected. The Creator did his job. He gave us enough. The Word and the light: *Now, my dear ones, go ahead and do what you will with them. And should one life prove too short, I am going to give you a few more – but you still won't get anywhere. Just like these people, with their science, they do what they do, and still end up in my courtyard.*"

Ricardo lifted his glass and drank up. Brian was seemingly no longer listening to him. Yet, when Ricardo stopped speaking, in order to pour into his glass the last drops in the bottle, Brian looked at him expectantly.

"Well, there's still art. And I think the Creator has a weakness for it. He is sensitive to interpretations."

"Ricardo, Ricardo! Aren't you coming? Look, the guests are leaving."

"Let them leave!" he whispered to Brian, hiding behind his deafness.

"Ricardo!" shouted Lya from the deck.

"Go and tell her I'm soused and would ruin her image, if I showed up like this in front of her precious company. Tell her, too, I suddenly realized I'm fifty and this piece of reality really hit me kind of hard. There's no way any serious man can remain indifferent to such a blow. Fifty years old! And I've got so much to do still!" chuckled Ricardo.

Brian stood up to take the message to Lya. He was tall and gaunt, with delicate movements, like those of a ballet dancer. Melancholy and mysterious.

"And on your way back, can you get us another bottle of wine, please?"

"I think I should also leave."

"To go where?"

"That I really don't know."

"Then stay here."

Lya gave up on the decorum of Ricardo's seeing the guests off. Anyway, he would have been morose and unpleasant. Better he should stay where he was. Leave him to his own devices, while she'd keep up appearances. Brian had returned with another bottle of wine from the refrigerator, strategically placed in the summer cottage. His friend the photographer was waiting at the top of the stairs.

"It's late and Gino is waiting for me."

"Gino?"

"The photographer."

"Ah, Gino! I thought you said you didn't know where you would go."

"I don't. I've crashed at Gino's place for the past two months. Now his girl friend is back from Italy, so I have to leave. He said he was going to try to talk to some neighbors of his, who might have a room in the basement…."

"Don't leave just yet. Stay a bit longer, so we can drink another glass before you leave. In fact, why don't you stay here, since you've got no place to go to?"

"What do you mean, stay here?"

"You just stay here. You can live in this little cabin. While it's not much so speak of, you've got everything you need in the way of basic needs. Electricity, heat, a bathroom, and a television set. Plus a refrigerator, filled with drinks," smiled Ricardo.

"No…. I can't…I haven't told you everything."

"You've told me enough. Shortly after you turn fifty you get the jitters. You left your job, quit everything and gave yourself over to ideas. Becoming a tramp, some kind of vagabond, as Lya, would say. Irresponsible. But I do understand. Life is so short and we do nothing with it. Got any children?"

"Oh, no."

"Very well."

"Family?"

"Look, I really can't stay."

"Nonsense! Come to the attic, and I'll show you what I do."

Ricardo led the way, holding the freshly opened wine bottle tightly by the neck. Brian followed in silence. When they passed Lya, Ricardo whispered into her ear :

"Gino can leave, if he wants. Brian will stay."

"Where are you two going?"

"Upstairs, so I can show him my latest work."

"Oh," said Lya, glad that finally he was showing someone his work.

This was a rare occurrence. Usually he wouldn't allow anyone into the attic. And he never even invited her to come up there.

"And stop drinking!"

"Oh, what a nag she is!" grumbled Ricardo, climbing with effort the narrow wooden stairway. She is stalking my every gesture; even counts my breaths. See, I am gagging now. That's what she's doing to me. I am endowed with an infinite patience. Infinite indeed!" lamented Ricardo, panting in rhythm with the creaking of the steps.

The attic was truly spacious, indeed like a church. Right near the entrance, a gray tomcat and a tabby were rolling playfully in mutual enchantment.

"Samson and Delilah," said Ricardo, introducing them. "For them this is a genuine paradise. The attic is full of mice."

Large as it was, the attic was jammed with things. It seemed as if the contents of several households had been removed and deposited there, helter-shelter-cardboard boxes, trunks, garden utensils, scraped window and door frames, clothing, pots and pans, sports equipment, lumber, plywood, mannequins, and all sorts of odds and ends.

"When we moved in, ten years ago, I couldn't settle in any room. They were clean, but small, with such low ceilings that I always felt my head would pop through. With the floors smelling of chlorine. Lya was dreaming of arranging for me a studio upstairs, in the large room, where everything would be tidy and civilized and where people could come and admire me while I was working, buy some paintings and generally study the artist in his own medium. The understanding was that I too would be clean, organized and tidy, wearing an apron with just a touch of paint discreetly spread on it, enough to convince the visitors I *was* painting, but with my palms perennially white and clean, ready to shake any customer's hand. Alas, I chose the attic!"

"It's a marvelous place!"

"You bet! Besides, here I can be all by myself! Lya comes up only when she needs to throw something away. Most of the mess you see in here is her handiwork! She does it all out of spite, to colonize my private space! She shuffles up here into the attic even as many as two or three times a day, under the pretext of having to stow away some old things, but in fact simply out of the desire to check up on me. Am I painting or am I idling? Do I keep the painting or tear it up in the end? Am I drinking? Or perhaps smoking marijuana? Do I feel at peace with myself? That's what she hates the most – that I can be happy without her. It is the worst kind of offence to her. I know she'll never forgive me for that. But you know, I had to fight for this solitude. It hasn't come cheap."

"I bet it isn't that easy to get," agreed Brian, rather absent-mindedly.

Ricardo poured wine into two dirty glasses and handed one to Brian. At that moment the door creaked open, banging against the wooden pillar, which was preventing it from falling. Discreetly, Lya put her head round, then stepped in triumphantly.

"What are you guys doing here?"

"Having fun and gossiping about you."

"Well, why am I not surprised! I just came to deposit these empty beer cartons and bottles."

"Wouldn't it has been easier to just put them in the trash?"

"You never know when we might need them.... Watch your drinking, Ricardo! All the guests left."

"Very well!"

"Your conduct was abysmal. Still, it was a good party, wasn't it?" she said, this time to Brian. "By the way, thank you for all your help. Has he shown you his paintings?" but did not wait for his answer, shuffling with her slippers down the wooden stairs instead.

"See how diabolical women can be? They are bent on keeping us under their thumbs, pestering us no end, pounding us into fine powder like termites, until there's hardly anything left of us!"

"I'm hardly qualified to offer any opinions on this...."

"This obsession about hoarding everything is almost like a disease. She simply can't part with anything, collecting instead whatever comes her way, restoring and neatly depositing everything. Her possessiveness goes far beyond the range of useful things. In fact, I bet she includes me in that special category she reserves for useless things."

"Ricardo, don't forget to switch the light off when you leave," shouted Lya from the bedroom door.

Ricardo shook his head, hopeless.

"When I first stepped into this attic, I knew there and then it was going to be my very own private place. From that day on, I've never regretted leaving behind our house in Italy. No more nostalgia. The attic seemed at first so vast and empty that I hardly knew where to place my easel. But it was full of mice, bees and pigeons. There were droppings everywhere. In the spring I would build nests for swallows, while in autumn I would lay out baskets with walnuts and peanuts, for the squirrels to help themselves to, as they gathered their winter supplies."

He poured himself some more wine, studied Brian cautiously and then pulled off the sheet that was covering a stack of recently-finished canvases.

"I've had quite a bit of success these past few days."

Brian took each of them in his hands, then held them out at a distance, so he could examine them as an expert would, tilting or lowering his head, to see them from different angles, under different spots of light.

"I don't know much about painting," he said at long last.

"Thank God."

"But I do like what you do. These things convey something. They are alive. They have a certain mystery about them. They stir up something in me. Certain states, recollections, feelings. I can see beyond them. I am experiencing a kind of joy, I don't quite know how to put it...."

"You see, this is precisely Lya's problem. She has no interest whatsoever to find out what's beyond things. She cannot see further that what the physical eye can see. She lives exclusively on the outside. And that's what's keeping her from being happy!"

"Who *is* happy?" inquired Brian, turning towards him.

"Well, *I* am!" exclaimed Ricardo, opening his arms as if he would embrace the entire attic. "Here and now. Every morning when I wake up and I have another day in which I can paint. I stand in this attic alone before my easel and I am happy. And the light comes through each day in a different color, with a different brightness, according to the season, to the atmosphere and to the degree of humidity. It is soft and mild, with orange tones on autumn mornings, reddish, blazing hues just before a storm. There are times though when it is so sharp I could cut myself on it. Or so cold and icy my fingers would freeze on the paintbrush. At dusk it is material and heavy, while in early spring it is rarefied and translucent. And at times it is dark, very dark, almost black, preventing me from seeing anything. I have a good relationship with light. I could paint it forever. In the scales of a fish or on a woman's thigh, in the eyes of the monks, on a knife's blade, or in this glass of wine. Ad infinitum. I never get bored, can never have enough of it. I only dread the day I won't be able to paint anymore."

"Ricardo! Enough of this! Let's go to bed! Put out the light," Lya's imperious voice could be heard from downstairs.

"Pay no attention to her," said Ricardo unperturbed. "As we have no children, I'm the only one she can bark orders to, the sole object of her torture. Otherwise, she's quite a decent girl. I guess each of us is aging according to his or her soul – I in silence, she shouting her lungs out."

By now they had drunk the second and third bottle of wine. Brian continued to study the canvases, as if he was going to buy one but couldn't make up his mind which.

"I like these two haystacks. One green, the other blue; one in the light, the other in the dark. This picture is so sad, so tenderly sad."

"Well, it's a composition...a sensual one. *The complementary pair.*"

Brian started, jerking his head sideways.

"My partner died."

"What's that?" asked Ricardo, remembering he was deaf.

"Two months ago my partner died. I quit my job and moved out of my rented apartment. I just couldn't face living there alone. You have no idea what it's like to lose your matching pair. Each morning is a punishment. I wake up defeated. Purposeless. I'm just waiting for the end. I can't see why I survived him. Where's the blame in this, if there is one? I will crawl all the way to the very end. I am too weak to put an end to everything, the way I ought to."

"Lya must not know this," warned Ricardo. "She sees things in black and white. Let this be our own little secret."

As of that evening, Brian moved into the summer cottage. The next day Ricardo woke earlier than usual, made some coffee and went over to Lya's bedroom.

"What's the matter with you?" asked Lya, frightened. "Did anything happen?"

"I just wanted to indulge you for a little while."

"Have you done something stupid?"

"Au contraire!"

"I'm sure you must have made some booboo and now you are here to smooth things over before I find out...."

"I told Brian he can live for a while in the cabin."

"Whaaat?"

"Calm down. Just think, he can help us with the house, the garden...."

"You mean help *me*! Because you won't lift one finger. You have no idea of the kind of world we live in."

"Precisely. It will make it easy for you. He's willing to do anything."

"So?"

"So that's it! He's going to stay with us."

"What about rent?"

"No rent, but we won't pay him for services rendered either. It's not going to cost us a dime, think about it."

"Well, come to think of it, said Lya, a bit more placated, we do need a man around this house!"

"See?" chuckled Ricardo. "It's going to work out great!"

Ten years elapsed since the party. Brian became a member of the family, and a daily witness to the cold war fiercely waged between Ricardo and Lya. He was constantly called upon to come to the defense of one or the other – a convenient safety valve for either of them. He did everything, took care of the house and the garden, too. But most of all, he listened. Both needed to be heard, pitied, encouraged, contradicted and, above all, allowed to speak, to get it off their chests. In a sense, he had become a kind of private shrink, armed with patience, and so quiet and forlorn, that he seemed understanding and wise. They were living in a kind of peculiar triangle. Lya and Ricardo could no longer imagine life without Brian. Lya kept selling jewels from the family's heirloom, in order to cover the household's needs. Ricardo went on, painting passionately in the attic pictures no one wanted. The monotony was occasionally broken by Ricardo's ideas.

"Let's take up bee-keeping."

Brian found for himself a protective suit, bought the beekeeper's manual and installed three beehives in the backyard. For a while everything went well.

"Bees! That's all we needed!" protested Lya. "It's like he's competing with himself to invent ways to drive me crazy! I can't even step into the garden these days, with all that humming. Besides, no one eats the damn honey. What a headache!"

In the end the beehives were gone.

"Let's plant garlic! Lots of garlic! Every fall in the next town they have the Garlic Festival. We'll win the big prize! The soil is great. Brian, why don't you till the entire garden?"

Brian dutifully complied.

"Have you gone raving mad? What in the world are we going to do with so much garlic?"

"Well, we win the competition and then we sell it."

"And where exactly do you plan to sell it?"

"Brian knows! He'll take care of it. I guess at Sunday's farmer markets. Didn't you say we should be practical? There, we are finally getting there! We're making some money."

"Selling garlic? You've got to be kidding!"

"Yes, selling garlic! What's wrong with it?"

"You men have gone insane. Except that I'm not going along with it."

The following year they harvested an impressive crop of garlic. It didn't bring them a prize, nor did they sell any of it. Instead they put it in the attic, from where it provided them with an ample supply of the pungent vegetable for years to come. Evenings Brian would cook potatoes with dill and garlic – a recipe the family proudly adopted as the specialty of the house.

In time they tried all sorts of things, like opening a boat-repair shop, although only a handful of neighbors had boats on the artificial lake. Then they turned to planting tea, a small vineyard, a pheasant farm and a silkworm nursery. Each of these enterprises lasted about a season, until Ricardo came up with another idea, only to see it fail, like the previous ones. Brian fulfilled his whims, worked hard and then abandoned each new project with the same speed with which he had taken them up. Lya had grown accustomed to the insanity emanating from the minds of the two men and eventually stopped protesting.

Ricardo spent his time in the attic, painting. Always grumbling about the outcome, but nevertheless happy. Only Brian was admitted into the attic. Ricardo would call him up on the pretense that Brian needed to sweep the place clean, or that he wanted to show him his paintings. Inevitably, each visit would lead to long spells of conversation that would end up stirring Lya's jealousy. He never tore up any painting Brian liked. In the evening they would leisurely drink wine, out in the garden, into the late hours of the night.

Most of the time Brian was quiet and resigned. He would catch cold often and didn't get well easily.

"Have you thought of getting some treatment?"

"What's the use? My partner followed a treatment. A useless agony. Brought him no relief. The end is always the same. Besides, I have no desire to go on."

"What?!" Ricardo burst out. "Life is a miracle! I would get myself several if I could. What about this brilliant autumn light or the scent of these crushed grapes, what about the chirp of the crickets, the rustle of the wind, the skies before the storm? Don't you like it here, with us? Why don't you try some medical help? You know, wonders never cease! There are miracles!"

Brian was silent. When he did speak, his voice shook gently.

"I like living with you two."

He spent mornings with Lya, helping her clean house, do the shopping, wash the dishes, take out the garbage; then he'd resume his garden work, which never ended. In the afternoons Lya brought her chaise lounge into the garden and Brian sat on a low stool next to her, massaging the soles of her feet. Lya would then launch into reminiscences about how happy she had been living with her former husband. How rotten spoiled she had been! Now she was paying for it, she would add. Both literally and figuratively.

"What would I do without you?" Lya would tell Brian. "All by myself, day in, day out! He doesn't even care to show me what he does. Never invites me up there, to inquire whether I like his work or to let him know what I think of it – you know, just to chat with me. He thinks I don't understand. He deliberately forgets I was married to an art dealer, that I traveled round the world at his side. All I'm good for is to always come up with the money. What kind of a life is this?"

"But, you know, he *does* care! He appreciates your opinions. It's just that he won't admit it, hates to show he pays attention to you."

"You think so?"

"Definitely. He loves you very much!"

"But why won't he organize a show?" said Lya, to change the tone.

"I don't think he has any interest in that."

"We live a quarter of an hour's drive from Manhattan, at the beginning of the twenty-first century, and yet, one might say we live outside time, cut off from society, avoiding the world."

"And what's wrong with that?"

"I don't know. It's strange. Do you think Ricardo is a failure?"

"Oh, no! He's wonderful."

"You know something? He never dedicated any painting to me. You know what I mean? He never painted one especially for me. All artists paint their wives. Instead, he just doodles on his canvass, his rafters and his haystacks, and his monks with those ridiculously distorted faces, and rotten fish. And now he's got another mania: collages! Have you seen some of the stupid stuff he's been painting lately?"

"I like it. There's so much force emanating from his works! So much joy! The way he applies color, the intricate forms he comes up with! With him, everything is imagination."

"I see," Lya nodded, unconvinced. "Everything happens in that mind of his. No connection with the real world."

"And what's wrong with that?" insisted Brian, in defense of Ricardo. "Reality brings only unhappiness."

"I don't know where you come up with such ideas. You don't mean to tell me you're unhappy. But why am I asking? As though I were any different…."

"No, with you two I'm OK," Brian would whisper as he continued to massage Lya's feet until she dozed off in her chaise lounge, with her chin resting on her chest, her mouth barely open.

One afternoon, Ricardo came down from the attic earlier than usual. Brian was fixing something on the lakeshore. Lya had gone to the bank.

"Brian, get your old self over here, we got us some work to do."

Ricardo's eyes glimmered with barely suppressed anticipation. Brian walked over, slowly, coughing hoarsely, nursing a three-week-old cold.

"I've got an idea. We're going to fly!"

"Fly?" questioned Brian, as if only the time was inappropriate just then.

"I've just found out how to fly. I wonder why I haven't thought of it earlier! It's so easy! You'll see."

"How did you find out?"

"It just came to me. It popped into my head," chuckled Ricardo. "Everything's up there! All we can ever invent is in our heads."

"So how do you do it?"

"Piece of cake. You bend down, stretch out your hands and rest on your knees, as if you were a bird."

Brian did as he was told, kneeling down, with his arms wide open and his head bent down. His feet sank into the tall grass. Little swallows were circling noisily above their heads.

"Yes, yes, like that. Keep it up like that. Now, I'm going to sit here, next to you.... Tense your legs and lower yourself a bit more. And concentrate. That's all it takes: concentration."

Ricardo stretched out over Brian's back, his arms resting on his. Then he closed his eyes and held his breath in. There they were, like a group statue, caught in a graceful movement.

"There we go! We're flying! Can't you feel we are floating in the air?"

Brian nodded in acknowledgement and followed Ricardo's example, closing his eyes. He barely felt the artist's weight pressing down on him.

"Flying does wonders for one's bones. In fact, it's good for every part in the body. So therapeutic! Every flying creature is healthy. Brian, can you feel we are flying?"

"Yes I can."

"Then you are going to get well. What can you see?"

Brian closed his eyelids tighter.

"Blue fields."

"Tell me more."

"A light from above is coming down on my eyes. I can see it. Bright and pure. I can even feel it. "

"Is that so?"

"Vast green spaces...."

"Good, good! What else?"

"The tree tops. And the golden grass."

"Can you see the ocean, too?"

"Yes, I can see the ocean."

"Then you'll be healed, Brian. Miracles do happen. Look, right now we are taking part in a miracle, we are causing it to happen. Think hard and tell yourself under your breath that you are going to get well."

They had been flying peacefully for a few good minutes, when Lya paused in the middle of the garden, looking at them perplexed.

"What the hell are you doing there?"

Her strident voice startled them and they fell in a pile. Ricardo slid off Brian's back.

"If I told you, you wouldn't believe it."

"Nor would you believe if I told you that I put myself through all sorts of hoops to pay all our bills for this month," retorted Lya.

"What did you say?" asked Ricardo, cupping his hand behind his ear.

"That I'm tired of all your stupid behavior. At least you should have the decency not to involve Brian."

"Sorry, I can't hear you."

"And I wish I couldn't see you!"

"We are flying! Would you like us to teach you how to fly too?"

"Stupid old fool!" snorted Lya, and then stormed out of the garden.

They would fly several times a week, with Ricardo invariably lying on Brian's back. And while they were in flight, they told each other what they saw. Lya would make the sign of the cross, disgusted. How ridiculous men can get!

"It's all because you have no job, not a care in the world! However, if you were forced to earn your own living, you would hardly find time for all your oddball ideas."

"You don't know what you're missing in life, just because you refuse to use your imagination," replied Ricardo sadly. "So many things you'll never feel, never see and never touch!"

"Sometimes I wonder if you are just a clown, or a real crackpot!"

Ricardo was now dividing his time between the attic and the flying sessions with Brian. In the evening they would drink wine by the lakeshore, braving Lya's nagging. They would get drunk, and then go to bed peacefully.

Except that Brian was getting more and more fragile as the days wore on. He would get tired easily, coughed constantly, lost weight and his eyes had retreated deep within their sockets. He slept late, collapsed whenever he exerted himself. The garden was now overgrown with weeds. Lya grumbled, discontented, while Ricardo defended Brian, attempting to conceal his own concern.

On that hot August day, Ricardo had had a premonition. Lya had gone to Manhattan, in an attempt to sell another of her famous rings, which would assure their survival. It was past noon and Brian had still not shown up in the attic. Several times Ricardo came down, under various pretexts, searching for Brian in the house and out in the garden. He was nowhere to be found. He pulled the chaise lounge by the lakeshore, covered his head with his large straw hat and started reading a book, while also watching to see Brian when he would show up. It was already quite late. Lya returned, agitated, following the incident where she was robbed in plain daylight by some black men in Chinatown. She was edgy and exhausted, with frayed nerves, showing all the wear and tear her martyr-like existence with Ricardo had caused her. She went straight upstairs, to take a shower and lie down for a while. In the meantime, Ricardo' grew more alarmed. At one point he stood up, walked to the summer cottage and laid his ear against the door. He couldn't hear a sound. He walked in. Brian was lying on his back, with his gentle eyes fixing the ceiling.

"I thought you were asleep, said Ricardo cheerfully, but then you are only meditating. What do you want to do? Shall we fly for a bit?"

"I can't."

"What's wrong?"

"Nothing. I just can't do it anymore."

"Come, we're going to switch places. Now you will fly lying on my back. It's going to do you good, you'll see."

"It won't matter anymore. I don't think I'll be able to fly again."

"OK, OK, just rest here for a while," said Ricardo, his voice shaking. "Not to worry. We'll fly tomorrow. Why don't come up to the attic with me, so I can show you my latest paintings?"

"I can't move," whispered Brian.

"All right. You lie still. I'll be back in a bit."

He crossed the garden in long strides, then climbed the steps to the attic two at a time, like in his youth. He returned quickly to the cabin, carrying a canvas he had painted that very morning.

"What do you say, old chap?"

He set the canvas in front of Brian's eyes, so the latter could see it without having to turn his head.

"It's Lya. She's so beautiful!"

"I thought of you, while I painted it."

"And you did a very good job handling the light over her face. She is exactly as she would have liked you to see her."

"But please don't tell her. She shouldn't know about it. Let's just keep this between us."

"Sure, it'll be our secret…."

"I'm scared, Brian."

"I know. I'm too."

"That's why I've painted Lya. I'm scared to be alone. Loneliness is different than solitude. You choose your solitude. To be creative, to put order in your thoughts. It's an energetic state of mind. But loneliness it's only a snake squeezing its head in your cap of tea, caching your breath. These days I was thinking of our trio. Our wonderful sad trio. My painting is not enough. I need both of you. Don't go, Brian."

Brian cast him a grateful look. Ricardo's hands were shaking. He put down the canvas and rested it against a chair beside Brian's bed.

"Should you change your mind, we can still go for a short flying session. You'll find me by the lake."

He left Brian's cottage exhausted. The sky was overcast. The swallows flew in low circles. They would dive, almost touching the treetops – sign of the storm's approach, as Brian had once told him. He sat down in his armchair and, for the first time in his life, felt helpless. The laurel bushes were writhing, in the strong gusts stirred by the storm. Two years ago he had had this idea of planting laurel and oleander shrubs, just like the ones they left behind in their Italian house. Brian had gone along with the idea. The oleanders froze when winter came, but the laurels adapted themselves quite well to the climate, growing their metallic-green tall bushes. Brian got to like them too. Sometimes he would add laurel leaves to his barbecue sauce. The first raindrops stung his skin.

"What are you doing there?" Lya's voice boomed from the window. "Can't you see it's raining?"

"What did you say?"

"It's raining!"

Lya came down into the garden, to pick up the wicker chairs and the chaise lounge, before the rain came down hard.

"OK, I understand you can't hear, but can't you feel either? No wonder you can't feel, after smoking another joint of marijuana.... Your glassy eyes give you away...."

"The storm is coming."

"Then get into the house!"

"Brian is not feeling well."

"You told me already. I can see for myself how weak he's been lately. What's ailing him?"

Ricardo touched her arm and looked at her dejectedly.

"He's going to die."

"What?"

"Brian is going to die."

"Cut it out, will you!"

"It's true."

"Look, I've had enough of your dumb jokes."

"I've always been afraid of this day. It's been our own little secret, his and mine. Ever since that night when he first stepped foot in our house. He didn't want you to know."

Lya surveyed him with a mixture of doubt and terror.

"What do you mean he'll die? What of? I'm going to go see him."

She entered without knocking. Brian was sitting on the edge of his bed. He had turned the picture Ricardo had painted that morning with its face towards the wall, having expected Lya would visit him in his cottage.

"You're going to get well. I promise you."

She was speaking in a slow, measured voice, quite unlike her typically loud and fast speech.

"We'll go to the best doctor. I know you don't have any insurance or money, but don't worry. I'll pay for everything. I've still got two rings left, that Ricardo knows nothing about. They'll fetch the highest price, by far. Then we'll find the best hospital, the best doctor. No matter the cost, I'll pay for everything."

Brian was smiling, as if to reassure her.

"Why didn't you tell me? You've got to get well! How could we ever live without you?"

Brian was no longer saying anything. Not a word. He made to stand up and Lya helped him. Both of them went out into the garden, Brian leaning on Lya's arm. Ricardo was waiting for them. Outside it was drizzling with small, hot raindrops. All three looked at one another, as if they had a hard time finding each other in the midst of a infernally crowded place.

Ricardo bent his knees, lowered himself and spread out his arms. Lya helped Brian lie on Ricardo's back. Both were holding their eyes closed, while Ricardo's palms held tightly to Brian's palms, as if afraid they would really lift off the ground. They were flying in silence, with Lya next to them. The raindrops were streaming down their cheeks.

"Can you see the treetops?"

Brian nodded as his face was lit by his customary gentle smile.

"Then everything is all right. And the ocean? Can you see the ocean? Beyond it, over there, there's another ocean. And so on, old chap, ad infinitum. Land, water, light, water, land...."

By now the rain had turned into a mighty downpour. Lya watched tenderly as they flew. She was almost flying with them. She too could see the wide blue water expanses, the treetops, the grass in flames, the gloomy light shoot down to earth.

After that day Ricardo didn't come down from the attic again. After a week Lya went into the cottage to clean it up. She found the painting, resting against the chair, facing the wall. Ricardo had painted it the very day Brian died. She stared at it, recognized herself and her heart flooded with tenderness. Except that in the corner of her mouth Ricardo had painted Brian's smile. She carried the picture to her bedroom, and hung it on the wall facing the bed. She stepped out onto the landing towards the attic, and called:

"Ricardo!"

No one answered.

"Ricardo! Ri-car-do! You deaf lout!"

"Come on up!"

*Translation by Dorin Motz*

# Post-Meridian

The devastating news reached the office of the Minister of Foreign Affairs on a Tuesday at 4 p.m. An ill-fated day for the entire diplomatic corps. Tuesdays are always doomed, but this happened to be the 13th, too, that unlucky number, a dog-day afternoon that overwhelmed the city with heat, drained its inhabitants of energy, melted the asphalt, maddened the dogs, and roasted the basements, causing thousands of rats to throng the streets.

For a few years now even the weather had gone off kilter in the capital of this Eastern European country. Or, to be precise, ever since the communist regime had collapsed, at least according to the superstitious old ladies counting their minuscule pensions in front of the shop windows overstocked with imported goods sold at prohibitive prices.

In the minister's office everything was copacetic. At the end of the day two ceiling fans were still blowing hard, ventilating Gloria's desk, where she'd just finished arranging all her folders. On the corner of the desk one envelope alone would have been left unopened until the next morning had she not noticed the red stamp on it that said URGENT. Gloria was a model secretary. She noticed everything. Nothing escaped her and everything passed through her hands.

Careful not to touch the envelope with her freshly painted fingernails, she opened it with a deft, rapid motion and cautiously drew out the letter. Her nostrils dilated abruptly, her chest expanded, she leaned her head backwards and broke into hysterical laughter. Then she reread the letter one more time, waving her hands through the air to dry her polish, but also to accompany the peals of laughter that shook her voluptuous beautiful body enveloped in a red mini. Oh, the beautiful women of this country!

"Holy Mother of God!" This, for Gloria, was the supreme exclamation. Giggling and sobbing, she wiped the beads of sweat from her neck with the back of her hand. Just as she was about to knock on the minister's door to hand him the ridiculous letter that had put her in such a good mood, three formidable-looking men with darkened faces burst into the office, one after the other. Gloria was not new at her job, and she knew what that meant. Something major must have occurred. Just her luck:

another crisis at the end of the day, ruining her evening; but how can you complain, international problems always outweigh personal ones, as they explained when she was hired by the ministry of foreign affairs.

Under normal circumstances, each of these men would begin innocuous, seemingly casual conversations with her – What a hot day it is! What a beautiful dress! What wonderful coffee those delicate little fingers of hers just made – and only then would they go into the minister's office. But this time the three of them charged in, shoving open the office's upholstered door and completely ignoring her, as if she weren't even there.

"Gentlemen, gentlemen, you can't burst in like that. I have to announce you, what if the minister is tied up? I need to ask him if he can see you…." "It's urgent!" the three shouted almost at the same time. Gloria glimpsed instinctively at the letter, which she was still holding in her hand, and realizing that the three ministers must have received the same, then once again burst out laughing under the horrified gaze of the Secretary of State, the scornful frown of the Chief of Secret Service, and the desperate eyes of the General Director of U.S. Relations.

"Urgent, urgent!" howled Gloria. "I received this URGENT letter, too. You can't imagine how ridiculous it is! Holy Mother of God, what a crazy world!"

"Miss," hissed the Secretary of State between clenched teeth, "I don't know what sort of a letter you got, and I don't give a damn, but it's imperative that we see the minister at once. Right now! Can you get that through your head?"

At that very moment the minister's door opened, revealing him standing at the entrance with a disinterested air, like a man used to solving the fate of humankind between two flights. He was dressed in shorts and had a tennis bag slung over his shoulder.

"Gloria, call the chauffeur," he addressed his secretary with a conspiratorial air.

Then he noticed the frozen faces of his three colleagues.

"Have we a problem, gentlemen?!" It was more an exclamation than a question. Being a cordial man with a sense of humor, the minister was used to treating the desperate cases brought to him by his subordinates, even the most desperate, in a sportsmanlike manner.

"Disaster!" shouted the three in near chorus.

"Ok, ok, c'mon in. Gloria, get your notebook and come in with us."

The three fidgeted with discomfort, as if in disagreement with the idea of Gloria being part of the discussion; but the minister, a young wolf whose eagle eye never missed a trick, ignored their reaction just to irritate them, opened the door wide and let his secretary in first, then without much enthusiasm dropped his shoulder bag in a corner and sank into an imposing walnut chair. Dressed as he was in shorts and tennis shoes, with a huge painting behind him, one would think his authority would seem compromised. But no, the three dignitaries trembled at the very thought of breaking the news to him.

"Come on, come on, gentlemen, out with it, it's 4 o'clock, for God's sake!"

The Secretary of State, an elderly gentleman who had seen a lot, both during communism and after, rubbed nervous palms damp with sweat together, and gripped his tie knot so tightly, it looked like he was asking for his own public hanging. The news fell like a guillotine blade across the neck of the Minister of Foreign Affairs.

"A snake penetrated into our diplomatic mission to the UN in New York."

The minister wrinkled his forehead, attempting to understand. Gloria broke into muted laughter. The General Director of U.S. Relations, a young man in a foreign suit with occidental manners, completed the picture by swallowing the gum he'd been conscientiously chewing ever since he received the letter.

"A boa. Four meters long."

The Chief of Secret Service dropped his head in shame.

"What?" The minister hesitated between a grave and an ironical approach. "Our mission has been penetrated by what?"

Gloria studied his eyes for a reaction, noticed his indecision, and smiled innocently, shrugging her shoulders: "A snake. I think that...."

The minister shot forward like an arrow. The three others sank deeper into their chairs and drew their necks into their collars.

"Have you gone insane?"

"What is even more serious is that the snake has disappeared," whispered the Chief of Secret Service.

"What do you mean, *disappeared*? *Where* did it disappear?" thundered the minister, lumbering across the room in giant steps on account of the sportsman's attire in which this news had surprised him.

"Inside the building of the mission. They can't find it."

"When did you hear about this?"

"Just now," reported the General Director of U.S. Relations.

"When did it happen?"

"A few days ago."

"Why wasn't I informed?"

"An attempt was made to solve the problem at the local level."

"Gentlemen, are you aware of what you're saying? Are you aware of the gravity of the matter? Recall all the diplomats! Beginning with the ambassador!" ordered the minister while performing nervous genuflections in the middle of the room.

"With your permission," dared the Secretary of State, overwhelmed by the sensitive situation, "it might not be wise to proceed this way. We could create a diplomatic crisis, a scandal.... It is New York, after all."

"Yes, yes, it's New York, that's the problem. Why the hell couldn't this happen in some hellhole in Africa, or someplace like that? This is all we need! In the middle of the war on terrorism! Just when our army is getting fighter planes, when our troops are leaving for the hot zones of the world, when the great powers are finally beginning to notice us, care about us, even accept us, WANT us! When we're struggling to win over America and make her our ally, gain her confidence, get our head out of water, these idiots lose a snake! What kind of diplomats are we sending to represent our country, gentlemen? And the damn security service, what the hell did they *secure*? Why do we pay these imbeciles in dollars?! We give them everything they need to make sure nothing gets by. The latest technology, western standards. They're goddamit wired, connected to the Internet, to the whole universe, gentlemen, the whole u-ni-verse! Armed, instructed, chosen from the best, and they, what do they do? They let a snake into the goddamn mission. At the United Nations yet! I can't believe it! Not only that, but they lose it without a trace. Have you ever heard of such a thing?" The minister's voice was turning hoarse. "And what about all my magnificent speeches, all those meetings, international conferences with the heads of state, all the work I put into creating a decent image for this country.... And gentlemen, I assure you, it's not easy to draw attention to a small country, even when it has, like ours, such gigantic potential. It is not easy. We were about to gain credibility, our voice has been heard from the Middle East to the White House, and look what happens now! This is ridiculous! Absurd! Unfair!

How can you have any self-esteem in the world, how can you pretend to be a trustworthy partner when the hallways of your mission in New York are haunted by a snake?! Keep the press away from this. No leaks! We're going to be the laughing stock of the world. Gloria, get the ambassador on the phone. And how the hell did a snake get into the building? Tomorrow, first thing, call a meeting of the Security Council!"

Feverish hours followed. A crisis committee was put together, a secret mission with the code name "Post Meridian" was launched though it had nothing to do with 4 p.m., when the news upset the order and priorities of the Ministry of Foreign Affairs. The Prime Minister was informed, too, but he decided that the president shouldn't be disturbed yet and gave those responsible 24 hours to find a solution. What's more, the Prime Minister was just too composed about the whole case, emotionless, which looked a lot like pure cynicism to most people.

Originally a journalist, essayist, and one of the heads of the former communist youth party, the Prime Minister was a powerful figure from every point of view. He had been schooled in Western Europe like all the children of the communist leaders, spoke three foreign languages perfectly and dabbled in a couple of others, loved to travel to exotic places, was a terrific skier and a passionate hunter. His poised reaction to the terrible news was due in part to the fact that he was an animal lover. He'd adopted two stray dogs, and he raised racehorses, chickens and ostriches on his farm in the country.

While the Minister of Foreign Affairs resorted to threats and forceful measures, the Prime Minister used a different tactic. The next day he assembled young analysts from the Institute for the Investigation of Conflicts, and within the framework of an open discussion, over a cup of Turkish coffee, asked them to come up with an essay about the historical event.

"Certainly, gentlemen, you will resort to symbolism and interpretation, to geo-political and socio-political analysis, you'll evaluate the situation, its long-term consequences and international implications. You'll forgive a little strong-arming here, but I want to bring everything into the light. I want you to prove your value to the utmost, and there's no better opportunity than this event of Borgesian, Marquesian magnitude. And, if we really think about it, our own mythology is full of monsters and dragons. In essence, excavate your collective subconscious, tradition, folklore, and the national spirituality."

The young analysts, a bunch of quick-witted young men with short cropped hair and glasses, fragile gestures and an intellectual air, who'd been carefully selected by the Prime Minister himself, drank in his words. Their ballpoint pens were already twitching impatiently in their pockets. One of them had developed the beginning of an erection, which instantly faltered as the Prime Minister urged them to prove their "potential." All of them kept half an eye on the half-smoked cigar, which the Prime Minister had put out in the ashtray.

For them this was the crucial moment to prove their mastery as essayists and specialists in delicate conflicts, and to advertise their Europeanism and capacity to analyze in depth the intricate traps of diplomacy and international politics. All of them would struggle to project a positive image of the Prime Minister who'd invested good money and a competitive preparatory program in them, along with great hopes, now that the general elections were knocking at the door. These genial young men would oppose the frozen mentality of communism with their dynamic thinking, flexibility, imagination, transparency and modernity, and change the country's image, still unjustly associated with post-communist phantasms of this East European state swamped in poverty and corruption.

Meanwhile Operation POST-MERIDIAN unfurled impetuously. The country's Security Council met the next day in an extraordinary session. Everything would remain confidential, behind closed doors. The Chief of Security had worked out elaborate protection measures for the members of the diplomatic corps in New York and advanced various alternatives for capturing the snake through methodologies specific to espionage and anti-terrorism tactics.

Nobody knows how the press got wind of it. The daily newspapers from the capital came out in special editions in which all sorts of scenarios where played out with journalistic brio building progressively into a paroxysm. The simple headline: "Boa Penetrates the Corridors of Our UN Embassy," became, in a mere few days: "Terror in New York." "Gigantic boa threatens our diplomats." "Children could be the first victims." "Sleepless Terror in New York City." "When will the families in danger be evacuated?" "Politics and diplomacy in a state of apprehension and fear." "The nightmare continues."

A few days later, the newspapers were filled with stories about the escaped snake, or depending on the particular story, the snake that sneaked in, the snake that came in the mail, the snake that infiltrated the diplomatic mission: "The wife of a diplomat was chased by the snake for over two hours in the basement, where she'd gone to take out the garbage"; "In his office on the 6th floor, the building administrator spotted the snake's head between two bottles of Scotch, recently delivered for a reception in honor of National Heroes' Day"; "The son of a diplomat was evacuated from his room in the middle of the night after a series of bizarre moans and hisses issued from the closet"; "The wife of the ambassador woke one morning with horrible muscle spasms. It seemed that the snake had been coiled around her all night long."

In a country so open to conspiracy and supernatural phenomena, new scenarios followed: Imperialism's duplicity; Jewish conspiracy; Masonic plot to weaken our country and manipulate us according to their will; a practical joke played by our diplomats in New York to distract attention from their cigarette smuggling.

The people forgot about the heat and the economy. Everyone had an opinion, a motive, a solution. TV channels broadcast documentaries about snakes, interviews with boa constrictor tamers, talk shows with specialists. The whole country became experts in boas, and especially the women seemed to know all about their practices, in great detail.

Even the president of the country felt it necessary to appear on television to appeal for calm, tolerance, universal harmony and understanding, imploring all the responsible powers to work together to overcome this difficult moment. The President, an optimist in his own right, yet again demonstrated his confidence in the nation's institutions, in the loyalty of the diplomatic corps, and declared himself firmly against any sort of violence or provocation, finishing his speech with the slogan that brought him victory in the elections: "Together we will succeed. May God help us!"

The only one who remained perplexed was Gloria, who still wanted to laugh, and was incapable of understanding the dramatic dimensions this piece of news had assumed: to her it sounded more like a farce. Nothing in the world could have helped her predict the national crisis that followed.

In fact, things became far more complicated. The snake, a splendid example of a boa, had been brought into the building by the wife of the ambassador of a South American country, who'd been invited to a reception on the occasion of a national holiday. The distinguished lady showed up with her husband and the snake wrapped around her neck. She had raised it from the time it was born and it was her pride and joy. It had sparkling yellow scales dotted with brownish stains. It curled around its mistress's neck, completing her long and elegant gown so well that it looked like an extravagant and generously pleated shawl. The security officers never stopped her, perhaps they hadn't even noticed the animal. In any case, there were no rules regarding the access of snakes into the building.

All evening Madame Ambassador ambled through the halls with the snake coiled around her neck, which everyone admired and commented on. She replied patiently to all questions and satisfied everyone's curiosity: "How beautiful and well-behaved it is!" "How old is it?" "How long?" "What does it eat?" At someone's insistence, she removed it from her neck and placed it on the sofa for inspection. When and where it disappeared, no one can remember.

At the end of the reception she looked desperately for it under the tables and feet of the guests, in the hallways, bathrooms, even on the terrace and roof. The alarm was turned on. The security officers panicked. Only Madame Ambassador kept her calm, accepting the idea that, for a while, she would have to live without him. She explained that she had lost the snake a few times before, once in the apartment of a friend: "He showed up again after a week. He hid under the wardrobe. It usually happens when he sheds his skin. I know he looks gigantic, but he can squeeze into the smallest places. I'm worried, but I know he'll show up eventually. Call me the instant he returns and I'll come and get him."

"Is it dangerous?" asked the officers, their faces disfigured by fright.

"Oh, no, he's the sweetest and the gentlest, he never attacked anyone. Perhaps out of love or pleasure he might surprise you…," but no one enjoyed her humor.

The campaign with code name POST MERIDIAN, under the immediate directorship of the Minister of Foreign Affairs, and in close collaboration with the secret services, decided to send a group of anti-terrorist specialists to New York under the pretext of repairing the ancient plumbing and sanitation, and the roof. It was a credible ruse because the diplomatic building was in a sorry state. It hadn't been renovated for decades on account of lack of funds, as the Minister of Foreign Affairs kept complaining. Certainly the costs necessary to bankroll the snake operation greatly exceeded those required to repair the building, but this was about international security, the circumvention of a diplomatic conflict with the United States, as well as with that country the snake originated from. Among the 18 specialists properly trained for such intervention missions, there were a few actual workers who could patch things up a little. And the Minister of Foreign Affairs, a practical and inventive spirit, came up with the idea of sending a snake tamer from the State Circus.

"I loathe this humiliation. Shall we allow ourselves to be terrorized by a creeping reptile? You will return with the skin of this snake waving from a pole! I want it dead or alive!" he shouted, plunging into his imposing chair, and contemplating the vulnerability of countries that find themselves at the crossroads of great empires.

In New York the tension reached a critical level. The families of diplomats slept by turns, no one switched the lights off anymore, they avoided being alone in their rooms. They were exhausted, anxious, their senses in a constant state of high alert, always suspicious of sounds or smells that might indicate the presence of the snake, though no one knew what smell or sound to expect from a boa. As they all agreed, the most frightening daily rituals involved using showers or toilets. They'd found out that boas feed on rats and the basement of that building would be a paradise for it. The basement was teeming with rats and mice scurrying along the garbage dumpsters and washing machines. No one went down there anymore, they threw the garbage directly out into the street and refused to wash clothes. The building entered a kind of quarantine. Diplomatic activities were reduced to a minimum, visitors were prohibited, and security cameras were installed everywhere to watch and monitor each particle of space. The diplomats cancelled all outings for fear that something horrible might occur while they were gone. New York, Broadway with its shows, the museums, all the attractions for which the world so desperately yearned, left our diplomats cold: the snake had monopolized their attention.

The antiterrorism team arrived in New York on a Saturday afternoon. After a short meeting with the ambassador, the 18 specialists spread throughout the building, searching everywhere, dismantling sinks, toilets, pipes, walls. The snake tamer followed them with a whistle of Indian origin and other tools of instant intervention. The tenants were happy to cooperate. At last they were not abandoned to confront the beast by themselves. The atmosphere grew more relaxed. Soon enough snake jokes began to spread, propagated by the younger diplomats who hadn't completely lost their sense of humor despite the professional rigor required by the situation.

After a few days, the building was in shambles. Demolished walls, dissembled pipes. The two workers didn't manage to piece everything back together or to repair what the anti-terrorist experts took apart, venturing even into the fabled "snake's mouth" in order to fulfill their mission. A television crew was sent to New York in order to broadcast news from the scene. Every news report opened with headlines like "Breaking news: Snake eggs found under sink on the 10th floor." There were updates called "Live from New York: The War on the Boa." Charismatic correspondents with frozen smiles promised the most balanced and fair coverage of the crisis.

The snake's mistress telephoned one day to find out if her favorite pet had made an appearance. Her husband had come to the end of his mission at the U.N. and they were due to return to their country. Though she was pained by the loss, she would console herself with the other three boas she'd raised since birth. She added, however, that if the snake made an appearance after her departure, it would become her gift to the ambassador as a sign of friendship between the two countries.

Then evenings became somewhat more entertaining in the building, the workers played folk music, got drunk and passed out dead-tired. Little by little, life grew more normal, though everyone was aware that somewhere, in a corner, a snake was stalking them.

After a month of detailed and exhaustive searching, only two days before the meeting of the Security Council in New York, the building of the UN mission was to host the head of the parliament, who arrived with his special advisors and ministers. The team of specialists was just about to give up, when, under one of the heating boilers in the basement, someone found the snake's skin. The entire building celebrated the event with a private cocktail. The sparkling yellow skin, dotted with tiny brownish stains, was placed in the office of the ambassador. People lined up to view it and everyone acknowledged that it possessed an unspeakable splendor spread over the sofa and glimmering with orange reflections. It was carefully wrapped, placed in a diplomatic pouch, locked with a secret code and transported back home under great secrecy by four anti-terrorist experts, the crème-de-la-crème of the POST MERIDIAN action team.

The next day, at exactly 4 p.m., the snakeskin arrived at the office of the Minister of Foreign Affairs. Gloria spread it out on the thick carpet, which had been a gift from the Iranian prime minister, at the foot of the sofa where the Chief of Secret Service sat next to the General Director of U.S. Relations and various other political advisors.

"Well, well, I can see the skin. But the snake? Where is the snake?" asked the Minister of Foreign Affairs, without being able to wrench his eyes away from the orange reflections.

"Disappeared without a trace," the defeated Chief of Secret Service replied.

"This means that it's still in the building?"

"I doubt it. Our men searched everywhere. Maybe after it molted, it managed to escape...."

"But we can't be sure, can we?" insisted the minister.

"We can't be sure of anything."

"You sound fatalistic, gentlemen. We cannot be diplomats if we are to be the victims of superstition and fatalism."

Unfortunately, through these affirmations the Minister of Foreign Affairs unwittingly stepped into a mine field – the territory of the Prime Minister, who was a thinker, a philosopher, and an analyst who couldn't stand failure. When he did encounter failure, his legendary tenacity pushed him to make the most out of it by polishing his image to perfection. So this time the Prime Minister exercised his authority and exhibited his qualities as a charismatic leader in a nationally televised live symposium. He called together the young analysts from the Institute for the Investigation of Conflicts who, in the meantime, had fleshed out complicated essays. He convoked the parliament, notified ambassadors, the president, the press, the unions, the regional party organizations; and within the framework of an impressive reception at the Summer Palace, he expounded his theory: "The Transcendence of the Political and Collective Unconscious." It was sublime, though hardly anyone understood a word.

The most talented of his disciple essayists, full of pride, presented papers and reports about cosmogony and the symbolism of the snake in the history of national culture, about the battle between Angel and Demon, the gap between East and West, the axis of evil surpassing the

European Union and finally, reaching our territory, the opposition of Ethos and Thanatos, with evident allusions to the infiltration of the diplomatic building of an ex-communist country by a snake. In their subtext, the essays could not forgive the failure to capture the symbolic animal, which was always imprudently associated with cunning, perversity, duplicity of diplomacy vanquished with its own weapons. The snake would continue to remain, for many, a constant threat; its presence, be it imaginary or fictive, would haunt them for many years in the corridors of diplomacy, in unhealthy basements or on roofs reeking of heat. The works created for the symposium were anthologized in a brochure, published with an excellent set of graphics under the patronage of the Prime Minister, who delivered the opening words, which no one remembered much of, except that these fantastic events, beginning in a small country with great ambitions, took place right in midtown New York.

After the symposium, the Minister of Foreign Affairs came back to his office a defeated man. Even though it was already late, he found Gloria waiting for him. The well versed and devoted secretary instantly discerned his state of mind and made him herb tea in a Chinese porcelain cup painted with a dragon. The minister furrowed his eyebrows in distaste.

"And the snake skin, what will become of it?" asked Gloria, pacing around it carefully but without hiding her admiration.

"Whatever you want," the minister capitulated and fell without much relish to the reading of the latest URGENT letter. "Nothing to do but move on."

Two weeks later Gloria placed a pair of shiny pumps and a marvelous purse on the minister's desk, both made of snake skin.

"For your wife," she whispered conspiratorially. "I hope she likes them."

*Translation by Julian Semilian*

# The Second Life

## I

## *The Reader*

America had settled for blooming prosperity. For a good while now, the stock market was riding high, unemployment figures had dipped spectacularly, newspapers had been filled with innumerable job offers, and gasoline prices had been negligible. People were building and traveling; they had money and were living well.

Andrei Roscov, a New Yorker naturalized more than fifteen years before, had won his battles with immigration. He had fought his way up the professional ladder and had reached as far as his training and capabilities allowed him. All that was left to him now was to savor his success. He was content and past his prime, with only retirement to look forward to.

As the great confrontations – in the family, at work, in his social life – were behind him, he started to think of ways to spend his old age. He was mildly terrified at the thought of inaction, which, he knew, could undo men his age, both physically and psychologically. In a way, he had already started to prepare for retirement, trying out hobbies, obsessions, dabbling in things that he would later practice as antidotes to alienation, to the punishment of having to stay at home all day, even if this home was their dreamy Upstate possession, complete with his relatively even-tempered and rather understanding wife.

He could travel, but then, how much can one really travel? How many movies can one see, how many chess games can one play (that is, if one finds a worthy adversary), how much can one garden, after all? Besides, he didn't play golf or tennis, he wasn't the athletic type. Then again, there were always books. One can read books forever. Reading is a sure thing, readily available and potentially endless. All he had to do was to recover all the books he had put off, all the books he had failed to read all those years he had to wage war with life, all those years he had to work until, late in the evenings, he collapsed in exhaustion.

And since he thought one should have some practice and establish a tradition early on, Andrei Roscov started to read right away. Not just randomly. Systematically. Books by classic and contemporary authors, expensive volumes, and cheap editions soon began to flood the house, which until recently harbored few books, mostly bought by the children during their college years. Andrei Roscov became a conscientious book buyer, a regular of local libraries.

He would read insatiably, devouring universal literature chronologically, from the Greek to the post-modern authors, going through all the major literary schools and periods. He was discovering fascinating writers, he was entering a world he never imagined to be so replete with all the humanity and the fantasy ever produced by reality or by the imagination.

Books had flooded his home. All the rooms, which had previously been divided according to fixed purposes, had sprung shelves, wall units, and all manner of custom-made or improvised book storage. Books were practically everywhere: on top of tables, spread on couches, in the kitchen, under the bed. His wife had shown herself puzzled in the beginning, but by now she had accepted the odd development as a harmless childish obsession or fancy: her husband had suddenly chosen to become an overeducated eccentric.

Andrei Roscov would use each free moment for reading. He would read on the subway, at the dinner table, on the toilet, in the garden, even at the stadium, when he would go to baseball games. He had been a passionate baseball fan in the old days, but now he was dismayed by the long-drawn out games, which would keep him away from his readings. The wasted time prevented him from enjoying spending his weekends at the stadium.

He would read during the weekends, late into the night and early in the mornings before leaving for work. He would read at work, too, during his lunch hour, while he was munching on a sandwich, or whenever he found a moment of peace and quiet. Since he had been promoted to head of department in the fiber optics company where he was working, he no longer worked in a cubicle in the large hall; he had his own office, away from his colleagues' prying eyes, from the constant shuffle of papers and the irrepressible chatter of computer keyboards. He was now free to read as soon as he was alone in his office, with major emergencies taken care of. He naturally hid his books in drawers and avoided being caught reading by his colleagues or bosses.

He would read avidly, thinking about how unfair it is to have only one life against all the millions of books ever written. He felt frustrated by all the volumes that would be left unopened, by all the books that would survive him, by all the authors he would not be able to reach. He adored the feel of expensive covers, the feel of freshly cut paper or of pages weathered by the passage of time; he loved to leaf through vanilla scented volumes and to behold the complex shapes of rare books. Many antiquarians began to know him. They would set aside for him editions they thought he might be interested in, even though Andrei Roscov was interested in everything, in every work of literature.

He had naturally acquired some taste, he already had preferred authors, genres, and themes, but his reading hunger obliged him to refrain from nothing that ranged from poetry to drama or from philosophy to fiction. He was riveted by reading, by the succulence of words. His hands would shiver on the spines of books and his eyes would race insatiably from one word to the next and from one line to the other. His desperate advance on culture had started to take its toll – not just in money, but also in sleepless nights, obsessive dark circles under his eyes, skipped heartbeats, eye infections, and exhaustion caused by his drive to conquer the libraries of the world.

He would check the stock market less and less frequently, even though he had been a successful investor with good intuition and a knack for brokerage. There had been a time when he called himself a market fiend. He had made substantial profits in the stock market and had achieved financial stability precisely because of it. Now, however, all he did was spend ever-increasing sums of money. He saw money in a new light – it seemed to have been made only in order to be invested back into books.

Old age no longer scared him. Neither did retirement, whose monotony and promise of decrepitude are so terrifying to so many men. He was now looking forward to his retirement, to devoting all his time to reading.

Roscov was not exhibiting any other bizarre behavior; he had not become moody or unstable. The only thing was, he had become the mirror of his own readings. Whenever he was reading philosophy or was deep into existentialism or minimalism, he would become sad, withdrawn, depressed, he would refuse to talk or eat. For him, just as for the dejected absurdist or pessimist writers he was reading at the time, the world would lose its meaning. On the other hand, whenever he was reading romances, he would become melancholy, even maudlin, his eyes turned tender, obscured by an avalanche of sentimental clichés. Then again, his condition got even more serious when he turned to fantastic or surrealist authors. At such times, he simply wanted to fly away, but felt unsupported in his child-like impulses. But all this was happening within the confines of normality. He continued to be in control of his moods, which appeared to be rather histrionic in nature. Roscov had become particularly skilled at walking the tightrope between reality and the ineffable. He had become a mime capable of playing all possible roles, and there seemed to be too little time for the countless roles and existential moods he was able to go through, from Bovaric boredom to Chekhovian nostalgia, from Hamletian indecision to the hallucination of life as a dream.

Most of the time, though, he would simply appear pensive or grave, since he was constantly under the spell of the events or characters in whatever book he happened to be reading. The angles of his face had grown sharper, his eyes had acquired a glimmer of wisdom, his fingers appeared longer, as those of a piano player constantly practicing his skills, maybe because Roscov himself was increasingly turning page after page in the grand score of literature. He was becoming mannered, aristocratic, meditative, and enigmatic. At times he would appear to plumb the meaning of life in depth, to penetrate the complexity of life, indeed of the whole universe, to ask fundamental questions, and to concern himself with the purpose and destiny of the whole mankind – where we come from, what we are meant to do, how, why, and until when….

Death, mysterious and incommensurable, a fat subject for most of the authors Roscov was reading, had also carved out a space for itself among his preferred themes for reflection. For him, death was both revelation and forgiveness, both end point and ultimate accomplishment, the doppelganger of our lives, the shadow awaiting to engulf us. When his thoughts bent towards death, he would be attracted by metaphysics, and would even partake in representing death as a wise woman, bored by earthly entropy, a cynical apparition in a smoky mirror or behind a closing door. Roscov was at times resigned, at times alarmed. He would strain to feel death's touch on his shoulder during those long autumn nights when everything is still and settled, when leaves rustle and daylight gradually slips away into the calm and cool night filled with the sweet smells of fruit and smoke. He would sit on his porch, facing the woods, and he would read listening to the silence and fancying himself as

Raskolnikoff, Mishkin, or Gregor Samsa. At such times, nothing in his future had the power to terrify him.

Literature gave him strength; it manipulated his personality and made him stronger precisely because of the flexibility he gained by inhabiting so many characters. He had room enough for them all, he could take any shape without losing interest in new readings, without being enslaved by any of his experiences, except by reading itself, by reading as a global phenomenon indispensable to life itself, by reading as a definitive, organic action. He grew increasingly certain that he would die without his readings.

All this, at a time when no one was dreaming of classic heroes anymore, when the contemporaneous characters with whom most people identified were superheroes, programmers, creators of artificial intelligence, brokers, corporate lawyers, computer nerds turned millionaires overnight. The world was turning into a gigantic dot-com, multi-media slowly replaced books, the space of literature was being bit by bit replaced by cyber-space, and myths, rather than springing from cultural heritage, were projections into the future.

Perhaps Andrei Roscov's role was precisely to keep classical values alive, to remember those powerful characters that changed the history of culture, to rekindle the glory of the words written by the great titans of literature. But Roscov's timing was ultimately bad, his passion was anachronistic and obsolete now that the world was consequently obsessed with the other, future, end of time. The fear of change, the threat of extinction could have been stimulating, just as easily they could have been conducive to resignation or feelings of emptiness, but, purely technical concerns aside, no one appeared willing to meditate on the possibility of the end. A handful of cults, fanatics, and operetta Messiahs reared their heads here and there, preaching to the hysterical, but a few superstition-ridden readers of Nostradamus did not amount to much in an otherwise robust context which ignored fatalism. America was prosperous, Communism was no longer a threat, and mankind was irremediably engrossed in a technological adventure whose glory overshadowed even the passage from one millennium to another.

Who would Andrei Roscov share all these thoughts with? Who would understand him, who would believe him? But then again, he had no need for anyone's understanding, he did not seek approval or appreciation for his gigantic gesture of spiritual elevation, of heightened, unique, and intense awareness of each living moment. He felt at home with his books, all he wanted was to read, to be left alone to read. He was conspiring with time as best he could, he made short order of his social, professional, and family obligations. The minimum, nothing more. What was left of his life was his own, and he would make use of it by reading. He had no screw loose, he was not alienated, though all that culture, stored higgledy-piggledy in him, could have easily turned him against the world. He was a pretty balanced man who had turned one of his hobbies into a vice – a vice both unhealthy and beneficial, a fabulous vice!

One night Jesus appeared in Andrei Roscov's dreams. Since Roscov had been born of a Jewish mother and Christian father, he at first thought that the dream made no sense. The apparition was doubtlessly owed to his readings, which leaned at the time more towards philosophy and history of religions. Anyway, Jesus was duly dressed in his famous white mantle with wide flowing sleeves; he was sad and benign, with an aura hovering over his head, a classic image derived from paintings, frescoes or naive book illustrations. He looked rather like a chosen beggar bathed in resplendent light. He was holding a book and a strange pencil radiating light from its tip. At each move, the tip of the pencil would spring words, themselves made of light, material words. They would unfurl in the air and, for a fraction of a second, Roscov could read them, but then they would disappear as if by magic. Roscov beheld words written on air for the first time in life; he was fascinated by their blinding pulsation, by how the words vanished only to be replaced by yet more others, endlessly poured from the tip of the pencil, held by Jesus like a sword.

He was at first scared by the apparition, especially since it was so faithful to the images he already knew. Jesus appeared real, true, living, and Roscov could not understand why he had manifested himself in his dream. He did not know the meaning of that rare encounter and he especially could not understand what Jesus wanted of him. He had read that only the elect few have such dreams, and he knew that the visions are rarely without consequences. Those dreaming are usually given messages, tasks to perform, duties to fulfill, destinies to follow, some kind of cross to bear, some kind of purpose in life.

He was relieved to see that Jesus was not speaking to him, that he was not pushing him to understand anything beyond the spectacle of his apparition, that he was not burdening him with any kind of cross or commandments, that he did not ask him anything. He was beginning to believe that Jesus had not even noticed his presence, when the Savior made a sudden move, pointing the shining tip of the pencil towards Roscov. He stretched out his hand, thinking that Jesus was offering him the pencil, but Jesus rushed on, piercing Roscov's heart with it.

Roscov instantly woke up, feeling his chest inundated by words. It wasn't painful. He even had a strange and pleasant feeling of plenitude. He close his eyes and almost saw Jesus walking towards a milky horizon, stepping lightly as if he was walking on water or flying low above the ground, as if he was walking on one of those gliding lanes in an airport. Roscov was left confused, his chest brimming with words, overwhelmed by the strangeness of the heritage the divine apparition had lodged in his heart. He did not seek to understand its meaning, though. Nor did he talk to anyone about it.

He went back to his books. He was reading perhaps more eagerly than ever, now that Jesus had clearly shown him that words were born out of light, that light and words were one. He had finally understood why God said that in the beginning was the word.... Roscov was now hiding under his shirt all the luminous words planted by the Savior straight into his heart. He discovered that it wasn't all that difficult to live with such riches in one's heart. Roscov's life hadn't changed in the least. Soon he would forget to think about his dream, caught in his web of minor and major readings.

* * *

Were his mother alive, she would have been so happy to see him buried in books. All throughout his childhood, she had unsuccessfully tried to encourage him to read. He had been born into a family of teachers, in a small town in Eastern Europe, where Hungarians, Germans, Romanians, and Jews lived peacefully together – except for those few tensions that usually sprung out of one too many drinks. His father, a history teacher, was an unsophisticated salt-of-the-earth fellow, with robust ideas about duty, family, and correctness. He was as conscientious about his work at the school as he was about his life at home. He was a man one could count on, but there was little to talk to him about, outside the specifics of his everyday life. Andrei Roscov kept invigorating yet vague memories of him. His father had left little in the way of an impression – he was just a reliable memory and nothing more. His mother, on the other hand, had been a real character, a complicated figure in his life. He was almost wondering how she came to be in that terse, unexceptional town lodged between the mountains.

She played the piano, she had a real talent for drawing; during the winter, she would paint in their small kitchen long male faces in surreal settings and short pudgy women with wings or unicorn horns. She spoke five languages. Andrei Roscov remembered her reading, always. She could do anything, a sophisticated lady who concerned herself with the arts and the ideas circulating throughout Europe. She would spring up with unexpected insights, she was subtle and humorous, a flying spirit in the sleepy provincial town where they were living.

Roscov was very proud of her. But he was sometimes intimidated by her tenacity, by her alert spirit; he had a hard time meeting the expectations she had of him, he was tortured and guilty about not being always able to rise to the challenge. He felt that he was disappointing her in being so normal, so unexceptional, so bent on refusing to read, so wayward and uninterested in anything else but his games and his friends, so lacking in any special passion, so exasperated by his mother's ambitions to see him become one of the elect few. He did not have it in him to collect prizes and it didn't look as if he had any chances of becoming any kind of champion any time soon.

It was because of his mother that their house was filled to the brim with books in all sorts of languages and about all sorts of things. Andrei Roscov, though, treated the books as furniture, not to be moved lest one tried to threaten the good order and tidiness of the house. The more his mother encouraged him to read, the more books she piled on him, the stronger Andrei's rejection and resistance.

When he was fifteen, Mrs. Roscov died. She passed away uneasy about leaving a disoriented and unformed child in this world, despite all her efforts to transfer onto him at least part of her genetic heritage. So far, it hadn't worked. Andrei Roscov took after his father, who for a while seemed to him an easier model to follow. He had admired his mother, without really understanding her. He never wanted to follow the ambitious dreams she had carved out for him.

This was all about to come to a head after the fall of the Berlin Wall. Up to that point, he had lived inside the communist system without ever trying to rebel, without ever doing anything courageous. He had resigned himself to the pervasive collective cowardice of his time and place. He had graduated from one of the technical institutes of higher learning, he had gotten married, and had brought forth two children. He was a member of the majority class of which little was expected other than quiet survival in the given historical circumstances.

But Roscov, instead of completing his unexceptional existence in the now liberated Eastern Europe, decided to challenge his destiny. He immigrated to the United States with his wife and two children, and started all over again. This proved to be a courageous, daring gesture, especially since he was no longer in the prime of his youth and had little to go on other than his unspectacular tenacity. But he succeeded. He was the first one in his family history to set foot in America; still, he worked his way into a middle-class existence and became a respectable citizen of the most important world power. He could imagine his mother smiling contently wherever she was – not so much because of his success in America, as because of the reading adventure he had recently dedicated his life to. That's one thing he was sure of.

* * *

In the evenings, he went to readings and book signings, to meetings with authors who were promoting their books in stores or book clubs. He had purchased a long white scarf that he twisted with studied negligence over his elegant coat, modeling himself after a recently discovered character with complex psychological makeup.

It was on one of these evenings that he met the great Alen Hunter, an established writer and author of several novels, some of whom had been awarded prestigious prizes. He was waiting in line for Hunter to autograph a copy of his latest work. When he finally reached the end of the line and spelled out his name so the author could add it to a canned formula such as "with regards," Hunter lifted his eyes inquiringly:

"Andrei Roscov?...The name sounds familiar."

"No, I don't think...." Roscov grew self-conscious. "I'm not a literary...type. That is, well, I mean, I don't think you could have met me before."

"Not sure, the name's familiar. Roscov with a C or a K?"

"C."

"You never wrote or published?"

"Never," Roscov assured him, a bit embarrassed by the long line of people waiting for autographs behind him. Alen Hunter couldn't have cared less.

"Still, Andrei Roscov – I definitely heard or read the name before. No writers in the family?"

"Well, my mother used to correspond with all sorts of literary types. But…I don't think, she wasn't really a writer."

"Where are you from?"

"That's not gonna help either. I'm from Eastern Europe."

"My grandmother was from Bukovina! Listen, if you can wait a few minutes, I'll finish up here and we can go have a drink. I know a place nearby. Of course, if you don't mind, that is."

Roscov was speechless. An invitation from the great Alen Hunter himself! He suddenly remembered the words of an old fortuneteller in his hometown, many years before. He had never given them a second thought, since he had no inclination for superstitions.

They had been to the wedding of a cousin. Towards the morning hours, when everyone's minds had turned cloudy with alcohol, food, and music, an old fortuneteller was brought in to go from table to table. His wife kept goading him to show his palm to the fortuneteller, and Roscov played along halfheartedly, incapable of going against the disordered, confused atmosphere. People moved languidly, disoriented, like women whose mascara began to run at the end of a prolonged party, like men mumbling with their ties loosened and their white shirtsleeves rolled up among cigarette smoke and alcohol vapors.

The fortuneteller told him that at the mid-point of his life his destiny was to suddenly break off and take an unexpected path. It looked, she said, almost as if this was another, new life, which Roscov was to experience with intensity, as if he had died and been reborn a new man, with a new calling, in a new world. He did get a bit scared right then and there, but later decided that there was no reason to give any credence to the old fortuneteller, who probably was saying whatever crossed her mind to the cheery wedding guests waiting in line for her prophecies. But she did tell him that his life would be influenced by his meeting a famous man, a celebrity, and that things would change under the spell of that man.

He had first remembered the words of the fortuneteller when he arrived in America; he thought that that was the change she had foreseen. Now he was making a different set of connections, though. Maybe the new life the old lady had told him about was his life as a reader, and the famous man was Alen Hunter himself. Or Jesus from his dream?

But beyond these speculations, superstitions, and coincidences, Roscov and Hunter were about to embark on a friendship with unexpected consequences for the destiny of the passionate reader Roscov had become.

* * *

The bar Hunter had mentioned was two blocks away from the Barnes and Noble bookstore were they had met. Roscov was still nervous, even though Hunter was treating him as if they had known each other forever. Hunter even introduced him to the bartender and the few customers he knew, who appeared to be somehow related to the world of literature or the arts. Hunter and Roscov ended up drinking scotch until late in the night, smoking cigars and telling the stories of their lives as brothers in arms meeting by chance years after the end of the war.

Roscov was overwhelmed by how natural his conversation with Hunter turned out to be, by the unreserved trust the writer had in him, by the fact that he was being treated as an equal in the otherwise pretentious field of literature. Hunter would ask for his opinions, would provoke him to comment on and analyze particular authors, books, or critical categories; he would correct or contradict Roscov only gently, like a teacher who wanted to bring out the best in his favorite student.

But the most interesting moments were provided by Hunter's confessions about writing. Roscov was proud to have been elected to hear secrets about writing, creative states, feelings, quirks and habits. It was so exciting to peek into a famous man's writing habits and motivations, to learn the backstage details of a kind of work usually surrounded by an ineffable cloud.

"I began to write too late. I was over forty when I published my first short story in *The New Yorker*. I had written only occasionally, for my own pleasure, until then. I was teaching at a Long Island college and was bored to death. I would read a lot, and it's very hard to get by only by reading. You start wanting to write. Have you ever felt this? Have you have felt that you too can do it, that you too have something to say, to add?"

"No, I don't think so," Roscov hesitated.

"Not yet," Hunter corrected him, smiling slightly ironically. "I can feel the writer in you."

Roscov's head spun for a second. He was both flattered and embarrassed by Hunter's suspicion.

"We keep being thrown traps. And we're happy to fall into them. After *The New Yorker* published me, I started to take myself seriously. My colleagues in the department were very impressed by my achievement. I felt it was my duty not to disappoint them. In fact, writing is just a way of satisfying one's ego. In the beginning, you write out of vanity. Then you write in order to flatter yourself. I don't discount passion in all this, but prose writing is hard labor. There's no pleasure in it. Some call it talent or gift. I think it's just about carrying out a task, a chore you are told to do. You fall ill with the duty to write, and everything else takes a back seat, as when you have to deal with a serious illness. Professional accolades are no longer important, even family becomes a second priority. In fact, in a way, you write for them too. Or, sometimes despite them, if you happen to have a needy wife or indifferent children. In the beginning, you're just trying to prove to yourself that you can do it. Afterwards, you can't stop. Of course, success and fame count a lot in this whole affair. You are always within short distance of arrogance or obsession. Every time you walk out there to get an award, failure is just around the corner. Fame can tickle your ego and drive you to all sorts of errors or compromises. It's like walking a tightrope. If your attention slips for even a fraction of a second, you find yourself lying flat on the ground. There are so many others who are at least as good as you that your fall might never get any notice. People record only success; no one has time for losers."

Roscov was looking at him with moistened, admiring eyes.

"I am overwhelmed by the strength writers have, by…."

"You should be overwhelmed by their weakness, too. And besides, there's only one small step between being a reader and being a writer. Only a matter of courage. Some readers do dare to take up writing. That's all. Just write your first line. Dare yourself to write the first line. Everything else follows automatically. What about talent? Yes, one could talk about talent in the same terms as one could talk about luck – you can make your own. In fact, what people admire in the best of us is perseverance, the ambition of seeing things through, irrespective of circumstances or costs."

All of Hunter's conversations assumed some fundamental contradiction as their basis. One got the impression that the only reason he sought company was in order to argue. He always positioned his discourse by contradicting his interlocutor. He then launched in a long demonstration that randomly amassed sometimes contradictory evidence. That was the only way he could communicate. Maybe he was a lonely man, Roscov thought – but then, how can a famous man like him be lonely?

"Most people write out of weakness or solitude. Those who write out of weakness are trying to provoke their destiny, to prove that they can overcome their complexes, and that they have a world all of their own, which only they can control, with no interference from the outside world. The lonely ones write in order to squash their fears. There is something pathological about every great writer. A chemical imbalance, a degree of deviation from the norm. Loneliness is a good way into writing, whether the isolation is imposed or voluntary, traumatic or optional, real or imaginary. There are so many forms of loneliness, it's not too hard to find one."

"Of course, metaphorically speaking, every writer is alone…," Roscov attempted.

"Metaphorically like hell! Who do you think would want to live with a writer? Oh, it might be pleasant to be around one for a while, to sniff the glory and the fascination that surrounds him, but who do you think can last though to the end? Writers are impossible people. They are finicky, bizarre, hard to take in the long run. Some develop a persecution complex; others, on the other hand, can get enamored with themselves. They can be boring or, even worse, eccentric. Listen to me, I know what I'm talking about, I saw a lot of things in my life, and sometimes I can even see myself. Tonight, I might be willing to risk my own life for you, but tomorrow I might pass you by without even a flicker of recognition."

Andrei Roscov looked at him askance.

"Well, that's just a manner of speaking," Hunter tried to mend things. "I mean that writers are unpredictable and their reactions often follow a different logic than for most people. They live in a disorderly universe created by themselves, which has a hard time following the general rules for cohabiting in this world. They like to pose so much that they fail to distinguish the model from the original, and they stop making an effort to avoid posing. They end up becoming histrionic and taking the shape of characters they themselves gave birth to."

Roscov was startled. Didn't he feel the same way, even as a mere reader? Maybe Hunter was right: what distinguished the reader from the writer was courage. Come to think of it, everything Hunter was telling him applied to him, too – he felt it, he lived it, even though he had never written a line in his life.

"Once, at one of these readings, I ran into this woman who went to junior high with me. She was living in Chicago, but had come to New York with her husband for a few days – he was attending some medical convention of sorts. She had seen my name in an ad in the *Village Voice*, so she showed up at the bookstore to see me again, decades later. 'I'm surprised you're a writer,' she said, kindly. 'I'm surprised you're not,' I answered politely. I tried, unsuccessfully, to convince her that being a writer was a choice, that I hadn't just turned into a writer, that I had chosen to be one."

"If it were really so easy, the world would be swarming with writers," Roscov said melancholically.

"But it *is* that easy. And the world *is* actually swarming with writers. I'm not talking about the established ones, or the ones who call themselves writers or aspire to be writers. I'm talking about those who don't write but could do it. We each have in ourselves an infinite number of latent little people gifted in an infinite number of fields. We just don't let them out, we don't allow them to manifest themselves – that's a whole other story. But it's up to us. They continue to wait there, patiently, fully prepared to spread throughout the world. But we are afraid of our own infinite abilities, and insist on keeping them locked up inside us, suffocated by our complexes and our cowardice, by the comfortable mediocrity which every day billions of people prove to be a viable way to make a living. It's against this complacency that that we must rise. Those who don't accept this insipid abandonment, the complacency in the general mud bath, are the elect few, the trailblazers, the mold breakers, the destiny carvers, those who push the world forward. For them, everything is just a horrible, permanent chore, a perpetual discontentment, a painful never-ending birth. They spit out exceptional little people on a daily basis, and cater to their well-being in this world so eager to chew up exceptional little people."

Roscov swallowed air. He was touched, hurt, defeated. He almost saw inside himself an army of little people waiting, disappointed by their host's inability to spit them out. He felt small, helpless, and guilty. It wasn't enough that Jesus had planted words in his chest, now Hunter was at it with his little people.

Astonished at what he was discovering inside himself and unable to figure out what he was supposed to do, he fell prey to the endless glasses of scotch the bartender kept bringing their way, as if he were trying to wash away all the words and drown all the little people who were trying to turn his life upside down. Right when reading had brought him balance and peace, everything began to change around again. He could hardly wait to get home, open the first book he saw, and start reading. Reading would certainly give back the confidence, peace, and security he had worked so hard to achieve by organized, systematic, passionate, and responsible reading. This way he could free himself of the guilt and reproaches so cruelly thrust upon him.

His mother's face came to mind. Her eyes were scolding him even now. Was he reading too much for her taste? Was there anything more she expected of him?

Hunter was going through the shot glasses fast. His eyes had grown moist, he had begun to smack his lips, and a rivulet of saliva had formed at the corner of his mouth.

"Look around you. Only lonely little birds."

He was speaking slowly, dissecting the bar crowd with his eyes, stopping on various groups of huddled patrons. He was speaking mostly for himself, even though Roscov continued to listen to him attentively, hanging upon his every word.

"The consequence of all this madness with sexual harassment: all poetry went to hell. What's the use of some of them being smart, others talented, and others successful? They all reek of ambition, they are merciless and sure of themselves, the macho kind – you know, they have money, they're accomplished, and they wouldn't give any of up that for a man, not for the world. Now that they got even the rights they didn't need, now that they have become superior to us, now that they're encouraged by this politically correct society, we don't stand for much in their eyes. Whatever we do, they can do too. Whatever we have, they can have too. They satisfy themselves – or each other. Oh, where are the love intrigues of yesteryear! Where is the suffering, the depression, the mad passion, the sacrifice, the suicides of unfulfilled lovers?"

Hunter issued a melancholy hiccup.

"We are going headlong towards violent and promiscuous matriarchy. Just think about all the pavements filled with toned legs in silk stockings and sneakers, running all over the place all day long, energetic and competitive. How horrid! In fact, it's quite sad, even for them, no matter how hard they're trying to play the champions. You know, I don't believe the easygoing air they put on when they chose their own solitude. In fact, none of these beer-drinking broads giggling to each other and casting glances at the lonely men at the tables is truly happy. They yearn for a real male who can drive them out of their minds. But the broads are proud and the men are timid, full of complexes, defeated before the race. Many men were castrated by this idea of sexual harassment! Sometimes I miss Europe so dearly, our old-fashioned granny with run stockings, with black-and-white photo albums and run-down walls. At least there you can pinch a woman's butt in the street without ending up in court. And women smell like women over there! And they can sniff a man from a distance, too. They let themselves be picked up, they expect manipulation and seduction. I so miss some European booty! What if we went to Paris on a lark? Or to Rome! Will you come to Rome with me?"

But he didn't wait for the answer, which Roscov was trying to construct to be as evasive as possible, so as not to ruin Hunter's mood.

"Our generation saw the death of the family. The generation right after ours dismantled the couple – what with feminism, on the one hand, AIDS, on the other hand, let alone alienation, egotism, survival."

"Are you married?" Roscov asked.

"I was. Three times. And all of the marriages were successful," grinned Hunter, his eyes still moist with the image of Europe, which was slowly fading in the last scotch glass downed under the admiring eyes of the bartender, who kept Hunter's photo on the wall, alongside of a few other famous patrons like Paul Simon or Hillary Clinton.

They wobbled into the street. Hunter hailed a cab. Instead of sobering them up, the cold wind rocked the two men ridiculously. Their cheeks were burning and their eyes had turned red. Each of them had other reasons besides alcohol. "Now what?" Hunter asked, balancing himself against the cab's door. "We're not gonna go home?!..."

Roscov's white scarf was fluttering like a symbol of surrender. It was past midnight.

"I live far upstate. I have to come in to work tomorrow.'

"Aaah! That's right. You have a job. What do you care about writers' insomnias!"

The cab driver motioned impatiently. Now Roscov was supposed to feel guilty for having a job, for not being an insomniac?!

"All right…but I'll see you tomorrow night at my place. 26 Green Street. The top buzzer."

Hunter fought his way into the cab, folding his coat. Roscov was left in the street, his arm lifted to hail the next cab and his chest laid waste by a pain never before experienced.

He found his wife awake and worried. He had never come home so late. He used to rush home as fast as he could, so he could start reading.

"I was afraid something happened to you. Are you all right? Where have you been all this time?"

"In a bar."

"A baaar?!" his wife yodeled indignantly. "You, in a bar?"

"With Alen Hunter."

"The writer?"

"You know him?"

"Who doesn't? He's in the newspapers all day long, he's on TV, in shop windows. Oh my God, you and Hunter?"

"What?! Me and Hunter."

"Where did you meet him? And how did you get to…?"

"Friends. We became friends. We have a lot of things in common. And then there are the grandmothers, both from Bukovina."

The look on his wife's face mixed distrust, irony, admiration, and jealousy.

"Oh yeah?"

"I'm seeing him again tomorrow night."

"Oh yeah?"

"What's with you?"

"Nothing, nothing. I was thinking that you started to have a personal life…. Can I come along?"

"I don't think so…. Not yet. And I think you'd get bored…we talk about all sorts of technical stuff, so to speak."

"Such as…?"

"Creating, writing, people, little people…," Roscov stammered.

"Oh, so you've become intimate," the wife took a stab at him. "Maybe you think I couldn't sustain this kind of conversation, since I don't have your extensive readings…."

"Ella, I'm tired. What if we continued this tomorrow? I have to get up at seven to be at work."

"You're still going to work after hobnobbing with Hunter?"

"Ok, ok, I get it that you're angry."

"I'm not angry, I'm bewildered."

"All right, you'll get used to the idea. I have to go to bed."

"Aren't you going to read?"

"Now? No way, I'm exhausted."

"Then let's go to sleep together."

"Now?!"

"I said go to sleep, I had no other intentions."

"Ok, let's go to bed – but you know I'll be snoring. I drank a lot and I'm beat."

"It's all right. You can snore. I'll use earplugs."

Roscov looked at her gratefully.

"Was it really Alen Hunter? Himself?"

"Stop it, Ella. It was him."

They fell asleep in each other's arms, with the alcohol vapors and Hunter's ghost floating above their bed.

* * *

The next night, eight o'clock sharp, Roscov pressed the top buzzer at 26 Green Street. He was holding a bottle of scotch. His long white scarf had been replaced by a burgundy one. He rang a couple of times with no response. He stood about five minutes in front of the building, ringing the buzzer a couple dozen times. It looked like Hunter had forgotten about him. He wasn't home.

Disappointed and even a bit humiliated, he walked away slowly, aimlessly. He walked into the first bar, ordered a scotch, and began to feel ridiculous. He regretted not having a book to read while sipping his drink watered down with ice.

Whenever he was tense, stressed out, or just tired, Roscov resorted to a relaxation method he had learned from an immigrant healer from

Kiev, the kind of transcendental therapist who was always in between paranormal aptitudes and convincing imposture. During a few friendly sessions, Igor, the healer, had taught him to stay in control in moments of crisis, to dig back into his memory and face the traumas of his past in order to free himself from emotions and obsessions, to concentrate on a particular point on a wall in front of him and imagine soothing colors. Above all, though, the healer had taught Roscov visualization.

Even if he was always afraid to relive shameful, painful, or humiliating memories, he was always fascinated by visualization. Once he had reached such an advanced stage that he was able to relive his childhood, with its smell of burnt milk, with its brighter colors, stronger tastes, and more terrifying heights, with the small accidents that appeared catastrophic, with its catastrophes passing him by without being understood, with its strange adults and devastating curiosity. Sometimes he was able to remember even things he had not experienced.

He could see vast milky fields through which his mother, herself a child, would run barefoot in a fluttering little dress, gathering flowers and singing in the thin voice of an angel ran aground on earth. He would calm down, his breath would become shallow and regular, and a sort of weightlessness would take hold of his muscles and joints. He would experience the floating sensation he suspected astronauts knew. He would close his eyes, let his arms hanging as if he were a discarded puppet, he would experience bright colors springing from his forehead like paint spilled from a bucket. This was a simple trick he could perform on the subway, at work, at the theatre, in the park.

Igor had taught him to enter a state of deep relaxation by imagining a sphere of light practically anywhere. Thus, Roscov, still in the bar where he was recovering from being stood up by Hunter, closed his eyes and tried to empty his mind of thoughts, just as Igor had taught him. This was the hardest part – emptying one's mind of thoughts. He could hear Hunter insisting: "Art is something optional. You either resort to it or not, you either need it or not, you either decide to dedicate your time to it or decide to do something else instead. In fact, art does not need an audience. It's an ethereal gesture, meant for an abstract eternity. Books don't even need to be read. But they do need to be written."

Then Hunter's words took a metallic undertone in Roscov's head: "You could be a very good writer. You are a skilled listener. That's the first sign – if you like listening to others, if you have the strength to listen to others. Then comes a stage when you begin to write in your head. You write tens, hundreds of pages in your mind. Putting that stuff down on paper is peanuts. I wrote my best pages all in my head. God only knows how few of them ended up being transcribed on paper!"

Roscov saw the sphere of light above his head and slowly lowered it on his forehead, then let it slide down his neck, caressing his thyroid, down his chest, feeling it slowly crawl along his stomach and then, very slowly, down to his toes. He then lifted it, just as slowly, all the way up to the top of his head. The sphere left behind it a trail of pleasant warmth. Roscov relaxed, he calmed down – until, having reached the top of his head, the sphere exploded, and a golden shower of shining light invaded his body, giving him so much energy that his body, now strong, fully recovered, was shaken by a powerful frisson.

He opened his eyes. The bartender was studying him, worried that he might be on drugs or about to have a heart attack. Roscov smiled back strategically, bottomed up his scotch, paid up, and left, his red scarf billowing in the air. He passed Hunter's house again, but did not give in to the impulse of ringing the intercom once again. When he reached home, the hand in which he had been clutching the scotch bottle was asleep. Ella was waiting in the hallway, among books, which had taken refuge from the overstuffed rooms.

"Well, how was it?"

Roscov averted his eyes.

"All right."

"All right? What's that? I was expecting superlatives. Tell me more."

Roscov's wife wet her lips, peeled her eyes wide open, leaned against the dining room door, ready to hang on her husband's every word.

"He wasn't home.... Maybe, I don't know, something came up...."

"He wasn't home? You mean, this whole story about Alen Hunter was made up? You flexed your imagination at my expense?" Ella shouted, grinning maliciously. She was hesitating between continuing to humiliate him or exercising some compassion. "You're either naive, or a liar, or a sucker. Or perhaps you're having an affair...."

"Stop it. I'm not having an affair. He just wasn't home. I rang the intercom like crazy. Maybe he forgot."

"Ha! I should have expected it. Nonsense, this whole thing about you being friends with Hunter! Just like that! All the confessions, the invitations to spend time at his place…. Nonsense! I've suffered though your reading mania, but I'm not going to take this! Are you very sure this whole thing is not about another woman?"

"I'm sure," Roscov mumbled. "I'm going to take a shower."

"Take two!"

Ella went back to the bedroom, slamming the door behind her.

That night Roscov went to bed earlier than usual. Once more, exhaustion overcame him, together with the dissatisfaction of his failure. Not a very consequential failure, mind you, but an irritating one, one that bothered his inflamed ego of betrayed reader.

He chose a book, opened it, and tried to lose himself in it. He tried to return to certitudes, to that part of his life that he could control, to that part of his life where no one was going to slam a door in his face. But his eyes began to sting after only a few pages. A tear rolled down his cheek. It must be exhaustion, he thought. He turned off the light and squeezed his eyelids tight together until those tiny points of light he knew so well from his childhood reappeared.

What if there was something wrong with his eyes? What if he was about to go blind? The very idea of darkness, and especially the thought that he might have to give up reading, terrified him. They were going to take his books away from him. An endless night would take hold of his soul and mind.

He could see himself useless and powerless, with all those words boiling over in his chest, with all his potential destinies unfulfilled. He remembered that once in a museum he had seen a gallery for the blind. There was this large room where copies of famous Roman and Greek sculptures were placed so that the blind could touch them and imagine what art looked like. He had found himself there by mistake, while looking for the Impressionist rooms on various floors, lost in the gigantic maze of the museum.

Only two men with dark glasses were in the gallery. They had let their white canes fall down to the floor. They both happened to have on white raincoats, which were fluttering on their frail bodies. They were feeling the cold marble, embracing the statues, caressing their ample shapes in silence. The scene looked like a pantomime, like a ballet without music, beautiful and sad.

Roscov relived the scene with some envy. At least the blind could feel the art – he, on the other hand, might never be able to read. He turned the light on, startled. He looked around. The objects were each in their place, but he continued to feel his eyes stinging. It had to be something temporary and unimportant, Roscov consoled himself, trying to escape his paranoid fantasy about losing his sight. He opened his book again and went back to reading.

The truth was, he wasn't happy with anything anymore. His readings were slowly becoming a burden and seemed to be less and less interesting, he was anxious and dissatisfied for no apparent reason. He would survey his books without feeling a strong impulse to pick up any of them. Had he gone too far with his readings, was saturation setting in, or what? He had exiled Hunter from his thoughts. He was no longer thinking about his Jesus dream or about the little people ready to take over the world. Nothing in his life had changed; there was no apparent reason for this feeling of discomfort. Still, he couldn't sit still. Something was amiss, something was torturing him every second of his life.

Had things stopped here, everything would have stayed within the limits of normality. But Andrei Roscov was about to cross into a dangerous and uncontrollable world.

# The Second Life

## II

## *The Writer*

It began one morning. As usual, he had woken up very early. He was sipping his coffee. A book, still closed, lay beside him. He was trying to slowly come to at an hour when most people were still lost in their sweetest dreams. The anxiety he had been feeling of late took hold of him once more. A strange and powerful feeling he had not experienced before took possession of him. It was almost like a panic attack. It seemed that an imperious, abusive, undefined, confused, but dictatorial voice was barking orders in his brain. He began to perspire. His head started to ache, and a shiver went down his spine, all the way to his slippers. He felt as if he was being pushed by something he couldn't identify. Nothing was clear, but everything appeared definitive. He could neither understand nor oppose whatever was happening to him.

He took the book, opened it, and tried to read. But, far from fading away, his anxiety amplified. He could not concentrate. Words became garbled and began to eat each other. He began to be truly frightened. What if he couldn't read anymore? Anxiety was clutching at Roscov's soul like a claw. His fingers were shaking, holding the book. The text of the book became an amorphous mass of letters. He closed the book and stared at the wall in front of him. He was feeling alone and endangered, powerless and vulnerable.

He held out his hand and picked up another book. He opened it frenetically and tried to read once more. Same effect. None of the pleasure he experienced before. Just towering anxiety. The chaos of words. Something was happening to him, his brain and his soul were changing. Something was being born inside Andrei Roscov. Reading didn't help anymore, it had lost its powers and its meaning. Or maybe it was no longer enough for him. All of a sudden, he understood. It came as a revelation, as a necessity, as a resolution, or a challenge. He should try to write something.... He had to write. He had been born for this. He had to start that very moment.

He remembered that Hunter once told him that the hardest thing for a reader was not to take up writing. But he didn't have the choice to resist the impulse. His biological and spiritual being needed the conversion of writing, the conversion from reader to writer. His destiny was claiming his rights. All Roscov had to do, scared and defeated, was to put himself in the hands of that choice, made for him from the outside, dominating and despotic, impossible to resist. It had become absolutely clear to him that he could no longer go on living otherwise.

Several forgotten pens lay on the table. There was no paper, aside from a few envelopes with bills and some supermarket receipts. He didn't have time to procrastinate, he couldn't afford to. So he started to write on the back on the receipts. His handwriting was nervous, fast, illegible – but so coherent and beautiful! It was at that moment that Andrei Roscov's life was turned upside down. We can even talk about a new Roscov and a new life from that moment on.

His first rebellion was the one against the day, which insisted on being 24 hours. A disgraceful thing from the perspective of a writer who still has social and professional obligations.

His job had become a chore, an absurd obligation that had no apparent motivation. Money? The safety of retirement? What good are all these when so much of the time Roscov could have used writing was spent in a fiber-optics plant, checking orders and drawing up contracts – occupations so devoid of any poetry and so inimical to the writing of prose. Roscov thus began to neglect his duties at the plant. He was distracted, inattentive, wishing that he could be left alone in his office to pull out his notebook from the drawer and write. O, writing, what a blessing!

This did not go unnoticed among his colleagues, and especially among his superiors, whose numbers were quite significant in such a prosperous institution. As he was to later find out, memos were piling up in his personnel file; this colleague or another would complain that Roscov failed to exhibit an interest in the efficient functioning of the plant and that he only sought to be left alone to write god-knows-what.

He was discovered writing during weekly staff meetings, and when he was asked to present his quarterly report he behaved like a stranger accidentally thrust in the middle of a board meeting, like a visitor lost among production halls and offices at the plant. Everyone noticed his detached, disinterested, and defiant attitude.

He had been seen writing in the restroom, during the lunch break, in the reception area, even in the office of one of the managers while the manager was on the phone trying to solve some vital problem. Roscov had taken out his notebook and started to write, forgetting where he was or why he was there.

Some launched the idea that he was a spy, others were saying that he had lost his mind. Most didn't know what to believe. They just pitied him, reminiscing of the days when Roscov was among the most efficient employees of the fiber-optics division. He was eventually fired. He didn't ask for an explanation, and he wasn't given any.

The loss of his job, which in the old days would have been a tragedy for him, came as a liberation. He sighed with relief, collected his personal things in two cardboard boxes, and left merrily under the astounded eyes of his colleagues. The loss of his income or retirement benefits failed to bring any trace of worry or sadness in Roscov's eyes, which could concentrate only on what he had to write. Hunter's words were true: the writer first writes all the pages in his head.

As a compensation, or a sign that he had made the right choice, Ella became very important in his life. She was the one who broke the news to the children and prepared the rest of the family for the big surprise: "Daddy is writing. Andrei has become a real writer. We must understand and protect him."

He was reading everything to her. In the beginning, she had been distrustful, but quite curious. She had thought this was just a phase in the development of any inveterate reader. But Roscov proved to be intent on being a serious writer. He had dedicated himself completely to the calling of being a writer.

He had brought tens of pens, colored markers, thin pencils he used to proofread his texts, whiteout, magic markers for those parts he still needed to tinker with, notebooks, notepads, plain letter paper, lined paper, colored paper, special memo pads in which he would just down ideas on a daily basis, thin long diaries, a desktop computer, some good word processing software, a printer, floppy disks, and finally a laptop he never parted with, a laptop he could always open on his knees, no matter where he was. He was in possession of an entire writing arsenal, switching between longhand and typing on the computer with the ease on one born for the technical empire of writing. Naturally, he was writing everything under the sun.

Ella began to like his sad, sophisticated poems, his robust, compact prose, his intelligent essays, and she came to be a conscientious and critical reader of her husband's works. Her reactions and opinions mattered to Roscov.

"You really have a talent!" she told him, and that was one of the happiest days of Roscov's life.

Ella was an educated woman, she had read and seen a lot. If she liked what he was writing, that meant that he could show the hundreds of pages he had written to anyone, without fear of embarrassment. Hunter had told him that embarrassment is what people should fear most. Still, he felt that the time to go out in the world had not come yet. He first had to have a real work and be convinced of its viability.

Ella protected him:

"Father's writing, he can't be disturbed now."

"Call later, he's working, he can't come to the phone now."

"Could you please lower your voice? Andrei is writing in the office."

"I'm afraid we can't come. Thanks for the invitation, but Andrei is in the middle of a chapter, we can't go out anywhere until he's done with this part."

"I'm sorry, we can't afford it. Money's a bit tight now that Andrei quit his job and became a full-time writer. It's a costly job. Naturally, now his work comes first for us, and he happens to be an exceptional writer. As it is, he's no longer interested in galas or any other events, except for the literary ones. I wish you good luck with your foundation, you're doing extremely important work, and we're really thinking of leukemia patients. Thank you very much, once again, for thinking of us."

"I think we're going to cancel the reservation. My husband is caught in this literary project and he doesn't want to travel…. No, no, a real vacation for him would be to spend uninterrupted time in front of the computer. Can we get a refund? I would really appreciate it, we're going though some tough times, financially speaking. You can imagine how hard it is to be a writer these days…."

All of sudden, he found himself lucky. He had an enlightened, tolerant wife who understood this need to write which had changed his life so radically. Beautiful people were everywhere. He did not regret anything, he did not wish for a different outcome. He was one of the few people on earth who were happy with what they had and who they were. He was looking upon his well-rounded life with satisfaction. God had given him a custom-made destiny. The Jesus dream had taken on a new meaning.

The glowing pen springing words, the pen that pierced Roscov's chest was now somewhere on his desk, among scattered manuscripts. The gifted little people had invaded even the most remote recesses of the room where Andrei was tirelessly typing on his computer.

He was writing day and night, as much as he could, until he fell down exhausted. His hands would hurt from all the writing. He had developed "writer's cramp," a dull ache in his right hand tendons that was so familiar to people in his profession. His eyesight was getting weak, as well. In just a few months, he had to change several eyeglass prescriptions. He was putting on weight. He was spending all his time at his writing desk. He was writing practically all the time, wherever he could, either by hand or by typing on the computer.

"Sometimes he worries me," Ella would confess to the children or to a close friend. "He sometimes writes as long as fifteen or sixteen hours a day. He's changed a lot, he seeks only quiet and solitude. He forgets to eat, sometimes he even falls asleep in his clothes before he can get undressed."

"I have to make up for lost time," Roscov would defend himself. "I began to write very late, and I have so much to say!"

"Have you published anything yet?" a more suspicious relative would ask.

"Nooooo...he hasn't even tried to. He writes simply for his own enjoyment," Ella would excuse him, herself suspicious of Andrei's disinterest in publishing and writing for an audience.

"And has anyone read these books of his?"

"I have. I read them. And I can assure you they are very good. He's got some talent. He's quite perceptive. He has ideas. He can structure all kinds of works."

But no one credited him all the way. What was he writing all that time? And why wasn't he publishing anything, so that people could see for themselves what he was working on?

One day Roscov rushed into the kitchen, where Ella was preparing his favorite potato salad. He looked devastated, his face disfigured with pain and his eyes bulging out of their sockets. He wanted to cry out, but all he could manage was a rather inhuman squeal: "I'm done for! I'm done for!"

He fell in the first chair he saw, crushing some lettuce leaves.

"God, what's with you?" Ella jumped up, dropping her chef's knife.

"I'm ruined. I've lost everything. Everything."

"What are you saying? It can't be that bad…."

"It's horrible! Everything I wrote on the computer during these last few days is gone! I don't know…what happened. I saved it – believe me, I'm sure I saved everything!"

A tear rolled to his chin. Ella let a sigh of relief.

"You can retrace your steps. You wrote that stuff yourself the first time around, didn't you? You can redo all that."

"You don't understand," Roscov's voice was trembling. "That stuff can't be done again. It's impossible, I'll never be able to be that good again. That was genius work, I don't know how I did it. I wrote it all straight into the computer, you see? Many pages, you understand?"

"How many?"

"About forty or fifty. I didn't keep any other record, I don't have a manuscript, and I didn't even make notes before I wrote any of that stuff. I hate modern technology, I really do. Computers! Nonsense! One should write only by hand, one should feel the sheet of paper!"

"Come on, calm down, you can write everything again. And, who knows, it might come out even better than before!"

Ella rose to her feet and resumed her work on the salad. Roscov was following her with his eyes, amazed at how insensitive she was.

"You don't understand anything, and you don't care."

Ella tried a potato with her fork. It was done.

"Fuck that stuff, I'm talking about a serious drama here, and all you care is mashing potatoes…."

"Drama? You say drama? Let me tell what the real tragedy is here," Ella burst out, in a tone she had not used since their youth. "We're almost broke."

"What are you talking about?"

"Broke, you heard me. I had to cancel everything, I sold everything I could, I sold the summerhouse in the Poconos, I canceled our last two credit cards, our vacation plans, and I cut down on everything I could. But we can't go on like this. My salary is not enough. We've got the mortgage, the car payments, all these expenses…."

"What expenses? I barely spend anything."

"But you're not bringing in anything either."

"You mean I'm a kept man, I'm a parasite? Who made all the money here, if not me? I wasted my years like an idiot in a stupid fiber-optics plant!" Roscov was babbling, congested with anger.

"But you left there a while ago, and all you did since then is waste everything you earned."

"Waste? Me, waste?"

"The thousands of books? Rare editions, old volumes, then computers, stationery, outings to tens of readings, expensive clothes – 'cause, well, you need to respect your position! And all this time, our income decreased, the stock market tanked…."

"It did?"

"See, you live in an alternative universe! The market is a mess. We lost everything, I sold the last stock we had a few weeks ago. Obviously, I sold it low. But are you interested in the stock market, in our finances? Noooo, you're an artist, a writer. Art comes before anything else. I kept thinking that I shouldn't tell you, that I should protect you. Not that you would have lifted a finger. You're lost in your little world. When you came into the kitchen just now and told me you lost everything, I thought for one second that maybe you had found out, that maybe you were curious enough to go to the bank or call the accountant and check our finances. But no way – you were all worked up about losing the pages you had written, not our money. What can I say, we're in deep shit and this time I have no idea how we're going to get out. I give up. This is too much for me."

Roscov listened to her attentively. He asked no questions, he had nothing to add, nothing to object to. Finally, he slowly rose from his chair, shuffled to his room, and closed the door behind him.

He reemerged shortly afterwards with two suitcases and the burgundy scarf over the jacket he had worn the night he had met Hunter. A potato salad bowl garnished with lettuce was now on the kitchen table. Ella had probably gone out shopping: the car keys were missing. He put down the suitcases, sat down at the table, took a few forkfuls of his favorite salad, then covered up the dent he had made in the salad. He was calm and content. He took a notepad out of his pocket, tore out a sheet of paper, and left Ella a beautifully written note. He pulled the door behind him, checking whether it was locked, just as he had done every other time when he left the house.

He took a deep breath. He felt the same way he did when, years before, he had left his little hometown for America. It felt like jumping into empty space. He was not afraid. He did not fear loneliness or poverty. The garage door lay open. He no longer had a car. Ella had thought it wiser to limit their spending by giving up his car, which he hadn't been using anyway, since he was spending all his time writing at this desk.

A cab was honking in the street outside their house. He slowly went down the steps. He didn't look back. He had no regrets, no nostalgia. He was only following his destiny. He was liberating himself. So that he could later liberate others. It felt like only now was he heading for the real America.

The driver helped him put his suitcases in the trunk. Roscov gave him the address of a hotel where he and his wife had spend some time right after arriving in the States years before. He was almost elated at the idea of living in a residential hotel in the Village. He wasn't considering any consequences. Most of all, he was elated at the idea of his new book. During the forty-minute ride to the hotel, he managed to write a few fabulous pages in his mind.

Yes, things were finally ripening. He knew how his future book would look. He knew it would be his swan song. The book of life and death. His great book, the one he had been preparing for all these years. Suddenly, everything he had written until that moment began to look like feeble attempt, like preliminary material. He was just warming up. Now he would be able to show what he was capable of. It would be like coming close to God. The thought frightened him. Didn't Hunter tell him, didn't all his readings warn him that creating only lifts us closer to the gods – a dangerous, uncontrollable path which sometimes ended up in insanity? The closer you get, the more uncertain and fearful you are, the less capable of commonsense you are; the universe can turn upside down in order to ease your way into unknown mysteries and hidden meanings, and your obedience to fate can turn to rebellion. God may remain elusive, he may recede further and further away from you while you keep quarreling with him and holding him accountable for you losing your way....

He managed to find a decent room with windows looking into an interior courtyard. The view was nothing to write home about, but the price was reasonable, and he charged his rent in advance to the one credit card he was left with after Ella's best efforts to restructure their finances.

He dropped his suitcases to the floor and laid his sheets of paper, notebooks, ballpoint pens, fountain pens and indispensable laptop on the table. He set out to write and worked for three hours uninterrupted. By the time he went out to get a sandwich from the corner coffee shop, the sun had gone down. He went to the same place where he had stopped for a drink after hopelessly trying Hunter's buzzer. He felt free and peaceful. Writing was good for him. It reinvigorated his muscles and excited his neurons. He was in good shape, he felt younger by ten years, more alive than ever.

He ate his sandwich in the buzz of the coffee shop, invaded by an all-encompassing sympathy for everyone and everything there. He could still see beautiful people everywhere. He experienced a diffuse love for the crowd of bodies, smells, noises, and gestures. It is from love that never-ending youth springs. When he was a child, he had managed to prolong the life of his terminally ill grandmother by telling her every day: "I love you, and please don't die today." His grandmother lived another three years on his love.

He went back to his room, which appeared a bit more austere in the evening, and continued the book of life and death. He was pleased, even amazed at the ease with which he was making progress, at the fluency of his language and the vigor of his storytelling. He was writing in the first person, which made everything come through more powerfully. He was convinced that each book should be testament for posterity. Roscov was writing motivated by the responsibility and duty to leave a trace behind him, to try to understand and untangle something of all this madness, to justify his birth and passage through this life, his choices and terrors, his waywardness or cowardice, his constant elation and amazement at the idea of having found himself elected, anointed, then thrown back into the ocean and made to fend for himself and discover his own survival skills and his own way of winning. He had come to all this by making efforts and sacrifices which he then wisely converted into passion and enthusiasm.

The first two weeks went by uneventfully. He was writing all day long, taking short breaks to get a sandwich from the corner coffee shop, where he had by now become a regular. He ordered the same thing every time: a sandwich, a vodka shot, and a beer chaser, which he ingested while eavesdropping on the conversations around him, studying types in the shop, and jotting down occasional notes for further development in his book.

He felt as if he had always lived alone. He had forgotten all about Ella, his children, or his spacious home upstate. He missed nothing. He already had over two hundred pages written of the book of life and death. He was making solid progress, his head abuzz with ideas. Everything he had read the years before, everything he accumulated was turning into psychological analysis, philosophical meditations, and strong characters drawn with vigor in the attempt to conquer time. He was writing everything in longhand, then transcribing his work into the computer, so as not to risk losing anything ever again. He kept his manuscripts under the mattress in his hotel room and carried the floppy disks with the saved texts in his breast pocket, with his identity card and the credit card, which was running on empty by this time.

He selected three chapters he thought representative, printed them in ten copies and sent them to the most important literary magazines and reviews in the New York area and the East Coast. It was his first run on the market. He began checking his mailbox at the hotel several times a day, looking for letters from editors and publishers. He subscribed to a whole lot of arts and letters publications, he had bought catalogs for literary agents and publishing houses, he began to manage his writing feverishly, waiting impatiently for the time when he would be published and known. He started again to go to readings, bookstores, coffeehouses in the Village, churches around town – but this time he was more self-assured, more patronizing in his posture as a writer, albeit unknown.

He was dressing up nicely, alternating the scarves he had thrown in his two suitcases among the bare necessities he managed to pack out of his four large clothes closets at home. He could still remember the time when he was a mere reader and was avoiding going out, obsessively saving all his time for reading. But now he needed life, accidents, gestures, reactions, facial expressions, words and idioms. He needed the living tableau of the streets, and the Village was the perfect place for satisfying that need. He sought the buzz of crowded bars and restaurants, paying close attention to stories told by unknown people. He was a good observer. He was still a good listener.

One night, when he was drinking his usual beer in his corner hangout, he found himself observed by one of the characters in his book, a woman with a controversial destiny, a whore who was supposed to become depressed and become a nun in order to escape her demons. He couldn't decide whether she would commit suicide, go finally insane, or go back to the streets.

He had discovered that he was not very adept at feminine psychology, so he took to frequenting bars of ill repute, trying to strike up conversations and steal as much as possible from the vocabulary, reactions, or laments of the kind of women who would hang out there. He found them much more complicated than he was willing to admit. Some of them had constructed solid justifications for their lives – usually having to do with survival, providing for a child or a sick mother, but sometimes dealing simply with the comfort of making their own money. Most of them tried to appear at ease when picking up tricks, though none of them actually enjoyed what they were doing. They had not become whores out of passion, but out of necessity or circumstance.

Roscov had learned a lot from books, from his personal experience, from his careful observation of the world around him. But he realized Hunter had been right when he advocated a writer's involvement in the facts of life:

"The writer is a historian, a sociologist, a politician; he must be all of this, as well as philosopher and a psychologist, especially in closed societies, in dictatorships where communication is monitored, where certain kinds of knowledge are prohibited, and the truth hides under successively censored layers of meaning. You should know about this better, you come from the Eastern Bloc, where great writing occurs only between the lines, behind bars, or in exile. There are books for which a writer must abandon his desk and begin documenting, researching, going down in the mines, on the construction sites, in the stacks of libraries, to the brothel, to the monastery, at the royal court, or next to a beggar's dirty shoes. Not everything can be written out of your own imagination or out of books. Our experience is limited and is filtered by our particular education and lifestyle. A writer needs to be authentic, he is constantly confronted with the personal truth of his readers – which, well, is impossible to predict. The only chance the writer has under these circumstances is to escape into fantasy and dream-like perspective, which can hide our flaws as writers. That's talent, indeed. We are asked to be historians and we insist on acting as directors. But we have to have genius in order to pull this off, to leave the impression that we know everything but we only say what is appropriate for a literary discourse. You understand?

There's a permanent life and death struggle between the writer and the reader."

The book of life and death had a complicated structure, complex situations, and countless characters which synthesized in their existence and relationships the entire burden of human trauma. It was a book based on myth brought into the present. It went through the stories of the Bible, the great Greek tragedies, and then the search for God through suffering, rebellion, and vanity. Roscov was pouring everything he knew and everything he didn't know into it. Day after day, he felt lighter, as if he was emptying himself of words on those sheets of paper. Sometimes he would be overcome with fear. Maybe he was giving too much, maybe he was giving himself up for good. In fact, his terror was the completion of his book itself, the moment he would write "the end" at the bottom of the page, and when it will become clear that there was nothing left of him.

He ordered another beer, touched by the image of him giving himself up so completely, to the last drop. He barely noticed the hand resting on his shoulder.

"And how are you?" He heard the woman's languorous voice in his ear, almost touching his lobe, making him shudder.

He withdrew, giving her a bothered look.

"I'm drinking."

"I see you around. Do you live in the area?"

"Yeah, somewhere around here."

"Will you buy me a drink?"

The woman was drawing out her vowels deliberately. Her sensuous hissing was annoying Roscov.

"You already have one."

"I want another one, from you," the woman giggled.

Roscov shrugged and asked the bartender for a beer. He pushed the glass in front of the woman and turned around, trying to signal that he wanted to be left alone, now that he had satisfied her request.

"I live in the neighborhood too. Right there!"

She pointed out to a small attic window. Roscov looked up to the window, nodded, emptied his drink, left some money on the counter, and tried to leave.

"What, you're leaving!" the woman called in a languid voice. "I want to have a drink with you. You're very nice, you know. I like your hands."

"My hands?" Roscov wondered, instinctively looking down at his palms.

"You have beautiful hands," she whispered into his ear. This time Roscov felt a shiver going down his spine.

"Thank you. I haven't thought about it."

"Are you sure?"

He hesitated. He took a second look at her. She was young and good looking.

"What are you doing?"

"I'm a writer."

"A writer? How exciting! And what do you write?"

"All sorts of stuff."

"Poems too?"

"Poems too."

"I love poems. I…knew another writer. Only he wasn't writing poetry. Just novels. Very long ones. I don't have any patience for that stuff. It's very boring. And difficult. I would never have time to read through one of those bricks."

The woman smiled mysteriously.

"I'm very busy, you know. That other writer gave me one of his books. Signed and all. I can't tell you his name, that's a professional courtesy, but he's famous, he's everywhere, I even see him on TV. But he's just as boring as his books. He talks nonstop, all sorts of nonsense. Now he says one thing, now he contrasts – oh, contradicts himself, I don't know which it is. He lives around here, too. He sometimes hangs out here. I can introduce you to him, if you want."

"I gotta go," Roscov decided.

"Oh no! You can't leave now! Can you tell me a poem?"

"I don't know any by heart."

"Then will you give me a book?"

"I haven't published anything yet."

"You haven't published anything?" The woman was sincerely surprised. "How can you be a writer if you haven't published anything?"

Roscov was irritated. He began justifying himself. "I haven't published yet. Some fragments of my book should come out soon. I've been writing a novel for the past few months."

"You too? How terrible. What about poetry?"

"What about it?"

"You don't write poetry? I want you to write poetry. I'm crazy about poetry."

"Listen, I really have to go. I've got work to do."

"Do you live alone?"

"Yes...."

"I'll come with you!"

The woman grabbed her handbag, jumped off her stool, fixed her hair, and waited for him to motion.

"I live in the hotel on the corner...."

"Perfect. Let's go."

"But I don't have any money or...."

"It's all right," the woman assured him. "I appreciate writers. I do it for free. I get more educated," she giggled merrily. She took hold of his arm and pulled him towards the exit.

Pages from the book of life and death were lying scattered all over the room. He had left the window open by mistake, and the wind had blown sheets of paper on the bed, on the floor, on the butter left on the table. It looked like the house had been ransacked, and Roscov rushed about the room shouting in despair.

"God, I've been robbed! They ruined me! They stole my book, I'm finished!"

The woman was quicker to realize what had actually happened and started to laugh. She tried to calm him down: "Better close that window. No one stole anything from you. It's just the wind." She placed her hand on his shoulder and tried to hold her body against his. Roscov pushed her so violently that she lost her balance and fell on the bed.

"Leave me the hell alone. Can't you understand? I'm finished. They robbed me."

He was unusually brutal. He was perspiring profusely, his face was congested, his hands were shaking, and his head was pounding. He was feverishly gathering the scattered pages, checking page numbers obsessively. His eyes were bulging out in terror. The woman watched him in bewilderment.

"Are you nuts? You're really insane. Who the fuck would want to steal your stupid stuff?"

"Shut up and get out of here," Roscov yelled, losing his cool.

He had managed to gather and order all his papers, and was slowly coming to, now that he knew nothing was missing. The woman had been right. It was the wind and the mistake of leaving the window open.

He was breathing more calmly now. He crumbled in an armchair. The woman was still watching him, scared but disdainful.

"What's the big deal with that stuff? Is it worth giving yourself a stroke?"

Roscov did not bother to answer her. All that mattered was that his book was intact.

"These writers are really out of their minds!" The woman was now soliloquizing. "That's why you end up in hotels and no one wants to be with you guys. Who has the nerves for all this paranoia?"

"Once I lost forty pages," Roscov confessed to the woman. He didn't know why.

"That's because you're stupid. Who could possibly be interested in that stuff?"

"I thought you said you liked writers."

"I said I liked poems." She took off her t-shirt, on which a snake with a forked tongue and an apple was printed cheaply.

"What are you doing? Are you hot?" Roscov was surprised.

"Stop playing the idiot with me. I promised you a free one, now I have to make good. How do you want it?"

"Want what?"

"Are you really an idiot or are you just pretending to be one?"

"Let me catch my breath.... Tell me a story. Something about yourself, your life...."

"I told you I was going to do it for free, not that I would tell you the story of my life. Come on, I don't have any time to waste. I've wasted enough on you. I'm not the charitable type. I don't give to charity. That's what I need now – for my john to catch me with a broke writer... Will you read me a poem?"

With a swift move, the woman took off her skirt, then threw her shoes across the room, and struck the pose of a model in a painting class. She was ready to listen.

"I told you I don't have any poems. I'm writing something completely different right now. The book of life and death."

"Well, well!"

Roscov began to preach.

"It's like a literary testament, a fundamental, capital work, a message in a bottle floating on the ocean. It's going to be a book that will shake the world."

"Forget about this nonsense! I heard it all before. You haven't even published anything yet."

Roscov grew irritated again.

"You're tragically stupid. Can't you understand that one of the most important publishing houses is going to pick me up? They'll print millions of copies. I'll be famous. And soon, fragments of my novel will be published in tens of magazines and reviews. I didn't want to go out on the market until now. I waited to do something grand and definitive. And I did. I'm a good writer. I write all the time. I don't care about anything else. I don't even need to eat, if that's what I must do to finish. I can't sleep anyway. It's fascinating, exciting, and difficult. I write all the time, and I write terrific stuff, can you understand that? You could help a little too," Roscov had changed his tone. He sat down on the edge of the bed.

"Me? You're certifiably insane."

"Tell me about you. I want to know how you live, what you're thinking about, what you think about this life of yours…."

"This life of yours!" she mocked him. "Like you have such a great life! What are you trying to say? Well, my life is normal and legitimate. I work and make money. I pay my taxes. You'd better pay more attention to *your* life," the woman admonished him. "You're the lost one. I have nothing to feel guilty about, I don't lose any sleep."

"Tell me more, I want to listen to you. I'm a very good listener. Please."

The woman withdrew to the head of the bed, casting frightened glances at him.

"Good lord, I stumbled upon a pervert!"

Roscov wanted to calm her down. He gently drew himself closer to her, but the woman shot upright, naked, and landed in the middle of the room, covering her breasts with her hands.

"Don't come close to me. I know your type. You're gonna turn violent on me any second now!"

Roscov felt humiliated. He raised his voice.

"Who do you think I am? I only want to know more about you. I want to know what you think about life, about your relationship with

God. Do you believe in God? Do you talk to him? Are you ever afraid? Are you afraid of him?"

"Look, I came here for free, but I'm not going to confess to you," the woman said, gathering up a bit more courage. "If that's what you want me to do, you'll have to pay me."

"I have no money. All I'm interested in is your own words, your stories...." Roscov was almost yelling, having lost all control. "I don't want you, I want your life story. For the book, understand? For the book of life and death!"

"You dirty pervert!" the woman cried, frantically dressing herself while keeping an eye on him. "Impotent! Why don't you jerk off with that book of yours! Paranoid! Let your mamma tell you stories!"

She slammed the door behind her, leaving Roscov, head resting on his palms, staring at the nicely ordered manuscript on his desk.

He knew he should have felt ashamed or humiliated, but he only felt relieved by the woman's departure. He went back to writing right away, happy to be alone again. He wrote for a few hours, without a break. He had become a writing machine, a perfectly functioning writing machine – just like he had been a perfectly functioning reading machine before.

In the evening, on his way out to the corner coffee shop, he checked his mailbox to see whether there was any response from the literary magazines and reviews he had bombarded with fragments of his book, now over four hundred pages long. Nothing. But the manager of hotel took advantage of the circumstance and politely reminded him that he hadn't paid his rent in ten days, that his credit card had expired, and that the payment couldn't wait any longer. The first Hanukkah candle was flickering in a menorah on the reception desk. He walked into the street, feeling tired and disoriented. Only now did he notice that the streets were decorated with Christmas trees, red bows, and colorful lights.

He was never one for the holidays. When the children were small, they used to celebrate Hanukkah and decorate a Christmas tree, just so that they would have a framework for the main ritual – the presents. Ella used to bake apple pie, the children used to make a lot of noise, loads of guests used to come for dinner and fulfill their duty to have a good time.

While so many could hardly wait for the holidays, Roscov could hardly wait for them to be over. The ubiquitous plaintive Christmas carols, the bells rung by security guards dressed up as Santa, the ridiculous shop windows filled with mechanical toys, the hysteria of the shopping countdown, the lunatics carrying packages, shopping bags, and gift boxes trimmed with candles and little angels, the boots swooshing in the melting snow, the insane traffic blocking the streets, the highways, and the airports, the stress of holiday sales or of preparing to take off for sunny Florida or the Caribbean, or for some ski area in the mountains – all of this irritated him. For a while, everything was topsy-turvy, and what one was left with in the end was only exhaustion, crumpled gift wrapping, empty boxes, dirty dishes, dry pine needles stuck in the carpet, weather delays, inappropriate gifts to be exchanged at the end of irritatingly long lines, a post-holiday slump, a feeling of disappointment with what could have been a better holiday.

He never cared about the holidays, so now that he was all alone, he had no reason to feel more unhappy than he felt all those years he had to spend his holidays with the family. The year before, he had spent the whole Christmas reading. He was still a reading machine at the time. True, people were bustling around him – Ella, the children, a few friends, a few neighbors. He was an active participant only in the Christmas dinner. For the rest of the festivities, they had decided to leave him alone.

The suicide rate goes up around the holidays. The lonely ones get depressed, mental disorders become aggravated, unhappiness turns to despair, despair becomes paralyzing – and people in that state don't care about much. Illicit girlfriends begin to envy the wives, who suddenly become divas who have the power to unite the family around them; wives, on the other hand, suffer at the thought of the presents that their husbands must be giving their girlfriends. Children can hardly bear the thought of spending time with their families, rather than partying with their friends. Spinsters mourn their childless lives. Patients in hospitals turn to God, and nursing homes decorate the daily boards with little garlands: "It's Thursday." The year is 2000. It's snowing. Happy Hanukkah and Merry Christmas." The happiest are the beggars, who finally receive decent dinners and donations from those who want to save their souls through charity.

Roscov thought of the woman. He had scared her. The saddest thing, though, was that he didn't seem to care about anything other than writing. Not only had he lost touch with the world, he had lost any desire or pleasure. All he had left was his overwhelming need to write. His wife, his children, his professional life, his home, the quiet life of years past – everything was just a beautiful memory. All he was concerned with these days was the life of his characters. He had no needs aside from writing. He didn't even need sex. He ate rarely, mostly because he had no money. The closer he got to finishing the book, the less he slept. The Roscov writing machine was functioning impeccably.

He stopped at a bank and tried, unsuccessfully, to withdraw some cash. For the past few days, he had been waiting for a miracle, so that he would be able to get at least some loose change. But miracles appeared to have abandoned Roscov. He was already running a tab at the coffee shop. He lifted the collar of his coat up. He was hungry. He felt weak. There was no point in walking the streets. He passed by the coffee shop, but did not have the courage to go inside. He returned to his hotel room and started to write. His entrails were howling with hunger, but he continued to write, pressing one hand against his stomach.

Once he tapped his inspiration and found ideas flowing over, on top of each other, he found himself unable to keep up with them and write everything down in his notepad. He was impatient to transcribe everything on paper, and regretted not being able to write with both hands, like a pianist. Had he been able to write with both hands, he would have been so much more efficient, he would have made so much more progress. He hung a tape recorder he had bought around his neck and began speaking into it precipitously, afraid that he would forget something. At night, he would transcribe what he had recorded during the day.

He had never worked so hard. As Hunter had told him, prose is hard labor. It wrings every ounce of energy out of the writer. One has to sit in a chair long hours and concentrate, trying to pierce through bizarre lives, to live and die through surprising characters, to experience various historical periods, civilizations, and social conflicts, to feel the whole range of sentiments and states. It is as if one lives several lives at once. If just one life – the one the writer is supposed to live – is so exhausting, can the reader even imagine the hell the writer goes through only to construct a viable illusion of verisimilitude and serve it, with garnish, for public consumption? Can the reader imagine everything that lies behind words – all the torment, the effort, the waste, the soul, the blood, the sweat, and the nervous energy behind them? The reader may buy a book nor not, he may like it or not, he may read for a while, abandon it, and then pick it up again or not – all without the slightest idea of the work that went into every single syllable. Roscov, on the other hand, had been a perfect, ideal, utopian reader, just as he was now a prefect, total, completely dedicated writer.

He was now writing driven by hunger, like a machine that can no longer be turned off. He fell asleep towards morning, fully dressed, at his writing table, with his head against the book of life and death. He dreamed that he was famous, that he was in a vast bookshop filled to the brim with his own books. He was sitting at a table signing autographs. Before him there was a long line of readers with thrilled, admiring, and respectful looks in their eyes. He raised his eyes and asked the name of the man at the head of the line.

"Alen Hunter."

"Hunter?" Roscov wondered. "I know the name. We've met before, right?"

"Yes, I'm also a writer. I published some stuff, too. Of course, you may not remember me. These days I am less known than I used to be, though I had my heyday," Hunter smiled ironically.

"Of course, of course.... I remember you very well. If you have some time, I'd like to sit down and talk to you after all this is over. There's a coffee shop I usually go to right around the corner. We can get a drink."

People on line began to motion impatiently. Hunter took the book signed by Roscov and slowly faded away, gently caressing the cover of the book of life and death with thin long fingers and nostalgia-filled eyes. Roscov's chest was spurting shining words straight onto paper. He woke up, his chest almost frozen against the cold writing desk.

He would write everything in longhand and then enter his notes in the computer. Each night, he would check the integrity of the printed manuscript under the mattress and then he would reach for the floppy disks in his breast pocket. Once reassured, he went back to writing. It wasn't long, he could feel the end drawing near, and the thought of finishing the book of life and death increasingly terrified him.

Unshaven and dizzy with hunger and exhaustion, he went down to the lobby of the hotel to check for any responses from editors. Maybe the post office was slow during the holidays. The editors might be on vacation, too. He found a stack of magazines and reviews in his mailbox. He began leafing through them, shaken with nervousness. He couldn't understand why editors hadn't noticed him yet. He was good. He knew he was good. He had read enough to know that his novel was among the best works of literature.

He wandered the streets aimlessly, shuffling his feet. He remembered he had seen a thrift store nearby. He managed to sell his coat for a few bucks, then he wrapped his scarf tightly around his neck, went back to the hotel and stuffed one of his suitcases with his sports jackets and expensive shirts, which he took back to the thrift store and sold for a few tens of dollars. He was happy that he could at least buy himself some food.

He ordered up a huge plate of kielbasa and fries, plus some vodka and beer. The bartender glanced at him with suspicion. Understanding the bartender's reticence, Roscov took his money out and slammed it against the counter demonstratively. The bartender took out Roscov's tab and the cost of the meal itself, and left the change next to the beer glass. Roscov gratefully pushed it back towards the bartender. He gobbled his meal up in a hurry and shoved the last two pieces of kielbasa in his pocket, wrapped in a napkin.

"How have you been?" the bartender asked him in a friendly way.

"I've been writing."

"You a writer? I had no idea. There's a bunch of writers around here."

A group of men were watching the end of a baseball game on the TV hung above the bar; they were focused and impassioned, drinking their beer without taking their eyes off the screen. Roscov was sitting next to them, but he wasn't interested in the baseball game, despite his having been a hardcore Yankees fan for years.

"What are you writing?" the bartender asked, trying to be nice.

"Right now, the book of life and death," Roscov answered naturally, as if everyone knew what he was talking about.

"Good one," the bartender commented, a bit distracted.

One of the men turned around irritated.

"Keep it down, will you! We're watching the game here, can't you see?"

"Maybe you give me one of your books," the bartender whispered.

"I don't have a book," Roscov heard himself shouting. Even he was startled by his aggressive tone. But he could no longer stop. "I am a huge writer. It's true. I've never been one to publish. I just write. Books must be written." Roscov was yelling.

All eyes turned to him.

"I am creative. Touch me! Come on, touch me! Through me, you can come in direct contact with God!"

For a second, the bar fell silent. Then the baseball fan grabbed Roscov by the arm and squeezed tightly until Roscov clenched his fist in pain. Tears welled into his eyes.

"No, not the right arm! Not the right hand!" Roscov yelled, losing his mind in terror. "I'll never be able to write!"

The man let go of his arm, staring at him with enraged red eyes.

"You nuts or something? I told you we're watching a game here! I asked you to keep it down, right? I piss on your books, idiot!"

"You're the idiots," Roscov began to shout as he beat a retreat towards the door. "I am a great writer. One of the greatest that lived in America in this century! I am creative. A creator! You imbeciles! I wrote the book of life and death. You ignoramuses! The book of life and death is mine – remember that when you hear about it, it's mine! I wrote it!" Roscov hollered, the leftovers shaking in his pockets.

He rushed through the lobby of his hotel, still enraged, checked his mailbox, still empty, went up to his room, locked the door, and swung himself at the writing desk. He could no longer communicate. He was no longer able to communicate with people, and there was no point in his trying to anymore. He swore he would never leave his desk. He would never talk to anyone again. Ever. He would refuse to speak, from that moment on, as a form of protest against ignorance, indifference, stupidity, and the general inability to understand what is important in this world. He would not waste another word. All words would be devoted to the book of death and life. He locked his door. He would not come out until he finished the book of life and death.

The hotel manager began to knock on his door every day, demanding money and threatening to call the police. Roscov would sneak out of his room only at night, so that he could pick up the reviews he had subscribed to and check whether anyone had published him yet. But after some time he gave this too up. He was constantly writing, without eating or sleeping. Seven days later, he had finished the book of life and death. When he finally typed "the end" at the bottom of the last page, he nearly fainted with elation, hunger, satisfaction, and exhaustion. He was weary and content, feeling that he had done his duty. His eyes were empty, like those of a man drained of life, drained of his soul, drained of his last word.

He printed the almost six hundred pages of the book, saved them on floppy disks, took the rest of the manuscript from under his mattress and packed it all in a suitcase. He wrapped his scarf around his neck and went down the stairs shaking with exhaustion. He waited for the manager to go into his office behind the reception desk and sneaked outside. The book of life and death was hanging so heavy it almost tore his shoulder out of its socket. He was crawling. A Chase bank was right on the corner. In the old days, he had kept cash, stock, and other valuables in a safe deposit box at that branch. With the little strength he had, he pushed the massive glass door; minutes later, he came out of the bank without his suitcase. He placed a small key in his breast pocket, next to the floppy disks.

He tried to take a deep breath, but managed only a hoarse cough. The effort nearly knocked him down. He was right in front of the coffee shop, but he didn't dare go in. He had no money and he was no longer welcome anywhere. He looked up to the little attic window where the prostitute had told him she lived. He nearly crawled up the stairs. He didn't even know her name. He wanted to cry out for help, but he had no voice. He fainted on her doorstep.

She found him lying on the doorstep a few hours later. She didn't get scared; she didn't call the police or an ambulance. She had seen all sorts of people and accidents. She pulled him inside, felt for his pulse, unbuttoned his shirt collar, splashed him with water, and had him smell some vinegar. She helped him up on the bed, cooked him some hot soup, and kept talking, while feeding him:

"Come on, you're gonna get back on your feet. How was I to know you are such a great writer? True, you did treat me like a jerk. But you're a great artist, you know. I didn't believe you that day. And I'm telling you, you're gonna be famous! What am I talking about, you're already famous!" She continued to spoon soup into his mouth, chatting incessantly. "The great writer I told you about was here to see me yesterday. He's a regular, but I can't tell you his name – professional courtesy. And, what do you know! He had the latest issue of *The New Yorker* with him, and he showed me your excerpt from the book of life and death. He was dumbfounded with awe. I, for one, got all freaked out. I didn't tell him I knew you – you know, professional courtesy. But my heart leaped up with pleasure. I was very proud, you should know. He kept praising you, too. He kept saying that you're such a great discovery, that there's so much glory in your future. He praised you so much that I got curious and started to read your piece, too. That was the end of our evening! We both sat down like idiots and started to read your piece. I really liked it, you should know. I hadn't read so much in twenty years. And I got it all. The client said that that's what great literature is – stuff that everyone can understand, stuff everyone likes. You must be very happy. You really scored!"

Roscov was following her with empty eyes, with no visible reaction. He was sipping the spoonfuls of soup diligently. Each time a droplet would run down his chin, the woman would wipe it off with a dishtowel. She was now looking at him, worried.

"But you can't stay here. I have work to do. My next one comes in half an hour. You have to go. You'll get better, you'll see. Do you have a place to go? Now that you're so famous, I imagine your family must be waiting for you. You have a family, right? What about friends? Neighbors? I'm sorry, but I have no choice. I have to make a living somehow."

Roscov did not utter a word.

"You must have somebody. Please, don't make this hard for me."

Roscov held his hand out and mimicked holding a pen. The woman understood right away and brought him a pen and a napkin to write on. Roscov wrote down a phone number and a name, followed by the word "wife." The woman began to dial the number.

"Hello? Hi, could I speak to Ella, please?"

She then listened for a long time, noting down on the napkin an address dictated by the voice at the other end of the line. She finally thanked and hung up.

"Well, turns out your wife no longer lives there. She sold the house and moved in a studio apartment in Queens. Here's the address. You want me to call you a cab?"

Roscov shook his head vigorously. He took a key out of his breast pocket and placed it on top of the napkin with Ella's address.

"What do you want me to do with it? You want me to send this to your wife?"

Roscov nodded contentedly.

"All right. I promise. But now you'll have to hit the road. I'd like to help you more, I know you're a great writer, but that's life."

He sat up on the edge of the bed. He no longer felt dizzy.

"Why aren't you talking? Speak! What, have you lost your voice? Or is this some creative mood of yours?"

Roscov took the floppy disks out of his pocket and placed them in the woman's hand.

"What the hell am I supposed to do with these?"

Roscov didn't answer, didn't even gesture. He buttoned his shirt and slowly exited the room, casting one last grateful look back at the woman.

"Good luck!" she managed to wish him before he closed the door behind him. She then threw the floppy disks on the refrigerator.

He found himself in the street again. What now? There was no way back. As much as he wanted to go back home, he couldn't. He couldn't go back to his job at the fiber-optics plant. No one wanted him anymore, no one waited for him anymore. Not Ella, not the children, nor the friends. He had lost everything. He knew he could no longer read. But he could still write. He would write another book. In fact, that's what he was living for, writing. He would start another book that's what he would do.

He wandered the streets aimlessly. He passed a soup kitchen. He was hungry again. He went in. Everybody stared at him, as if they knew him. He drank his soup out of a cardboard cup, under the inquiring eyes of veteran homeless men.

He reached Battery Park towards the evening. He found an abandoned cardboard box and made himself a shelter for the night. He smiled at the thought that his world had been reduced to paper and cardboard. He felt good, almost strong again. He found a forgotten notebook and a pen in his pocket. He pulled them out happily and looked towards the Statue of Liberty, standing victoriously at the feet of Manhattan. He jotted down an idea. Strange. He had written it before. He remembered something else and rushed to note it down. He then reread the sentence, troubled. He had written that before, too. The next idea had been used in the book of life and death, too. He began to feel frightened. Everything he put down on paper was something – a word, an idea – he had used in his book. He was paralyzed with amazement. He was invaded by powerlessness. He couldn't write anything new. Nothing. Everything had been said before. He had given everything he had. He had emptied himself out. The Roscov writing machine had been broken. He had written everything and now he was working on empty, repeating the same words endlessly. There was nothing to add.

Roscov searched for God in despair. He used to be there, in his chest. From under his cardboard box, Roscov could see Ellis Island surrounded by water and the Statue of Liberty lifting her arm menacingly. There was no dry land in sight, no territory to be conquered, no land to be reached. Just darkness, slowly coming down.

In the early hours of the morning a police patrol made its way through Battery Park, knocking the cardboard boxes around. Some of the homeless people managed to run away, some were loaded into a van, others tried to negotiate, promising to go to a shelter or reciting their rights. One policeman kicked the box where under which Roscov had found shelter. It was empty.

*Translation by Mona Nicoara*

# Parking

At long last I was going to meet Lisa, having postponed our introduction several times. Something would always come up, either with her, or with me, and at the last moment we'd have to cancel and reschedule. This evening, though, I called to confirm that I'd definitely be there. At 8 p.m. sharp I'd show up on her doorstep. "Don't be late," she cautioned me. Was it perhaps because she knew I came from a country where people were not exactly famous for punctuality? Maybe she had no idea where I came from. Maybe my accent wasn't so thick on the telephone.

In any event, I don't like to be late. For that reason, I decided to drive there in the used car I'd just bought from a dealer in Queens. I filled my pockets with quarters so I could park on the street, tossed a thin book of some of my poems that I'd managed to get published with a small press in the Midwest into my bag. I wanted to write a dedication to Lisa on the book's title page, but realized I didn't know her full name. All Dominique had told me was Lisa. And I hadn't asked for any details. "You have to see Lisa."

I was looking forward to our meeting with more than a little anticipation. Lisa had assumed all sorts of dimensions in my mind, as I was investing in her a great deal of hope, albeit ill-defined, enveloped in mists of illusion that played playing tricks on my mind. I even thought I would achieve my dream, for wasn't I coming from a world where everything was possible? After all, the world of Eastern Europe – my world – was ridding itself of communism and its horrors, and that in itself was miraculous.

However, you don't have to be an immigrant to experience, on a rainy Sunday afternoon, moments of uncertainty and dread, to feel loneliness crushing in on you, to lie in bed, phone on your chest, waiting for it to ring; to open your address book, leafing aimlessly from letter to letter in search of someone you might call at that impossible hour, someone who would participate in your slightly depressed, slightly pathetic conversation. Someone who would also be an interesting, intelligent person, who could tell the difference between a bad case of flu and a mere common cold mixed with feeling a little down. Someone who would neither ridicule you, nor throw you into deeper depression.

So I called Dominique. Usually on Sunday afternoons he reads or translates the German romantics, and only after dusk is he inebriated enough to compose surrealistic poetry. When I called he was watching a Fellini movie. I began to complain about this and that, saving my pet peeve for the end. It was really bugging me: my identity crisis, this swinging between two worlds; my inability to write directly in English; this nagging nostalgia for the home I'd left behind, and all that it conjures up; the difficulty of making it as a foreign writer in a foreign language, moreover a minor one, for which there are so few translators, editors, readers…. Dominique heard me out patiently, then offered me just enough sympathy to dry up some of the dramatic effusion pouring out of me, making sure I got enough confession time, then gently led me on to neutral territory, and fell purposefully into clichés.

"Do you know how many people are on Prozac in this country? Did you see how many talk to themselves on the street? The alienation of big cities is not just a soap opera title. Well, you're in the most powerful of city of all. You need time to attune yourself to its madness, its magic. I know, you'll tell me it's consuming you. Yes, it can crush you, but it can also offer you every opportunity. You're in the right place."

I grumbled, I heard this speech about New York all the time. Dominique sensed my disappointment and changed his tone.

"After all, it's just a rainy Sunday. They're the same everywhere."

He was clearly eager to return to Fellini.

"We, the exiled ones, are built like nomads, we dream in atrophied languages, and, naturally, sometimes we're overwhelmed by a sort of uselessness, a kind of fatigue. The search is never over, especially when you think that you've found what you're looking for. Stop thinking. Even this exile can be simplified somehow. Some are meant to leave, just as others are meant to stay. And the one who leaves is not necessarily the one who's having a hard time in his native land, and the one who stays is not necessarily the privileged one. We're wanderers. But something might come out of our drifting after all…."

I wasn't following him anymore. I was sick of theories. While I was talking on the phone with him, I watched 3rd Avenue, completely deserted that Sunday afternoon. The rain had cleaned everything, the pavement sparkled, and the people had disappeared. Only a few cabs drove by, and, occasionally, the siren of an ambulance, the police or fire truck, soothing sounds for me, covered Dominique's voice. A Korean arranged flowers in vases in the small corner deli. A gray-violet light reflected from the glass of the facing skyscrapers. An old black man pushed a supermarket cart filled with empty plastic bottles. A sort of languor overcame me. This city belonged to me, too.

I heard Dominique telling me imperatively: "You've got to see Lisa."

"Lisa?"

"Yeah, a friend of mine. Very talented, intelligent, with lots of connections. You'll like her. And I believe she could help you."

After living in New York for a while, Dominique had moved west a few years ago, to some college in California, where he taught art history. From time to time he would come back east to give a lecture or to attend a translators' seminar, and then we would talk for hours, blissfully ensconced in some East Village bar, chain-smoking and reminiscing about the old country, where no one gave a hoot about the ozone layer, cholesterol, jogging, fitness, body-building or anything of the sort. No pressing concern there to have one's annual check-up. Back then life was a long, wholly satisfying conversation, over glasses of cheap wine and overflowing ashtrays.

I couldn't think of anything in particular that Dominique had told me about Lisa, but in my mind I somehow associated her with the literary world. I was left with the impression that she might, possibly, offer me some advice, some precious bits of information on how I could make it through the seemingly remote, inaccessible world of publishing. Or, who knows, she might be a writer herself. And so there I was, dutifully taking her my book of poetry, published by one of the lesser literary outfits – the only real breakthrough I could lay claim to since immigrating to America.

I arrived in front of Lisa's apartment building on the Upper West Side by seven-thirty, then searched in vain for more than half an hour for an empty parking space with a meter. When I looked at my watch again, it was well past eight and Lisa's warnings against being late rang out in my ears, now with bitter irony. Embarrassed, I telephoned her.

"I'm terribly sorry. I've been looking for a parking space for 45 minutes. I'm really sorry, but I'm going to be late."

"No problem." Lisa said calmly. "We'll be waiting for you. Don't worry, you'll find a parking space soon."

Her words were strange. I wondered if there was someone else with her in the room? Her husband? I'd barely hung up, when the jeep in front of me pulled out. Letting out a sigh of relief, I quickly parked my car and blessed gold-mouthed Lisa. Then I crossed the wide avenue to the building's entrance and in less than two minutes was ringing the doorbell to her apartment, panting with sheer exhaustion, nervousness and conflicting emotions.

Lisa gave me a hug and told me to leave my coat on the sofa in the entrance hall where the other visitors' belongings were. She was small, moving forward with graceful movements, displaying the most mysterious smile I'd ever seen. Her face took on various expressions as her smile gradually spread all over her face. It didn't start at the corners of her mouth, but rather in the middle of her slightly pursed lips. Her eyebrows arched over her eyes, and two lines creased her luminous forehead. Narrowing her eyes almost to a slit, she kept switching from a child-like air of innocence to the stiff image of a stern teacher. As her smile broadened, her cheeks took on a rosy hue, and her face relaxed, enhancing the delicate shape of her ears. The base of her nose took on a becoming, sensual shape.

It seemed that Lisa could morph from a shy teenager, exuding candor and naiveté, into a wizened, skeptical French intellectual, hovering between curiosity and irony. In the end you felt as if a little Asian woman were scrutinizing you inquisitively beneath a not unfriendly but condescending smile, belying a mixture of complicity and haughty understanding. As her eyes grew larger, her lips pursed again, Lisa's smile melted into an air of stern authority with which she studied me over the black rims of her glasses.

She took my hand.

"We've all been waiting for you," she said, leading the way into the living room.

About a dozen women turned their heads toward me, all at once. They were sitting on sofas and couches, in front of low coffee tables. Suddenly I was gripped by fear. So many women gathered in one place, all waiting for me? I almost felt unable to take another step, but Lisa gently pushed me forward. The ladies were sizing me up, as if to assess if I measured up to their expectations, if I was exactly as they'd imagined me. I sat on the nearest sofa, eager to avoid more scrutiny, having already committed the sin of arriving late. It was only then that I realized that the blonde next to me was barefoot. I looked around. They were all barefoot. All their shoes were aligned in a neat row along the wall. Do I really have to? I shot Lisa a quick, apprehensive glance and she, as if reading my mind, nodded a benevolent "yes" to my unspoken plea. No problem, you can keep your shoes on, she indicated.

Lisa was seated on a tall chair, a kind of stool, dominating the entire group. She also had kept her shoes on. Full of mystery and intrigue, she broke into another broad smile, which I didn't know what to make of. Then she went around the room, asking everyone to introduce herself – more for my sake, since the rest of the attendees seemed to know one another quite well. A photographer here, a social studies teacher there, an editor, a retired go-go dancer now comfortably transformed into a distinguished-looking housewife, a real-estate agent, a singer, a fashion designer and so on. Dominique had been right: Lisa did have lots of connections! The room was permeated by the atmosphere of a classroom or a conference hall, which at that moment was the last thing I needed! Hadn't I come all primed up for an intimate tête-à-tête with Lisa? Instead I'd dropped in on some sort of enclave. Could this be a meeting of some feminist consciousness-raising group? At that moment, I could imagine myself strangling Dominique, or at least bolting from the room.

Each of the participants stated her name, age, profession, family background, her idea of a good time and other information, peppering their presentations with bitter, caustic remarks about their past divorces. Others betrayed their deep-seated fear of aging or the usual dread of loneliness, which explained why they were here tonight. Lisa came over and laid her hand softly on my shoulder. Her gestures were natural and tender.

"Do you chant?"

Caught unprepared, after brief thought ("what kind of a weird question is that?"), I responded, with a smile, "Of course I chat. Everybody does it, right?" I asked, reassuringly.

It was Lisa's turn to give me a gratified smile, "You think so?"

"Isn't that what we're doing right now?"

I had no idea what I was talking about, but my words were making a good impression anyway.

"And who taught you to do it?"

"Oh, it runs in the family," I answered confidently. "I've been doing it ever since I was a little girl, with great results. I've always had a sociable nature, boosted, no doubt, by my Southern blood, and, naturally, by my Latin temperament." I was trying to sound good-natured and jolly. But I simply could not understand why they were elevating the simple art of conversation to such heights.

"I didn't know that Southern blood was an advantage," came the comment from the lady next to me, as she rubbed her bare feet against each other.

Then Lisa put an end to all the whispering, buzzing and rustling that usually goes on whenever a bunch of women get together, and announced, in a tone of underlying authority, "Well, shall we start, then?"

It sounded like an order. She lit up two sticks of incense and opened some sort of wooden box attached to the wall. A deep hush fell over the audience, all eyes fixed intently on the box. I rose, meaning to take a closer look at it, but the blonde next to me stopped me with a gesture that brooked no opposition. She whispered into my ear, as if to quash my curiosity, "It's a gohonzon."

"A…what?" I inquired. My English was getting worse.

"I don't know exactly what it is myself. They call it gohonzon. I believe it's a Sanskrit word."

"An icon of some sort?"

"I guess! Something like that."

Each of the women pulled from her handbag a little book, turned to the first page and wrapped a string of colored beads around her fingers, then settled into a more comfortable position. Lisa, the conductor, with an incense stick in her hand, clinked a little bell, and all of them started chanting in unison: "NA-MIO-HO-RENGE-KYO; NA-MIO-HO-RENGE-KYO." The same syllables, repeated again and again. Always the same syllables, sung in the same cadence and rhythm, while the ladies were rubbed the strings of beads between their fingers. I realized they weren't chatting, as much as chanting. I'd blurted out that I was an expert at chanting, only to reveal now that, actually, I was totally out of the loop. I'd dropped in on this Buddhist session like the proverbial fly in the ointment and was now forced to play along, lest they should discover the embarrassing truth about me. So I kept mumbling on, the best I could, trying, but not entirely succeeding, to stay in tune with the initiates, sometimes failing miserably, skipping many beats, all the time hoping I could hide from them the unpleasant truth that I hadn't the foggiest idea what in the world was going on here – I, who had never ever chanted in my entire life.

The blonde next to me held out the little book halfway between us, pointing each line with her finger as it was being chanted, encouraging me to fall into step with the other chanters. Then she placed her string of beads on my fingers, hoping this might somehow improve my performance. Alas, it was no use! I was a complete disaster. The women kept uttering those dreary syllables, in increasingly loud, shrill voices, in a chorus whose dirge sounded at once dramatic and languorous. They kept this up for the better part of twenty minutes.

That little book contained nothing but those same syllables, repeated over and over, with certain pauses and changes of rhythm in between. How I would have liked to see additional words of that strange language, but the chorus wailed on its lugubrious chant, some of the women uttering the syllables in a high-pitched voice, while others apparently fell into a deep trance. Here and there a voice had become irritatingly hoarse; one or two had lost their saliva, and nearly all had eyes that threatened to pop out of their sockets, as, with a fixed stare, they diligently followed the enigmatic string of words.

I thought they would never stop. I was definitely an ignoramus, unable to see anything magical or metaphysical in their chant, and felt ridiculous in noticing only superficiality and hysteria instead of deep meditation or spiritual uplift, as I was supposed to feel. Although this female choir had at first amused me, now it was becoming boring as hell. My only hope was that their Sanskrit chanting, or whatever, would somehow rouse the ire of the neighbors.

More than half an hour later, Lisa clinked the bell again and the chorus came to an abrupt stop. They all looked exhausted, but happy. Lisa beamed her benign approbation over them, pleased with their overall performance, and, from the haughty elevation of her chair, asked me:

"How was it?"

"Very good."

"How are you feeling?"

"Oh, great, just great."

"You may come every week, if you want."

"Sure…we'll talk about it on the phone," I mumbled and attempted to rise.

"We'll stay a little longer," Lisa explained. "These are the choicest moments."

The women seemed quite relaxed, content, and, above all, relieved. Some of them kept their eyes closed, smiling their angelic smiles, as if they'd just awoken from a very pleasant dream. Others were staring open-eyed, as if they were seeing the world for the very first time. Obviously the chanting had had a different impact on each of them. Only Lisa maintained the same controlled expression, the same mysterious smile.

"It's in our power to save ourselves," she told one of them, handing her a book on Buddhism.

They started to talk chaotically. The word harmony popped up several times. A cell phone rang and its owner turned it off in disgust.

"He doesn't understand that my life has changed," it wasn't clear who, but she was probably referring to the man who'd just telephoned; but several others nodded, smiling sympathetically. "I'm a free woman, I've recovered my power, and I'm in tune with the universal harmony."

Lisa watched her contentedly. I fumbled around, betraying my impatience, and handed the string of beads back to its owner.

"You may keep it, if you wish," she said, generously. "I have several more at home. There are a hundred and eight in all. Do you know what they stand for?" she tested me, taking obvious pride in having this bit of information she could impart to me from her fountain of knowledge. "They are earth-bound wishes chanted away into the realm of cosmic energy."

"Do these wishes ever come true?" I asked politely.

"Of course they do. Look, when you called earlier, unable to find a parking place, Lisa asked us to chant for you. And sure enough, shortly afterwards your wish came true, didn't it? Miraculously, you found a spot right away, did you not?"

"It's true," I said, bewildered.

She looked at me triumphantly. "You'll see how many problems you can solve by chanting," she added.

I said my good-byes to the barefoot ladies, thanking my sofa-mate for her kindness, and giving Lisa a hug. She walked me to the door, unable to conceal her displeasure at my leaving so soon. I couldn't bring myself to look her straight in the eye. Just as I was about to walk out, she planted a kiss on the corner of my mouth and smiled mysteriously. I forgot all about giving her my book of poems.

When I arrived in the parking lot, I found a 55 dollar ticket under my wiper. My time had expired. It hadn't crossed my mind to chant for that.

For a long time afterwards, I never gave loneliness another passing thought. But a few months after my Buddhist experience, I saw Lisa again. Ironically, it was on another rainy Sunday. I had been walking for a while, the rain intensified, and I went inside an almost empty Upper West Side church to rest and light a candle. A woman was praying in front of the Virgin Mary. I drew closer. She stood frozen, completely transfixed by the prayer, her eyes closed, and her lips moved rapidly every now and then. But the smile didn't belong to her….

*Translation by Dorin Motz*

## Concession

Like the majority of sculptors, he could have tried his hand at so-called decorative art – busts, statues, fake columns, flower baskets, little angels – or, reaping an even better profit, garden sculpture: giant cast-iron frogs, artesian fountains, stone-tableaux of does, lions, birds, little boys peeing or reading a bronze book on a cast iron bench.

Sasha, however, continued to sculpt what he pleased, only for himself and his friends. The viewing of the work was a ritual, Russian customs persisting in New York; it was, in fact, just like Russia, which you had the impression that everyone had escaped back to, since all you heard everywhere was nothing but people speaking Russian. They showed up at his studio, ate eggplant salad, marinated mushrooms and herrings and onion with boiled potatoes and drank a few bottles of vodka. They talked late into the night, nostalgically recalling how horrible life had been under communism and at the same time how great it had been, a paradox only Eastern European immigrants could understand, and this only when they were honest with themselves.

Here, as it had been in Russia, their art was preserved in a kind of underground. If over there you had to resist political pressure, to stay far away from the mutilation of art during the socialist realist period, here you had to go against the ignorance resulting from freedom of expression, culminating in kitsch and commercially driven taste. The monumentality of Stalinism, so much despised in the East, found countless disciples here. Being easily confused with grandeur, it satisfied the needs of this world of gigantic dimensions, its majesty and triumph.

Sasha was content with his job; it allowed him to make a living and develop his favorite ideas. But his wife reproached him for not trying hard enough to promote his work, for not working at getting an exhibit, claiming you couldn't be an artist just in your home, the world had to get to know you, to see what you were doing; what was so wrong with that? You had to sell something! So, in order to shut her up, on his day off he shoved his portfolio under his arm, wrapped three sculptures in blankets and went uptown to the galleries that a friend had told him were interested in acquiring contemporary art.

The first place he saw made a good impression on him. Both rooms had works by Chagall, Matisse, and Picasso, while in the center were some small sculptures by Diego Giacometti and Henry Moore. Perfect, thought Sasha; and after strolling leisurely through the rooms, he took advantage of the fact that he was the only visitor and approached the elderly lady behind the beautiful rosewood desk who seemed to be in charge.

"Sir?" the lady said to him before Sasha had time to open his mouth. "You're interested in one of the works?"

"It's a very beautiful gallery," began Sasha awkwardly.

"It's British!" she apostrophized, as though British were a synonym for "very beautiful."

"Of course, British, I realize that," Sasha stuttered, smiling in order to break the ice.

"Sir, I have work to do," she replied, barely moving her thin lips. "If there's nothing else I can do to help you, then please excuse me...."

"I'm an artist as well" Sasha jumped in.

The lady's face grew icy.

"Sculptor."

"So?"

She looked bored as she picked up a cup of antique English porcelain and sipped her tea. Sasha unwrapped two of the statues and placed them on the British desk.

"As a matter of fact, I'd like to show you some work." "Why?"

"You might be interested."

"I'm only interested in the dead, young man. Certainly you must have noticed that we only exhibit the dead here."

"Don't you think you're limiting your public?"

"Public?"

"The buyers, I mean."

"We're not interested in what you call *buyers*. We have our *clients*. *They* prefer the dead. They are the only secure investment."

"And you don't want to discover new artists, still in the prime of their power, or at the height of their artistic potential? Perhaps they too would one day be a profitable investment, don't you think?"

"That day you're referring to comes only after they've passed into the next world."

"Ma'am, it's not like that. There are plenty of famous artists who are still alive, very highly valued, and whose pieces are bought by agents and collected by galleries."

"Perhaps, but I'm not aware of it. Our gallery isn't interested in them."

"Please forgive my insisting, but you can't base your entire collection only on the dead."

"That's exactly what I've been doing for forty years, sir."

"Well, then since I'm alive, what do you expect me to do?"

"That's your problem, sir, I'm sorry I can't help you."

Sasha returned her strange look, wrapped up his pieces, which the lady hadn't even bothered to take a polite look at, thanked her and left.

The spring's cool wind filled his massive chest, billowed his long hair and reddish beard. He lit a cigarette and felt powerful and healthy. He loved New York in the spring, despite the withered ladies hidden in British galleries of the Upper West Side, who took an interest in you only if you were dead. And he had no desire to commit suicide. Not today.

He went into another gallery, which was certainly an American one. The young lady inside smiled incessantly and had a square plastic water bottle next to the catalogues on her desk. She wore comfortable and practical shoes, which allowed her to spend the day on her feet, sauntering from one room to the next, handing out information, engaging visitors in conversations, acting distractedly cordial. When you spoke to her she looked at you but wasn't there. She smiled at you but didn't understand exactly what you were asking, she stared at you, through you, into the void, with an exaggeratedly amiable manner.

"Hi! Can I help you?"

Sasha unwrapped his pieces and set them on the desk, one by one.

The woman smiled encouragingly.

"I am an artist. Sculptor. I was thinking you might be interested in my work."

"Oh great, great! Where are you from?"

"Russia."

"Wonderful. Fabulous."

"Would you like to take a look at my portfolio? These are some of the pieces I've made in the last three years."

"Certainly. Oh, they're fabulous. Great."

"I have others like them in bronze."

"Hmm, hmm. Cool."

"What do you think?"

"They're really…interesting," she said, even before she had time to look. "I like this wolf," she continued, running her hand over one of the pieces Sasha had set next to her square plastic water bottle.

"It's a wolf, right?"

"Yes, a wolf," said Sasha, happily.

He also liked this piece very much. He turned it to face the woman, who continued to study it thoughtfully. Sasha was excited. Something was about to happen.

"Bronze?"

"Certainly, bronze."

"Well, you know, I might just have a buyer for it."

"Great. It would be great…." Sasha's eyes sparkled.

"There's just one a little problem, I hope it won't bother you too much…. Can I make a suggestion?"

"Certainly, certainly," Sasha encouraged her, feeling like he would promise her anything.

"Could you add a little girl?"

"A little girl?"

"You know, like in Little Red Riding Hood. I wanted to say it but I thought it might shock you. Could you sculpt a Little Red Riding Hood next to the wolf?"

"Ma'am, miss, I don't understand…."

"I know it seems weird to ask. And I don't mean in any way to offend you as an artist. But if it's not too much trouble to ask, I've got a great buyer for you. For over twenty years he's been collecting Little Red Riding Hoods. He's a reliable client, I've already sold him fourteen pieces. He's got an impressive collection. He'd buy your piece right away, at a price, believe me, that you'd never get anywhere else for one of your works. All you have to do is to add a Little Red Riding Hood. Wolves alone don't interest him."

Sasha's ears were turning red. He stared at the wolf, which he'd worked on for several months, and tender affection filled his body. He wasn't angry or insulted; he simply loved his piece more than ever.

"Well, what do you think?"

"Miss, I don't know what to tell you. I don't do Little Red Riding Hoods."

"I know, I know, but try to understand what I'm asking. A little, how can I put it, concession, I wouldn't call it a compromise, just a little concession. How can it hurt you, just to add a Little Red Riding Hood next to this wolf? It wouldn't cost you anything, and the return would be phenomenal. Besides, you may come up with a Little Red Riding Hood that you'd love yourself. Don't you think there could be Little Red Riding Hoods that are masterpieces? Think about it."

"I've thought about it for a long time. For twenty years I've been thinking about it. Certainly, what you're asking is no big thing. A little while ago someone suggested that I need to be dead before my work can be taken into consideration. You only want a Little Red Riding Hood. Maybe I can do it…."

"Fabulous. Great. Wonderful."

"I would do it if I had a few lives ahead of me. I would spend one of them sculpting only Little Red Riding Hoods."

The woman withdrew a few steps, continuing to smile nervously.

"I hope you didn't take this the wrong way. I honestly wanted to help you."

"Are you interested in any other of my pieces?"

"I'm afraid not. Though they're fabulous. Absolutely fabulous," she said nervously.

"I thank you very much."

"Good luck. Have a great day."

As he was about to walk out of the gallery, Sasha's eyes fell on the inscription hanging above the door: "True artists speak about themselves as if they were dead."

"Can you tell me who said this?" he asked the lady while a shiver ran down his spine.

"I don't remember his name. British, I think," the lady answered. The billboard smile still on her face, growing….

"British, certainly."

Sasha crossed the street, more alive than ever. He held his heavy pieces to his chest, protectively, possessively. Through his clothes he felt the cold metal that had taken the shape his hands gave it.

*Translation by Dorin Motz*

# The Russian Fur Hat

Bob is a good, caring husband, though a bit boring. Case in point: When Betty went out to Manhattan this morning, he made sure he told her several times, “Don’t forget to put a scarf around your neck. It’s bitter cold outside.”

“My pullover will cover my neck just nicely, thank you,” retorted Betty.

“Still, you should take the scarf as well. That collar is not nearly enough to keep you warm.”

“All right, all right, I’ll take it,” Betty sighed.

“What about the overcoat? Aren’t you putting it on? “

“No, I’ll take the fur jacket instead.”

“Your knees will freeze. Besides, that fur jacket is no good – not without a hood, anyway. Better take your overcoat.”

“What do I need a hood for? I’ll simply put on my fur hat.”

“Well, you may put your fur hat on, but you should also have a hood. You never know. “

“Bob, that Russian fur hat is all I need. I bet it would keep me warm, even out there on the frontline.”

“All right, but take the overcoat, too. Do me a favor, will you? I don’t want to worry myself sick over this.”

Betty gave in, as usual. She was headed out to the Lenox Hill Hospital where a cousin of hers – also well past sixty – was recovering from a hip-replacement operation. She was going to bring her some pies and poppy seed coffeecake she had picked up at a Russian store in Queens, the borough where both she and Bob had been living for more than twenty years.

“And, watch your step. It’s slippery out there,” he added, for good measure, as Betty was positioning the fur hat on her head, wrapping the scarf around her neck and pulling the hood on – all under Bob’s protective gaze.

“Jewish men make the best husbands,” her mother had told her on several occasions. “They are good, decent family men, down-to-earth and full of common sense. They just know how to take care of children and will not leave you, even though they might, on occasion, cheat on you.”

They had had a pretty decent marriage, even though there had been no children. Bob had taken good care of her, practically spoiling her, in spite of his occasional annoying possessiveness. He was a thoughtful, careful man, full of foresight, always trying to avoid danger in whatever form, lest he should tempt fate. He was fearful and prudent, avoiding the unknown, a man who felt at ease only in places and among people he knew very well. He was steady and prosaic, not given to adventure or overexcitement, preferring instead the security of the commonplace, the blandness that made him feel he was in control.

"You're boring me, Bob," Betty would say to him quite often. "Boy, you're such are nag!" And her voice, otherwise soft and pleasant, took on a Bovary-like tone of desperation. "You know what? I'm quite capable of taking care of myself. Anyway, we can't go on living like this."

"Like what?"

"You know what I mean: this programmed kind of life, down to the smallest detail, always trying to avoid the slightest mishap; dodging everybody and everything."

These outbursts of rebellion always managed to put Bob in a blue funk. Thoroughly frightened, he would ask her in a plaintive manner, "Aren't we living the good life, Betty dear? Are you not happy?"

Such moving tenderness was too much for Betty. She could no longer remain indifferent.

"But of course we do, my dear. Ours is a very good life and you are very kind man," she would continue in her mind, but very carefully, lest he should hear her thoughts.

"I haven't had a chance to know anyone else. It's rather depressing to reach old age and realize you've been sleeping with the same man all your life. Having shared a desk in high school, we let our romance blossom in college and ended up getting married just before we graduated. What a beautiful woman I used to be! And now look at these bony wizened hands. What a dreadful trick life plays on us!"

These were the kind of thoughts crossing Betty's mind as she was riding the F train into Manhattan. The air was quite stuffy in the car, so she unwrapped her scarf and let her hood down. As for the fur hat, she decided she might as well keep it on. Why let people see the discolored, thinned-out, anemic remnants of her former luscious blond hair? No doubt she had been a coquettish woman. She gave a sigh and put her cheek next to the cold glass of the window, studying the faces around her. Riding the Queens train is quite an experience. In each car there must be at least ten nationalities. Most of the passengers were wearing drab, grayish clothes. They had long faces, marked by fatigue. Some of them napped, with their heads bobbing up and down, trying to hold onto to a book or a newspaper printed in some outlandish language. Overhead were all sorts of advertisements – most of them in Spanish – offering lawyerly assistance for accidents or medical injuries. In the end Betty fell prey to the same winter afternoon drowsiness. She dozed off. It was just a few minutes, yet they felt like an eternity.

When she opened her eyes, she was perspiring slightly. Her face was flushed and a thin rivulet of saliva had coursed down her chin. True, she had only slept a few minutes, but voluptuously. The air in the car was getting hot. Across from her sat a tall, heavy-set man, whose face looked Russian. He had a vacant scowl. No doubt he must have come aboard while she was sleeping. And, then she froze. Quickly she reached for her head and felt a lump in her throat. The hat was gone!

She looked around, felt for it on the floor, but it was all in vain. The hat was nowhere to be found. And, then she saw it. The man sitting on the bench across from her was wearing her own Russian hat. He must have snatched it while she was napping. A fresh wave of perspiration inundated her – this time caused by vexation and fear. She stared fixedly at the passenger. He was a hulk of a man. Should she ask him for her hat back? Could she afford to cause a scandal right there in the train? What if the man responded violently? Naturally, he had not pilfered it from her only to hand it back to her in the presence of witnesses!

Bob would go crazy when she would tell him the whole thing. Of all things, it had to be the Russian hat he treasured so much that was stolen! It was so warm, so comfortable! He had been wearing it for ten years, but another ten years would not make it look a day older.

The train was pulling into the station. The man was dozing along with the other passengers, the hat sitting proudly on top of his head. Betty screwed up her eyes, tensed her body, the way she used to in her youth when she competed in the long jump. Then she chose her time very carefully. At the last moment, before the automatic doors closed, she pounced like a feline. She snatched the hat from the man's head and dashed out just as the doors of the car closed off behind her, leaving the man agape and numb with surprise.

She ran as fast as she could, deciding to abandon her visit to her cousin in the hospital. Instead, she walked across the platform and boarded the train in the opposite direction, for home. Seeing her return so early, Bob suspected something was amiss and, naturally, panicked. Betty dropped down in an armchair, drained of all energy, clutching to her bosom the recovered Russian fur hat.

"You won't believe what just happened to me. I bet you would have died of fright, if this had happened to you. Just like in the movies."

"When I say you are naïve; that life is a dangerous thing, not to be trifled with; you merely laugh at me," mumbled Bob in a voice choked with emotion, trembling at the foot of the armchair from which Betty was ready to roll out all the details of this "made-for-the movies" story.

"A huge, sinister-looking man – boy, you ought to have seen him! A mountain of a man, with a glassy glint in his eyes, sat down right in from of me. And, can you believe it?" said Betty, letting suspense build up. Bob was almost in tears at the thought of what was to follow.

"Now wait. Wait just a minute," he implored. "Take your coat off first. And, your boots, too. Breathe deeply. Shall I fetch you a glass of water? Oh no, I think I am going to pass out."

As Betty took off her coat, out of the hood came the Russian fur hat, falling onto the floor. Bob picked it up, showing it to her triumphantly: "See what a good idea it was to insist you take the hooded overcoat? There! If it hadn't been for this hood, you'd have certainly lost the hat."

"What're you talking about?" snapped Betty. "Where did you get that hat?" she asked him, while continuing to clutch against her bosom an identical Russian hat, only perhaps a little larger.

"It must have dropped into the hood, while you were asleep," said Bob, smiling smugly at the thought of what he had managed to prevent by insisting she take the hooded overcoat. Betty looked at him in horror.

For several weeks, the local Queens paper carried an ad about the Russian fur hat that had been stolen off a man's head in the F express train. No one ever called to claim it.

*Translation by Dorin Motz*

## Three For Inferno

## I

### *The Last Day*

All I had to do was imagine my own funeral to get the perspective on the exact relationship with the two women in my life. And what each of them was going to be left, after my death. I could already see myself divided up between them. But I did need this hilarious, lugubrious picture if for no other reason than to satisfy my own vanity. So that I could sort out the unending stream of feelings, reactions and decisions that are constantly expected of me. And, all along, I proved to be nothing more than an expert in the art of procrastination, unable to break with or launch into anything new.

I was living on useless memories and expectations, in the hope that time would solve them. Or muddle them up for good. I was not a man of spectacular gestures. I was hoping that some powerful outside earthquake would shake up our little universe so full of meanders and confusions. And, as nothing devastating was showing up in the social or cosmic spheres, all I was left with was my own funeral as an absolute reference point against which to get some sort of assessment of the plight into which I had slid.

So, here was Claudia, my legitimate wife, surrounded by our three children. Claudia, at the head of the coffin, overcome with sorrow, yet stiff and proud to be the main heroine. Finally the center of attention, among candles and handkerchiefs and all that pathetically baroque Orthodox resplendence which makes even church beggars weep and howl at each service, only to be drowned out by the impromptu chorus of professional mourners. Claudia would accept condolences with dignity, displaying the demeanor of a modest, intellectual lady. She would stoically bear the brunt of yet another drama, herself part of her husband's life and death, going through this tragic but survivable moment by dint of her thoughtfulness in thinking through her new responsibilities as distinguished widow and mother.

And then, over in that corner, quite far from me, was Dana, who would not even look up, let alone get closer to the coffin. Rather, she seemed keen on blending in among the mourners, as withdrawn and unnoticed as she could possibly be in her conspicuous black hat, black glasses and black shawl which, by the way, looked so good on her that they seemed yet another insult to my honorable wife.

Dana seemed to have been struck by the same grief. Yet, because of her youth, it was a different kind of grief. And thus, in spite of the second fiddle role she played in the general scheme of this funeral, she was nevertheless drawing alternately lustful and defying looks, ironical or merely tolerant gazes, at worst judgmental appraisals from the ones who might have been in on our secret relationship. As for Claudia's relatives, if looks could kill, Dana would be devoured in an instant!

Naturally, I dread the embarrassment I might suffer, should both of them enter the rent-by-the-hour chapel, each with their own private pain for the one neither of them could envisage in the double life with the other. And I cannot deny that my pride has already been satisfied. Just thinking of the muted dispute raging between these two supposedly grieving ladies, obliged to face this unexpected event, namely my death – this uncontrollable situation of such drastic consequence which would, all of a sudden, upset the formal order of things in their lives.

And while Dana might perhaps have wanted to avoid these rather embarrassing moments caused by her attending the funeral service, Claudia wouldn't for the world have missed the opportunity of participating in this special event. The wife in black, before who people bow, take off their hats and encouragingly shake her hand. All eyes turn towards her, as if boring holes through her skull, barely concealing their pity and perhaps just a tiny bit of admiration for her courage in braving this new trial, after having faithfully stood by her man all their married life. As for her, she would immediately fit the bill of the heroic wife. My death would be but another sacrifice she would have to make. She would emerge stronger and embellish her memories of me with mawkish stories of "a really special character," yet careful to mention also his slight imperfections and shortcomings, but overall "a devoted father and husband," as I was to read in the flawless obituary published in the papers.

Of course, eventually, my disappearance would only emphasize her martyrdom, as she would have one less paycheck to depend on and would have to look after the unsettled children all by herself. But she would cope with all this in the manner of the woman so prevalent in classical literature – the lone, hardy widow who never shirks her responsibilities, no matter what, the lioness to the bitter end. She would feed on the memories of a happy marriage, of a special husband who had been spared what might have been the debilitating years of old age, even when they are spent alongside one's spouse.

Therefore she would choose the better side of my death. It's so much better that I did not get to experience the decaying of my body, the decrepitude and senility, the humiliation and grotesque aspects associated with old age, which some are forced to suffer while waiting for the eternal release from that condition one can call anything but life. To feel how your muscles go flabby and all your bodily functions slow down or begin to malfunction. To see the scornful, disgusted looks of those around you, impatiently wondering when you are ever going to that great unknown, while no doubt making a pretence of caring for you, out of a sense of duty or maybe even love.

Claudia would also regret that I had not lived to see my grandchildren. She would put all my clothes in cardboard boxes, which she would deposit in the attic, with a heavy heart or even compassion, either because I had not lived to wear some of them or because I had had too many. And so, again, I would come out favorably in her memories. I had never valued things too much, always assigning them a secondary place to my needs. Instead I had plenty of other sins! I wonder how many Claudia was aware of. Was it really true that, as one of her colleagues had suggested to her, I had had an amorous liaison with a writer's daughter, much younger than me? Could I have displayed such crass insensitivity, such a propensity for duplicity? How could I be so ruthless, so base, after all she had done for me?

Fortunately, Claudia is unspeakably vain. The thought would be promptly dismissed from her mind. For she could not bear for one minute to suffer such humiliation just as, throughout her life, she had been far more concerned with her standing in the eyes of those around her, than what was really happening to her.

I mustn't push my luck. All my reasonings stand up only if someone, perhaps a well-intentioned confidante of hers, would do her the required favor and whisper into her ear, as if in passing, a little bit of gossip such as is regularly spread about any man of consequence. A mistress. A fleeting affair, they would cynically hasten to add. In any marriage any man is bound to have at least one mistress.

What I'm afraid of, though, is that should Claudia suspect I'm having an affair with Dana, she would react in the most natural way women do: she would simply refuse to believe it. Not because she would trust in my honesty or in my simulated correctness – as it is – but rather out of a sense of self-preservation, in order to shield herself from biting sarcastic remarks, expressions of pity or possibly the chicanery those around her would stoop to. It might just be possible that the world for which Claudia lives and tries to preserve at all costs, the world which is the only thing that matters in her relationship with the universe, would tacitly approve of me. Or even take pleasure in my affair. Or even envy me this late-blooming folly and try to protect me from my wife's possessiveness, giving me and Dana blanket approval, which would really be the last straw for Claudia!

It's not her suffering that matters, but her humiliation. The damage to her reputation, the wounding of her pride. It wouldn't be me she would grieve for, but rather her own defeat. I can't tell exactly how the funeral would pan out and I'd rather not have to witness any of it, not if I can help it! Although I do not foresee any violent or unsuitable reaction from my wife upon Dana's entrance into the chapel, due, no doubt, to the presence of the other participants, whom she really wants to impress with her dignity, with her studied indifference to rumors. She would ignore Dana, would refuse to let her participate in the smallest detail associated with the funeral procession, reserved for the exclusive participation of the immediate family and their circle of friends. And on me, though no longer alive, she would heap her choicest scorn, happy at last that she could have me all to herself.

She would dominate the assembly, fighting back her tears, but evidently convinced that I got my just deserts. Me, the unrepentant villain who had had the audacity to cheat on her – naturally doing so only at the insistent nagging of Dana! For that's precisely where Claudia's problem lies. She might perhaps be willing to put up with a love affair, as long as I had been the seduced party, the loved, raped victim of an obsessed woman, the poor hapless man who had had no choice but to sleep with some crazy woman whose clutches he had been helpless to resist. What mattered was that I did not love that woman, that I had no desire whatsoever for her, that I did not take the initiative to woo her – something

Claudia would consider me incapable of, anyway, since she was securely installed as my wife, with the proper papers to prove it, the upshot of it all being that she owned me. From here on things are becoming clear: she has a hold on my feelings. O, yes, I may have affairs, but when it comes to loving, I am allowed to love only her. She was born to be the sole object of my affection.

Besides, my death would offer her a loophole out of this impossible situation where everyone had been talking about the other woman in my life – something utterly absurd from Claudia's point of view. She had decided many years ago she was not going to share me with any other woman, would never part with me, no matter what. Not only that, but her concept of marriage ruled out any possibility that I would leave her or choose someone else. That I might err along the way, preferring someone else or simply falling out of love with her, that I might no longer want her, growing tired of her or going mad, in my old age – that would be simply out of the question from her perspective. Since she was the one who always had to make sacrifices, evidently she had eternity coursing through her veins. She was a pillar of strength, jealously but with infinite long-suffering guarding me and making sure I would be entirely hers. Hers alone. Regardless of the passage of time. Conveniently ignoring the fact that this world is strewn with all kinds of temptations, pitfalls, errors and snares.

Sure, I had my own part in encouraging her to reach such a level of self-confidence. Through my cowardice when faced with surprises. Through my refusal to get involved in any adventures. Through my mediocre temperament, which lent me an air of stable domesticity, which might easily pass for seriousness, for poise or for sternness in the face of the sensational. I strike people as a harmless, reconciled or passive character. Philosophizing about vanity only to the extent it covers my weaknesses. In short, the perfect type to be manipulated by an ambitious, energetic, possessive and domineering woman.

What is awful though is that I am speaking only about Claudia, when, in fact, it's Dana I care for. I take a paranoiac view of Claudia's reactions at the funeral, when all the time my real concern is what would Dana look like, how much she would suffer. Not for me, but because of me. Which might mean that Claudia would emerge a winner again, vanquishing us once more. She insinuated herself permanently into us, transcending death itself. And she will continue to make demands on me, ad nauseam.

In Grand Central Station where I've been waiting for Dana for over twenty minutes, all these troublesome thoughts have a way of taking horrifying proportions. A showdown, that's what she's after! One final meeting to sort things out. I am looking at the big, black electronic screen listing the arriving and departing trains. I dread the discussion that will follow. Besides, I don't know why we had to meet at this particular place, amid all the confusion which wears me out and further tangles my nerves. I wish she had selected our little Second Avenue restaurant, where both of us felt encouraged every time the waitress offered us, at the end of the meal, cupcakes on the house, simply because she wanted to show her approval of the idea of a couple, even when this couple met clandestinely, as we did.

Scores of people are brushing past me every minute. I can't spot Dana among them. She may come from any direction and I feel ridiculous standing by myself in this big hall, expecting a tap on my shoulder any minute or waiting to sense her approach by the fragrance of her tangy lemon and lavender perfume. Maybe she is deliberately late. I have already prepared several speeches in my mind but, most likely, none of them with measure up to Dana's hopes and expectations. And everything is going to go back to square one. Another deadlock. Unfortunately I am unable to make the very move she expects of me. She knows this very well. And I can certainly understand her desperation.

In these two years since we got involved Dana has suffered more than she has been happy. While I shielded Claudia as much as I could, doing my best to hide from her the existence of another woman in my life, Dana obviously knows I'm married and has always lived with Claudia's ghost in her mind. I would leave her alone when she needed me most, during the weekends, holidays and vacations. But she made no demands on me, never protested, never reproached me. She seemed resigned to being the other woman, always putting on a convincing show of high-brow open-mindedness, modernity, emancipation and seemingly absolute defiance of conventions.

She kept saying my love was all she ever needed, that she was mindful of the risk of divisions or break-ups; that she hated causing other people to suffer. She didn't care for drawing up any legal papers. No abandoned children for her! No scandals, no tensions! All she wanted was to be with me, all I am and all I can be. A simple, unencumbered affair for any man, one might say. As for me, I loved her all the more, awed by her great wisdom.

How was I to know what she was cooking up for me? One night, after about two years during which I had considered myself a lucky, spoilt man, we were dining at that same restaurant on Second Avenue when she asked me, out of the blue, to divorce my wife. She loved me so much, she explained, she could not bear to share me with Claudia anymore. She wanted me all to herself, till death do us part.

I was surveying them both from that vantage point where they had laid me out in that stiff, full-length position, arms folded across my chest, with the little icon stick between my fingers, in my perfectly fitting evening suit, wearing my favorite tie, whose knot they had been unable to get right. It was far too large, making me look a bit outdated. If I were to open my eyes, my field of vision would be filled with Claudia, icy and grieving, with lips forming a smile dripping with a mixture of irony and malice. Studying me triumphantly, but deeply hurt. Her pride was all but useless to her now, as was her victory over me, which she had desired for so long, indeed had dreamed of, except that it would only have mattered to her if I were alive. I can hear Claudia hissing through her teeth, "You ungrateful beast! You're such a coward. You didn't have the guts to confront me."

And of course she is right. I did kick the bucket at the very moment she felt she was finally going to humiliate me. And she would do so either through her generously forgiving me, so she could then dominate me forever, or by blackmailing me with her cruelty for my having cheated on her. She, the virtuous, devoted wife who had borne me three fine children.

As for Dana, I could only see her if I rolled my eyes backwards. She was far away, hidden among those bodies in mourning who were standing on their tiptoes so they would not miss a single detail of the funeral ceremony.

I loved them both, God is my witness. It's just that I loved each of them differently. Claudia with tranquility, but also with fear in my heart. Just as I had loved my mother, when I would do something bad and was afraid of her wrath, which was sure to follow. But I still loved her even when she scolded or punished me. Dana I loved intensely, passionately, nervously and chaotically. Unsure of myself, awkwardly, just as I loved my daughter, afraid lest I should do something that would upset her or harm her, always trying to anticipate her whims, to read her mind, to never disappoint her. And each of them was assured of my love.

I tried to be a decent man, both in the matrimonial relationship and outside of it. In fact, I don't think I was deceiving either of them. I was giving one hundred percent of myself to each of them. It never occurred to me while I was sleeping with Claudia to imagine that I was actually sleeping with Dana. Or to make love with Dana and suddenly to remember some intimate moment I had spent with Claudia. They were not forced to share me because each of them had me entirely. I never blurted out the name of one while in the presence of the other. I was living two perfectly separate parallel lives.

But then these women were so different from each other, in age, temperament, psyche, in their reactions and in the way they behaved. Each had her own distinct cultural background. I seemed to be the exception to the rule that every man spends his entire life running after one type of femininity. Contradicting the pride he is so famous for, man is said to always seek his ideal, being instead condemned to always run into the same woman.

Actually, there are men whose mistresses look suspiciously like their own wives. Others go through two or three divorces and, if you put them all together, both their past and future wives seem to be but one and the same woman. The only thing different about them being their hairdos. It's enough to make one sink into depression, like Don Juan who fell into the inferno after vainly seeking the perfect woman. He, the hapless victim of perennially unsatisfied women, used by a long string of look-alikes, all of them grumbling, suspicious, jealous, wanton, shallow females for whom he would never amount to anything but an object of pleasure.

This certainly did not apply to me and I thanked heaven for this! For the life of me, I can't say what caused Dana to shed the typical image of an ideal lover, opting instead for the pattern of an ordinary, average woman seeing a married man. Perhaps she is going to tell me now at this, our last date, for which she is inexcusably late. In my mind though, she has deliberately and abruptly turned from a lover into a mistress. I still love her, but I'm now also afraid of her. Especially after her patently flimsy argument that she is thirty-five, that she wants a husband in her home, that she needs to start a family, to have her own children. Namely she wanted all the things I had.

But I simply could not leave Claudia or the children. I don't have what it takes to be either a hero or an adventurer. Naturally, I was flattered by the bitter fight each of these two women was putting up to have me exclusively for herself but, at the same time, it filled me with mortal fear.

I had been afraid Dana would push me into getting her pregnant, thereby forcing my hand. But she didn't do it. Did not beg me, did not threaten to get even with me. She didn't even try to blackmail me. Instead, she came out with something I would never have guessed: she took another lover who was only two years her senior. A free, unencumbered man, who was going to marry her. A man she never breathed a word to about our relationship. With whom she had probably lived for quite some time, even while she happily carried on with me. Could I protest? For did I not have Claudia?

However, I couldn't help suspecting this was but a cheap trick to make me jealous or to cause me to take a rash decision. I was trying to tell myself it wasn't true, that there was no such man in her life. That it was all but a passing whim, of the kind women often have. They build up an imaginary world of their own, living out a haunted, masochistic life within this cocoon, all wrapped up in themselves, playing their part in what is anyway, most of the time, but one huge farce.

Still, I was quite apprehensive. I explained to her, desperately, that I was past my prime, that she would only get to live with me in wedlock after years and years of legal wrangles caused by Claudia, who would drag me before all sorts of courts, would crush me financially and psychologically, leaving me a spent man. Basically, I was trying to convince her that my refusal to accept her plan was all for her own good.

I have no idea how sincere or crass my arguments sounded, but I was terribly afraid I would lose her. Or that Claudia would get wind of it and I would be left alone. I dreaded the future, the present, old age, death itself. I was going to see her for the last time at Grand Central, while there was still time to act. It was up to me to decide whether I would stay with her or whether she would become the honorable wife of someone else, in the manner of the wife I myself had back home.

They laid the lid over the coffin, hammered in four nails and, from that moment on, I could see nothing. Totally dissatisfied with the way the funeral had turned out, but relieved that Dana had not kept our date, I climbed down to the subway station, pleasantly surprised with my sudden jovial mood. Once aboard the train, I grabbed the overhead rail with a quick, youthful gesture and bravely suffered the apparently admiring looks of a lady about my age, who was probably thinking at that moment that each of us was aging in different ways.

Men who've topped fifty, if they are unable to preserve their strength for much longer, at least do a convincing job of faking it. They are less worn out than their female counterparts who give birth to our children, rear them, put up with us, bear the brunt of household work, love us and preserve us with Olympian pride.

Was I just imagining it, or did that respectable lady actually give me a curt nudge with her elbow, as if by accident, surrounded as we were by all that mass of people? She must have done it out of spite for my apparent lack of interest in her. Or perhaps she envied me my seemingly tranquil outlook on life's vicissitudes, especially after that outburst of athletic energy evidenced by the way I jumped into the car barely a second before the doors closed.

She had something of the silent, unspoken reproaches Claudia would often treat me with. The barely suppressed, malicious glint in her eyes as she gave me the once over after I had just bought a particularly well-fitting coat that made me look much younger. Or the coolness with which she would treat me whenever I achieved some outstanding professional success. Her jealousy is not confined to women but extends into some sort of competition with everything that belongs to me, something for which I am totally inadequate. I simply do not wish to compete with Claudia. I simply don't care one way or the other whether she gets ahead of me or not.

Come to think of it, the lady in the subway train definitely has something in common with Claudia's attitude when faced with things that go against her preconceived order of things. I could have sworn that woman in the subway was habitually possessive and jealous, a flaming feminist, easily hurt by the jaunty gesture of a man who feels on top of the world, oblivious to the drama experienced day in, day out by women grown old before their time, disagreeably soured, insufferable, irritable, aggressive but so deft at turning that weariness into a virtue.

Could it be that I'm so obsessed with Claudia that I've come to a point where not only is she filling my every thought, every waking moment, but now it turns out I find myself discovering striking similarities between her and perfectly strange women riding the subway, walking in the park or shopping the stores? Or perhaps my sense of guilt over my infidelity to her is what's making her even stronger? The fear I experience lest I hurt her in any way is boomeranging on me, assailing me with all kinds of complexes and panics.

I'm turning my eyes from the woman who is now looking at me almost scornfully, or should I say reprovingly. I deliberately gaze out through the window into the underground blackness surrounding the speeding train with an unavoidable sense of doom and foreboding, with taut nerves. I barely manage to keep my balance in this fast train, hanging on to the overhead rail, jerking every which way the car is swaying. I can feel a certain weariness, a numbness in my bones, as I get closer to home. I fear Claudia. No doubt about it, I am afraid of her, hence this fatigue, this sense of being haunted. Marriages born of love only end up in fear – at least that's what I remember having read somewhere.

I can picture her threatening me with suicide, with the suffering I would cause the children or, what's worse, with the stubbornness of never giving in.

I imagine myself riding the elevator alongside these two women, rushing down scores of flights. Space is tight around us. We can feel one another's breath. Dana's perfume of lemon and lavender is mingling with the aroma of the freshly woven wool in Claudia's pullover. We are silent. How oppressive this silence in the elevator can be! I stare fixedly at the tips of my shoes, so ill at ease and increasingly tense. The elevator continues its downward rush, carrying within it our petrified bodies. Frozen into one position like the dummies in a store window.

Each of us is looking into the gaping bleakness, as if we were inside a clockwork box. And each is alone. Claudia suspects nothing, while Dana feels crushed. Filled with despair, I steal a glance at their waxen faces. They seem so completely alien to me, inanimate. I feel absolutely no link with them, no relationship. I wouldn't dare. I'm overwhelmed, filled with fear, although this time frankly I don't know why I feel guilty. The women I loved or, anyway, the ones I'm supposed to still love are ignoring me. Nay, they are even hating me. In this tense silence I can feel their hatred. Finally they have found a common uniting thread while the elevator is forever descending. It may never come to a stop. Perchance we will descend with it into the abysmal inferno.

But fortunately I do get off. I buy some newspapers at the corner stand. When I arrive, I find the elevator is stuck between floors. So, less sprightly, I climb the three flights of stairs to our apartment. I don't bother searching for my key. Claudia's got to be home. Yes, she is. There she is opening the door to me, with a kitchen apron in her left hand, meaning she's just finished cooking dinner.

It smells so good, this moussaka! I drop my newspapers on the little table in the hallway. We will eat by ourselves in the little kitchen and will tell each other the day's events. I will tell her all about it, in graphic detail – this being another symptom of my fear. I will give her all the details she pumps me for. She is under the impression that these sweet little nothings are conducive to intimacy, are drawing us to each other, keeping us jointly linked to a world of common interests. I dutifully submit to this daily dose of idle talk, overcome with guilt over that something I will never be able to disclose to her. Something that might kill her, if she knew it.

Claudia is so serene she looks sad. I leave my coat in the living room. I wash my hands and then join her at the table. It's comfortably warm in the kitchen, so I undo the top two buttons of my shirt. She is not looking at me, busy with the task of getting the casserole out of the oven. She sets the table, lays out everything. I get ready to start married life as a couple. But Claudia is one step ahead of me.

"Some woman called Dana phoned."

I freeze, with one sleeve half turned, unsure whether I should bother tackling the other.

"Dana? Here?" I listen to myself stammering out panic-filled words.

"Yes, here. Why are you asking?"

"And?"

I don't know what tone I should adopt. I can feel a lump rising in my throat as I watch Claudia's reactions. She fills my plate with three spoonfuls of moussaka, then calmly hands it over to me, totally at ease, albeit somewhat sad. How much does she know? What does she know? I can't stand these tense moments when I am faced with a sudden, unavoidable danger.

"She said she couldn't make the date."

"Date? What date?" I burst out, almost shouting.

"I don't know. I didn't ask."

She said all these words evenly, in measured tones, as if to avoid irritating me; in rhythmic cadences, enunciating every word as clearly as she could.

"Ah! That's what you're talking about," I say, with relief in my voice, deliberately absent-minded, as I feign a ravenous hunger, ready to pounce on the still hot savory moussaka.

My stomach is tied up in knots. I feel a wave of nausea working its way up, and my chest is constricted by an acute pain. A pain that grows stronger and stronger by the minute, as if an iron clamp were tightening its jaws around my heart.

"She's on her way to a funeral," adds Claudia, and then spoons some moussaka on to her own plate.

I stop, my fork in mid-air, as I look at her pleadingly.

"A funeral?"

"Her lover died."

"Her lover?"

I'm about to go mad. Claudia slams the knife hard on the table, the noise startling me into deep despair. She looks at me guiltily, as if apologizing, but all I can read in her eyes is a weary resignation. She almost smiles now, as she waits for me to tell her how good the moussaka is. The pain in my chest has become unbearable. What's going on? Am I dying?

"That's what she said. Her lover."

"Did she mention any name?"

"No. I didn't ask."

And the pain is killing me. Am I really dying? Is it so easy to die? Of fear? Of guilt?

"Poor woman! You know what it's like at such moments…."

"I know…," is all I manage to say.

I can not stand it anymore. Where are my pills? I fall down on the floor.

I am back to square one. Deadlocked again. With both women descending in the elevator which would most likely never stop. As if swallowed by the earth, yet continuing to go on our way. Each of them is expecting a gesture from me, a word, a clarifying move. Space is so tight around us. I can feel their breathing. Dana's fragrance of lemon and lavender mixed in the savory smell of hot moussaka. They take up all the air.

The elevator is continuing its descent. Now I can't feel anything. Only a deep silence. Come to think of it, I feel fine with them beside me, these two women keeping me silent company. The door opens. Dana is pulling her black shawl around her neck, adjusting her black hat, which fit her so well, and she steps out, vanishing into the crowd. Claudia carefully flicks a few pieces of lint from her black overcoat. Then, stiff and proud, she cuts through the crowd, making everyone step aside.

Left behind, I am looking towards them, as a feeling of cold and darkness is washing over me, just like it did in my childhood when I would happen to get stuck in the elevator. But my panic is gone. The door swings back, closing with a clang. From there on nothing can be seen anymore.

*Translation by Dorin Motz*

# Three For Inferno

## II

## *The Wife*

Suicide? Who's talking about suicide? I may have threatened to commit suicide, certainly, but only in anger – doesn't everyone, when pushed over the edge? – merely to scare him, or punish him, but never have I entertained the thought of actually doing something like that! Thank God, I am a well-balanced woman, I've been spared those deep depressions and useless exultations. Even menopause, I've gone through it with relative tranquility, as I have gone through, in fact, every other major change in life.

I don't understand women who on account of trivialities become either hysterical or fall off the deep end, and then try to find a psychiatrist, whom they pay through the nose just to have him listen to their endless lamentations. I would feel completely ridiculous to lie down with my eyes to the ceiling and blabber to a stranger about all the intimate details of my life, the frustrating and shameful instants of my childhood all the way to petered out bedroom episodes, hoping for him to pull out of his sleeve the magic recipe for happiness.

And why, may I ask, are we so obsessed with *happiness*, when, in fact, we've managed to exhaust it of meaning? It's probably the most abused word in the language. We use it at every turn, for the flimsiest excuse, in connection with the most insignificant, trivial acts in our lives. We should be more careful, more decent, when we utter it. We depleted it of its mystery and subtlety. Happiness is a powerful state of being, at once grave and rare – a revelation, a sacred normality, a catharsis, whereas we feel no embarrassment in being happy all day long. I have always resorted to synonyms instead, avoiding, out of respect, to touch the depth of this word fearing I might thus cause its ineffable aura to dissipate. Instead, I would simply say I was glad, content, satisfied, at peace, anything other than happy! Once I thought I had understood it sensually. For me happiness is finding things in their proper place, neatly sorted, just as I have always intended them to be.

Psychologists hold their sway over you by constantly feeding on your insecurity, by always prodding you to relive the chaos in your life. They want you to dredge up all your failures, the countless humiliations you've gone through. Just bring them all out and talk about them, they claim, and you'll instantly be set free. You might, presumably, rid yourself in the end of your obsessions, only to take on those of your own therapist. Soon you'd run the risk of becoming addicted to his comfortable couch, on which he urges you to relax, to let your hair down. From that vantage point, life in the real world seems such a rosy-colored bright picture, drawn with bold strokes, which you seem to think you can easily modify at will, here livening up a color, there softening another as you see fit. Nice, but things don't quite work that way in life. Alas, there's no bridge connecting the blithe musings and revelries you have lying on your shrink's couch and the big world out there, where the rubber meets the road. You get cured of one disease, only to end up contracting another. It's not unheard of to come across cases where patient and therapist lived inextricably connected like this to the very end of their lives. And psychologists could be sometimes more troubled than their patients, which is an other story!

I read an ad in the newspaper: "Are you sad, melancholy, pessimistic? Nothing pleases you any more? Can't sleep? Are you tired and can't concentrate? Are you irritable, nervous, etc.? Don't like to socialize? If you recognize yourself in the above, then you're suffering from depression!" I smiled. All it said is that the whole world is depressed. For sure this profession will never run out of patients, if one were to believe the description in the ad. You get the impression most psychiatrists choose this profession to get rid of their own depression and loneliness.

Ah, loneliness – another word that gives so many women the shivers! All the literature written on this theme! All the energy expended by "expert" couple counselors in analyzing the causes and faces of loneliness! And all the pills people swallow and in the end you still end up with nothing but compromise! Everything ends with compromise. Unhappiness, marriage, loneliness, unfulfilled dreams – all get stranded, or better, saved, in compromise, which gives us the illusion that we have attained what we longed for. Of course, those who are faint-hearted cannot accept compromise, in which case you can talk about suicide. But it's not for me. I'd rather kill someone else than myself. This is something, yes, that I have considered seriously. Say, for instance, if he were to leave me. Or if I found out he's cheating on me. Then I would probably kill him. But why would he do such a thing? I'm not the kind of a woman you cheat or abandon.

All these years I've run the ship of our marriage in a masterful way. Our children are in college. We have a comfortable home, a comfortable checking account, a retirement fund, we respect each other and there are, doubtlessly, tender moments between us. We were in love when we were young, and even you could say we love each other, in a sportsman-like, quiet and tonic fashion, under that serene atmosphere that settles over people in their advancing years. All I expect is to reap the rewards of my labors. To lie comfortably in my favorite lawn chair and pat my grandchildren's heads, while my husband, resigned and shuffling along in his slippers, brings me cold lemonade. A well-deserved scenario.

Thanks to me, our marriage survived. If for nothing else, that should be enough to make him grateful, once in a while. Everywhere you look all you see are divorces, traumatized children, lawyers pouncing on both parties, broken homes, loneliness and desolation. How many husbands whose lives were destroyed by divorce! And all the crazy women in this world! I've given him confidence, I've protected and understood him or, rather, made him feel I understood him, even though he at times he goes off on his flights of fancy. It's no insignificant thing to have someone who can cure you of your utopias. In his case, he found in me both a devoted woman and a wise companion. Life is what it is. You need a strong constitution to survive.

Sometimes I've been reproached for being too telluric, with my feet too firmly planted on the ground, too practical, too much of a realist, that I don't know how to fly, or I appear to be missing those secret, necessarily unfulfilled dreams, which would lend me that nostalgic, a la Bovary air, a delicate melancholy, a sadness one might take for sensitivity. But it is not sensitivity that I have a need for in this life, it is resilience.

Perhaps I too thought at times that I deserve more or something else, that the trajectory I might follow could be existentially a little more spectacular. But it's just that I understand my destiny and I am reconciled with it. I do not hesitate to accept compromise over drama. And I've done my best to protect him of dramas, of temptations, paths that meander. Not so much to shelter my pride, or to protect myself – because I would have managed somehow – but rather to protect him from situations which no doubt would have crushed him. It's so easy to fall prey to temptation, but what about afterwards? I know he's not the stuff of heroes. And in fact this brings him closer to me. He doesn't have the adventurer's blood and courage won't kick him out of the house. And this, actually, brings him closer to me.

I like his weakness. Some might call it cowardice, but I think that goodness itself can make you weak. I am strong enough, and it's good he keeps a certain candor, I need his helpless, awkward way of dealing with those tensions that sometimes pop up out of nowhere, despite my constant care to keep him as far removed from confrontations and decisions as possible. I know he hates having to make decisions. Uncertainty and change frighten him. He operates perfectly within a given scenario. And I am the creator of this scenario. I could not have dreamt a better, more docile player for a husband, so careful lest he make a mistake and wound me. I think that is precisely why our marriage has turned out so good. He is forever on his toes, careful not to make waves or arouse my anger. I tread firmly, to guide his path and scatter his fears.

At times, though, I have the feeling he is afraid of me. Or perhaps he is merely respectful, grateful or admiring of me. All these put together may be confused with fear. Does he really know me? What does he know about me? Certainly, he knows only as much as I let him know. Nothing of my own fears or failures. Nothing of my vulnerability. I was always forced to play the stronger role, the one who has all the answers. I can remember his desperate eyes whenever one of the children got sick. "He is going to be all right," I would assure him, in the hospital, from the child's bedside, and all the while I myself was paralyzed with fear, except that I couldn't afford to show it to him.

Along the course of our lives we had our share of critical circumstances, deadlocks and crises and each time he would expect me to come up with a miraculous solution. And I did. His eyes implored me, each time. "It's going to be alright. We're going to make it." When we couldn't pay our mortgage, when for a time he was without a job, when we were forced to move, when our oldest experienced a turbulent period during his adolescence, when our parents died.... "It will be alright." There was no basis for me saying it. Only his fragility caused in me a mysterious upsurge of strength. I would detest it for someone to tell me I'm strong. I know I am strong, but I also know the price I've had to pay for this strength.

Sometimes I have erotic dreams. I'm not a woman who's hard to satisfy. In any case, I have never complained. The best orgasms I had were in dreams, which is not to say that he has not given me, on numerous occasions, sexual pleasure, or that I didn't do my best to satisfy him. Whatever remains unfulfilled or unconsummated passed into the subconscious. That is where everything finds its solution, it is not my concern. I can be happy even in my sleep. Perhaps that is where I draw my strength from.

My husband, absent-minded, as he appears to be, or naive, always trying to appear indifferent and resigned, knows only too well that I compromise nothing when it comes to seeing my family content, fulfilling all the requirements of my job, or giving him confidence and stability. That's not to say we've reversed roles, that I have taken on the role that comes naturally to the man. I'm not interested in ruling, just being in control. I have no desire to exercise my strength, I just want keep things balanced. This doesn't detract from my femininity. On the contrary. I am thus a complete woman, determined to defend her husband, her household, her children, her purpose, in this world without values and purpose.

I, too, have had my share of doubts. A few years ago, the company where he worked kept sending him on business trips. I would watch him pack at night, before we went to bed. I sat in front of the mirror, brushing my hair at length, so I could observe his packing ritual. And what a veritable ritual it was! He would open the closet and for several minutes survey the rows of shirts, neckties and trousers. Then he would pick out the newest, fanciest ones. He would pack them neatly, placing them one by one with gentle care in his capacious suitcase, barely touching them, lest they should break. Uncharacteristically, he would buy himself expensive after-shaves for the trip – totally out of line with his usual aversion to buying extravagant things. The ritual would end with his dropping in, surreptitiously, the eau-de-cologne and after-shave he had set aside. Naturally, I couldn't help thinking there must be something fishy here. Since at home he didn't seem to put an undue value on these things, hardly even using eau-de-cologne, all this sudden interest in fine clothes and fancy cosmetics made him suspect in my eyes.

Later in the evening, after he had finished packing and left his suitcase in the living room, I would sneak in and remove the eau-de-cologne, replacing his fancy shirts and ties with less elegant ones. To his credit, he never once lashed out at me for doing this. Who knows, my jealousy might have even flattered him or perhaps he was merely trying to avoid a scandal. He is a wise man, whose thoughtfulness might easily pass for resignation.

Nevertheless, one day he asked me, "Why are you doing this?" "Because this gives extra security," I replied, which elicited no further comments from him. He would look at me with an air of gloomy defensiveness, which would bring up a surge of tenderness in me. When we were younger, after such a glance, I would walk over, and begin kissing him. Then I would unbutton his shirt and we would make love.

Sometimes I would have to intervene, so as to tamper his bubbling enthusiasm and bring him back from the clouds, to the earthly reality, lest he would upset the rules of our game or try to change the balance of power in our relationship. He would buy a new coat and then admire himself in the mirror. He would nonchalantly stick his hands in his pockets, the way mannequins do, trying on various poses. "How do I look?" "Well..., don't you think it makes you look a bit older?" I would ask.

Other times he would come back from work and with sheer delight tell me, "Guess what! They published my article. They liked it a lot. I'm being swamped by congratulatory letters and telephone calls!" To which I would gingerly respond, "Honey, let's not kid ourselves. It's nothing but a second-rate magazine, which nobody bothers to read, anyway. People are just being polite. I hope you are not reading too much into these congratulations. You'd only be deluding yourself."

When they made him chief of section, he wanted us to celebrate big time. He rented a good restaurant, to which he invited his workmates, the management and his friends. He felt and walked like a star, as he feverishly planned every minute detail of the party. Unfortunately I couldn't make it since that evening I had been hit by an awful headache.

Once in a while, he would come up with suspect ideas, such as, "How about if we ask Lisa and Julian to join us this weekend on our trip to the mountains?"

"We're going to the mountains anyway, aren't we? After all, we did rent a chalet."

"Why don't we take them with us? They are very simpatico. I mean, don't they say, 'the more, the merrier'?"

I prevented myself from asking him whether he'd had enough of being only with me.

The night before our departure we had a row. We were in the car, on our way home and the radio was on full blast. "Would you turn than music down, honey?" I asked. He complied. Next they played a favorite oldie, from the seventies, a romantic love song from our youth. He turned the radio back up. He can't have enough of oldies from the seventies. Only this time I sensed that particular tune held a special significance for him, turning his face melancholy and inattentive.

"Please turn it down," I insisted.

"Why? I happen to like this song. It turns me on."

"Turns you on?" I screamed, quite hurt. "And which part of you does it turn on? Your soul, your stomach or what? No doubt it reminds you of something, or should I say, someone?" And then I reached out and turned the radio off.

All of a sudden I was caught in a frenzy of jealousy, hit by an immense pique, which had coalesced, seemingly, out of the blue. He turned the radio back on and the love song was still blasting its heart-wrenching tune out of the speakers. "Stop the car! I want to get out. Now, you hear me? Right here!" Of course by now I lost any desire I might have had to go to that mountain resort with the happy bunch he had wanted to foist on me and so we ended up calling off the whole thing, canceling all the reservations.

In less than an hour he'll be home. I am cooking his favorite dish, moussaka in tomato sauce, with sour cream, like we ate in Greece once. We were young and went on vacation on a little Greek island in the Mediterranean. Our first child hadn't been born yet. In fact he was conceived on this trip. We made love three times a day, goaded by the sun, by the oysters and all the other seafood. In a tavern we ordered moussaka, which he liked so much that I asked the chef to let me have the recipe. We were young, good-looking and serene and couldn't be denied. Even then I was already pampering him, without being maternal in my protective gestures, as might be suspected at first glance. I deplore energetic, willful and domineering women. The secret is to have your way, while simulating fragility, as you settle yourself discreetly on the control seat, gauging the correct measure and science of button pushing.

Every now and then I cook moussaka for him, a form of affection, which he is sure to appreciate. He is fortunate to have me. Had he happened to marry a woman more like him, things would have certainly taken a downward turn. I know he thinks me a forceful hand, but what he doesn't see is the velvet glove. I have been discreetly watching over him and one day he will thank me. Or perhaps he feels I have smothered him with my love?! Perhaps he sees nothing else in it but my tenacious will to preserve him over the years.

Once, during a particularly tender moment, I told him I wouldn't want to die after him. At first he was flattered, but then he inquired ironically, "On account you're afraid to be alone, or out of selfishness?" Odd, it didn't occur to him I might have said it out of love. "Out of selfishness," I replied, with equal irony. "I couldn't bear the thought of having no one to torture, that there was no one left to be afraid of me." We both laughed, but a little bitterly.

Sometimes I feel as if married life is a "dog-eat-dog" kind of fight, a race of competing vanities, which is apt to bleed one dry by the time one gets to the finish line. Under the circumstances, the winner is no more than a crumpled, worn-out champion, just as exhausted as the defeated opponent.

After I gave birth to our oldest son, our sex life began to go downhill. I was constantly tired, without any desire left in me, exhausted by the breast feeding, and the nights I had to stay up, I was afraid to be alone with the baby, so entirely tiny and helpless. I focused all my energies on him. At two-year intervals I had the other two boys. By now I had become an expert, but that didn't save our sexual relationship. I turned from woman to mother, from woman into companion, my hips broadened and the fire in my eyes grew domesticated. But towards him I remained as vigilant as ever, like a form of self-protection, always watchful lest I should lose what I had sacrificed so much for.

Several years ago we were invited to a party at his former boss's. A huge house, with an interior garden, swimming pool and all the accoutrements. Beautiful people, decked out in beautiful, stylish clothes, living the good and contented life. We were trying our best to appear relaxed, although we were definitely out of our element. The women were especially resplendent. You could tell they spent most of their days at the fanciest beauty salons, exercising at the best gyms, attending all those fancy shows, and eating at the priciest restaurants. I watched them without envy.

After my second child, I lost my hair. After the third, I never bothered to shed the twenty pounds around my hips and on my thighs. What was most agonizing, though, was that after each new birth I had to relearn how to be a woman all over again. For nine months I would be without a period, and therefore safe from being at the mercy of hormones, from whims and imbalances, from those outbursts of anger, jealousy or suspicion. During my pregnancies I would flourish, I was calm and tolerant, concerned exclusively with my belly growing bigger by the day. As soon as I brought the child into the world, all sorts of crises would be unleashed.

Old age doesn't scare me. I do not suffer from the horror in front of the mirror most women over fifty face. You wake up one morning. You pull the curtain. There's snow on the ground. You want to brush your hair and beyond the mirror a woman stares at you, who looks strikingly like you. Only around her eyes the skin wrinkles in crow's-feet, around her mouth the wrinkles rise and fall in tandem with the movement of her lips, the forehead is lined by scores of tiny furrows, and the light in her eyes is so pallid it can be taken for gentleness. I do not rebel before this woman in the mirror. She is not my spitting image, she is me. I don't have to resort to tricks or games to delude myself.

At that party we were introduced to a writer's daughter. She had come alone. She was single and seemed just as lost as we in that that crowd, but for different reasons, and the hosts had hoped we might keep her company till the atmosphere warmed up. I urged my husband to help out.

I, too, enjoy looking at a beautiful woman. I have the strength to recognize the other's beauty, or her youth; it doesn't humiliate or intimidate me. My husband kept avoiding her eyes, I don't know, he seemed ill at ease, and it annoyed me he didn't pay more attention to her. He ignored her, spoke with her absent-mindedly, indifferent to the movement of her eyes and elegant fingers through the air. Perhaps he was afraid I might be jealous. I was not. Quite the opposite. I wished him in those moments to be a seducer, hated it that he was not the stuff of a conqueror of hearts. I would have wanted him to play games with both of us. In any case, it was I he would go home with. I had nothing to lose. I was certain of myself. And of him, too. On a perverse impulse, or perhaps in order to see if I still had a hold on him, I wanted him to flirt with her. I can't exactly recall her name, Dana? Diana? Something like that.

Several couples began to dance. The girl would not unglue herself from us. She knew no one else at the party and, besides, I was being exceedingly amiable to her. In a way, she inspired pity in me. These unfinished girls, who can't make up their minds, always fumbling about till they end up with nothing!

My husband had become very tender with me, sliding his arm over my shoulder, or round my waist, the only gestures which appeared suspicious to me. Something was wrong, something made him feel insecure. What was he feeling guilty about? I know his reactions when he wants to prevent an explosion of anger from me or when he feels tension in the air. But this time he was wrong, I truly wanted to be generous, to help that girl – Diana? Dana? – feel good and at the same time to let him run around and play a bit.

I pushed the both of them into dancing together. Of course, I had to insist, and even throw him a dirty look. He wouldn't budge. In the end he gave in, without conviction, and they danced. When they stepped past me I smelled her scent of lemon mixed with lavender. She wasn't beautiful but there was something gracefully perverse about her, which was very attractive to men. But not to mine, who took it all like a thankless chore.

They were trudging their legs along. His palm wrinkled the back of her dress. Her right leg was rubbing against his trousers in the rhythm of an Argentine tango. They were a good-looking couple, I had to admit in the end. Still, they didn't look like a winning couple, did not emanate anything powerful or lasting, rather they seemed like a vanquished couple, forced together in order to share each other's defeat. And yet there seemed to be something between them, more like some kind of a sadness, or rather a kind of touching melancholy. I am not saying this out of malice, but pity.

In those moments I even imagined what it would be like if my husband and that girl were lovers. I took a new look at them. Perhaps that's what our marriage was lacking. A lover for him. Something to kick him out of his inertia, to sharpen his senses, to arouse his virility. I even believed this would have had a beneficial effect on our sex life. And, finally, he – who always tells me everything in the greatest detail – would have had something to hide from me. He would have fought for each of us, would have given his best. Would have displayed some attributes that otherwise I would never see in him. Or am I perhaps investing him with an undeserved aura? This is what I'm thinking about as I place the casserole of moussaka in the oven, while he still hasn't showed up. All our life I pampered him. Maybe I don't appreciate him enough. I play with the thought that he might actually have a lover. I smile at this thought and raise my eyebrows with my finger. I straighten my back to drive away the fatigue. I would like to read his thoughts, to find out how he sees me, what he thinks of me. Although, I am certain, he is grateful for all I have done for him. And faithful. I must be on the side of his good side. His domestic aspect, his stable aspect. I could have chosen a more distinguished man, more powerful, spectacular, who would have sprung on me who knows what later on. At least he is predictable, passive, lacking in surprises. Shortcomings may turn to virtues, if you know how to view them.

The telephone rings and I hope against hope it is not him, telling me again he's going to be late. He works too much overtime and he is not young anymore. Lately his blood pressure is up. The doctor prescribed him pills in case of an unpredictable heart crisis.

"Hello? Good evening."

"Good evening."

"Claudia?"

"Speaking. Who is this?"

"Dana."

"Dana? Dana who?" I shout into the phone, irritated that I can barely hear that faint voice.

"We met two years ago at a party in Long Island. I danced with your husband. Do you remember?"

"Yes, I do," I answer without conviction and suddenly my nostrils recall the lemon and lavender. "Yes, of course I remember. How are you?"

"I am here at Grand Central, watching your husband. He's standing a hundred yards away from me."

"My husband? What is he doing there?"

"Waiting for me. We have a date. One of our regular dates. We've been together for over two years."

I untie my apron, clutching it in my left hand, as if to defend myself from something, from someone.

"What are you talking about?"

"We were already a couple, at that party where you kept pushing us to dance.... But this is our final rendezvous. It's up to me to decide whether he leaves you and marries me or, if he goes on dragging along for the rest of his life with you. You're in the second place, Claudia, you're the outsider. Look, I am staring at him right now. His eyes are searching the crowd for me. I am very late. He's stressed, scared, at the end of his rope. He looks like a dead man. Dead with fear. Will I force him to divorce you? Or will I leave him? Hold on to yourself! Yes, I am going to leave him. I have another lover and I decided it is him that I want. I'm running out of time. I've got to make a choice. Slash into raw flesh. You understand this panic, when you feel you're running out of time. I realized I wanted something else and in any case I don't want him anymore. I'm looking at him right now and can't believe I've lived with him all these years. He looks so vulnerable, so helpless, the way he stands peering eagerly at all those faces. Except that I'm not going to show up.... He's all yours, Claudia, all yours! Do whatever you want with him. You know best what to do with him."

I listened to her to the end. I didn't interrupt her, didn't slam the phone down, I didn't scream or contradict her, I heard her out and at the end I slowly hung up. Then I turned off the oven. The aroma of moussaka was choking me. I sat onto the nearest chair, incapable of thinking or doing anything else.

All of a sudden the walls began to shake violently. At first it felt like an earthquake. I was numb, stared at them unable to react in any way. And, strangely enough, it was deafeningly quiet, as if time had stood still. Only my room was in the throes of a muffled trembling. Not a sound, though. Then the walls began walking. Seated on a chair, I saw them draw near, engulfing me, squashing me in the middle, cutting off my air supply; about to crush me, to wall me up within them, to swallow me and then regain their position up as if nothing had happened. Had I batted them, I'm sure my eyelashes would have touched the wall in front of me. It was so close I felt it pressing against my chest.

With my last ounce of energy, driven by sheer determination and willpower, I managed to get up from the chair and let out a throaty, inhuman scream that scared the wits out of me. I could see myself, but was utterly incapable of stopping. I heard myself, but could not drown out my screams. My body kept on banging against the walls violently, and I continued to roar like a cornered animal. I began to strip, dropping my clothes one by one, until I was stark naked.

With enormous effort I dragged myself to the bedroom, where I was horrified by what I saw in the mirror. That grossly overweight, dirty old woman, moaning lugubriously, was unspeakably ugly. I wouldn't be caught having anything to do with the wretched hag! At that moment a deafening noise unleashed itself within me. My insides were churning up. I started hitting myself with furious abandon all over my arms, my thighs and my breasts. Contorted with pain, I fell in a sorry heap on the carpet. I had shouted myself hoarse.

I lay on the floor, exhausted, thoroughly spent, frozen in time. The noise grew softer, until it faded out. My heart gradually regained its normal beat. I discovered I could now breathe regularly, but felt terribly cold. I stood up, did my hair, took out fresh clothes from the closet, put on my shoes, and tied the kitchen apron around my waist. I took in a big gulps of air and from the corner of my eye glanced in the mirror again. I looked okay. No one would suspect what had just occurred. The walls were back where they belonged. I moseyed to the kitchen, turning on the oven, to finish the dinner. My mouth was wide open and in my stomach was growling, as if a big rock was inhabiting it.

I hear him outside the door, I go to open it. In my left hand I still clutch the apron.

"Hmm, something smells good," he tells me, he drops his coat in the living room, washes his hands and walks into the kitchen. I find it hard to look him in the face. I take the casserole out of the oven, and lay the plates for dinner, expecting him to say something, a story, an excuse, a confession.

"I am dead tired!" he murmurs.

I can't stand it any more so I start.

"Some woman called. Dana."

"Dana? Here?" he asks. There is panic in his voice. He avoids my eyes. I can almost see a lump rising in his throat. I pour three spoonfuls of moussaka on his plate.

"Here!"

"And?"

"She said she didn't show up for the date."

I slam the knife on the table and the noise makes him jump in fright. He eats the moussaka, and it is clear that nausea swamps his stomach. I dish out two more spoonfuls for him to eat and stare at him calmly, as though I didn't suspect anything, didn't know anything, as if I just wanted to make him feel good.

"Date? What date?" he almost shouts at me – something he has never done before. He is scared, I can see him shaking and turning pale. Bluish circles begin appearing around his eyes and his mouth.

"She said she was going to a funeral."

"A funeral?"

He brings his hand to his chest. He is livid, his face contorted with pain. His eyes seem to grow out of their sockets, He's having a convulsion. I can't stop now.

"Yes, her lover died."

"Her lover?"

Should I get him the medicine from the drawer? Should I call an ambulance? Or should I just let him agonize a little longer?

He collapses to the floor, pulling after him the table cloth with the moussaka and everything.

*Translation by Dorin Motz*

# Three for Inferno

## III

## The Mistress

I remember well the moment I decided to leave him. Big things grow out of nothing. You may overlook a host of serious, crucial incidents, but sometimes all it takes is a mere trifle, a word or a gesture to trigger a break up.

We were in the same restaurant on Second Avenue in which we used to meet in the more than three years we'd been together. Christmas was just around the corner and I was anxious as I usually am around the holidays. Holidays were invented for wives. They gather their families around the table and start exercising their strength, their assurance, their supremacy. Looming ahead were empty days, unending nights, and the annoying jingle of bells and fast-paced songs played incessantly by radio stations, blaring out of the speakers along the streets, in stores or at train stations. If I only had the money or the strength to do it, I would certainly head out for some other place. But you can't run from loneliness. It clings to you.

No one talks about the loneliness of the mistresses. They are either envied or despised, but never allowed to have existential crises, simply because they are thought to cause crises and breakups in otherwise perfectly honorable families. Nobody breathes a word about the good they bring into a man's life. Especially the wives, if only they were honest, ought to put them on pedestals, sing their praises, dedicate odes to them. Moreover, they should found a non-profit organization, titled "The Grateful Wives Foundation." Frankly I don't see why not, given the fact that we have such associations as "The Foundation for the Protection of Wolves"! Mistresses play a useful part. Just think of all the saved marriages, of the men whose virility has been restored, their lives ridden of anxieties, weaknesses, fears, obsessions, and humiliations! And don't forget all the wives who owe their happiness to some mistress in their husbands' lives! Anyway, they outnumber those couples who separate for the same reasons.

It's not easy to be a mistress, for this, too, is a profession. One that involves risks, experience, talent, dedication and, of course, hard work – lots of hard work! You need to know how to keep a man, how to make him find something he would never find at home, how to compensate him for the tensions in his family with respect and admiration. They adore being admired. Unconditional admiration is an essential part of the male pride – something most wives fail to give them.

I loved my profession. And I lasted as long as I did because of certain rules and moral principles I strictly adhered to. I stuck to married men, so as to avoid messy complications. It may sound paradoxical, but you'll feel more secure with a married man, who is determined to keep his wife, children and house, than with a single man, who is always liable to botch things up by asking you to marry him. I never brought into my house a man with whom I was romantically involved. Instead, we always met on neutral ground, so I could be free to come and go as I pleased and have complete control over the situation.

Once in a while I did fear one of them might one day think of leaving his wife and turn up on my doorstep with two suitcases in his hands, with kids he needed to visit every Sunday and a long list of relatives to take over, along with all his idiosyncrasies, his cholesterol-reducing pills and his sciatica. Or, after a bout of love-making, he might want to stay late, luxuriating in my tub, using my towels, my terry-cloth robe. Or I might hear him suggest next that I cook something and play out a domestic scene, sitting in front of the TV in the absence of a fireplace.

They say every wife dreams she will one day become a man's mistress, while every mistress hopes to one day become a wife. Not me, though. Having found the proper framework for our relationship, I made sure we stuck to it. Marriage is a serious business one should not enter into lightly, out of mere passion. It's a highly complex institution, which must be built with care, not under the pressure of feelings, emotions or obligations of any sort. To bring up the subject of marriage can also be a test for a man acquainted with the comfortable setup of concubinage or adultery. This was precisely the moment I decided to part with this latest of my lovers. This reaction triggered in me some of the most alarming signals.

Somehow I felt life would go on forever, hovering somewhere between the age of twenty and forty. Youth grants you not only strength, but also illusions. You think you can control time. And, desperately, you live life to the fullest, denying yourself nothing, intensely pursuing happiness and the acquisition of a career. By happiness I understood whatever was new, surprising, unusual – the challenge of every new start, fresh, unexpected situations, fortresses to explore and conquer. I wasn't placing too much trust in the future. The intensity of the moment – that's all I was interested in.

That day – I can't make up my mind if it was a good or bad one – I turned thirty-eight. I hadn't slept a wink all night. I kept reading into the wee hours of the morning, on the sofa in the library. I was alone as usual those nights before Christmas, when I could smell the scent of fir-trees and the aroma of hot cakes. I could picture in my mind all the hustle and bustle of families as they were getting ready to open their presents. I don't know whether they were happy but they were together and for the first time I felt my heart pierced by a dagger. All of a sudden I was jealous, very jealous of him, of his wife, of his children, of his domestic tranquility – genuine or contrived. I threw the blanket off me and sat on the edge of the sofa, feeling dejected, hurt, defeated and useless.

I glanced at my naked legs, on which thin, bluish-purple veins were breaking out, drawing tiny rivulets under my no-longer youthful skin. Am I growing old? Could this sudden pique of jealousy be a telltale sign of something to come? And the deep quietude of my room, in which until a few days ago I had felt so comfortable, but which had of late become something like a prolonged sound, such as only loneliness can create, could all this be but the fear of aging?

In an attempt to get a handle on my emotions, to bring my panic under control, I walked into the kitchen and poured myself a glass of red wine, which was quite sour. The table was dominated by the bouquet of flowers he had sent me, along with the usual card on which were printed conventional wishes, followed by his signature and the eternal "love" – a word used by everyone ad nauseam. People no longer say what they like. Instead they "love" everything. They love everything. I constantly hear, I love this, I love that, i.e. foods, shows, animals, cities, books, words, situations. No discrimination, no decency. Thus how easy it is to empty love of its true meaning, in this belittling and unconscious manner! The word "love" must be quarantined! Its use ought to be allowed only under special circumstances, after a careful scrutiny of the speaker's motives.

I returned to the library and went back to sleep. Under the blanket, pulled up to my chin, I sensed my body trembling. With fury. With helplessness. With fear. Could jealousy cause all these feelings in a bundle? I remembered the Long Island party, when I also felt something of what I was going through now. I had been invited by the owner of a company with which I had once collaborated and for which my lover continued to work. I knew he would be there with his wife. I only went in order to see her. I had wanted to feel, to smell, to study her movements, to see the color of her eyes, to hear how she spoke, ate, and laughed. I badly needed to see her. He told me theirs was a marriage of convenience, in which they hadn't been making love for years, more exactly from the moment I had shown up in his life. This all married men tell their mistresses.

I had arrived early and sat down at a table on the fringe, so as not to be immediately noticed, while being able to watch the entrance. I wanted to see them when they came, to observe how they behaved when they thought they were unwatched. They came in walking slowly, Claudia several steps ahead of him. The wind blew her shawl off and he reached quickly to put it back, arranging it with quite tender movements. She did not cast any glance at him, but whispered something, to which he smiled the way he smiled to me whenever I told him we were lucky we had met.

Then we were introduced. Naturally, we both pretended we were meeting for the first time. Claudia was nowhere near the type of frigid shrew I had been led to believe she would be. As for him, he was quite fearful. He seemed to me smaller, older, weaker, dependent on her, quietly rebellious, as a teenager taken out into the public by his mother. Claudia though was even nice, even graceful, bearing her age well. O, how I hated her. I looked them both over. They were an ordinary couple. Tacit understandings were at work between them; they resonated at some word which had identical meanings to both of them. They were communicating. Through hints. Through gestures. Through their skin. There was between them a sort of complicity which only intimacy can create, the concern of each to protect the other. Perhaps they no longer had the passion of their former youthful days, but were still making love. I was in no mood then for metaphysics or psychology. Or it might be that the motive for the times they did have sex was their vanity, his capitulation, her need to dominate, or his determination to perpetuate the illusion of normalcy. It didn't matter. That picture made me suffer terribly. Subconsciously I think this was when there popped into my mind the idea of punishing them. Both of them. To hurt her and to leave him.

He brought us two glasses of red wine. All three of us clinked our glasses. Claudia and I studied each other quickly, while tasting the wine with elegant gestures befitting worldly women. He dropped his glass, which shattered against the concrete, spilling the wine into our shoes. He apologized; Claudia was magnanimously understanding, "It's nothing, dear; shards and red wine bring good luck." Then softly, only to him, with irony, rather than irritation, "Are you tired? You might try and get a hold of yourself!"

I tried to guess Claudia's perfume. She did not seem to have any suspicion about my affair with her husband. She was being kind to me, looking at me benignly, as she intuited my curiosity, and, bending her head over my shoulder until her forehead almost touched my cheek, said, "Magie Noir." I chill ran down my spine.

I went home early. That night I dreamed of Claudia. We were at the circus, watching the show in the first row. In the middle of the arena: Claudia. It was a dressage number. Claudia, whip in hand, was taming not animals, but men. I recognized her husband, my lover, the one both of us shared, without her being aware of it. Him she was causing to perform some of the most spectacular feats. And my lover, with an agility I could hardly have suspected, was jumping through fire, passing through narrower and narrower rings, crouching at her feet. The floodlights came on. I was alone in the entire circus.

The day I turned thirty-eight all of this came back to me with frightening proportions. What was I going to do with my life? I turned off the lamp and remained numbed with my eyes closed under the blanket, listening to my heartbeat. It was dark and quiet. My senses were at their most taut. And suddenly I felt light, as apparently I lifted myself off from that position of lying down perfectly, blanket and all, and was able to see my body still lying on the bed sheet.

I was thinking of myself with anger, but also with an overwhelming compassion. I had been such a squanderer. I gave everything I had to the men I got involved with. Youth, love, energy. There are several age thresholds in life and I was just crossing one of them, as I listened to my biological clock ticking away an ultimatum. Pervasive fear invaded me.

I remembered the words Claudia had told me that evening at the party. We were having a formal conversation, when the host approached us, urging us to have a good time, "Come on, eat and dance. It's a perfect summer evening. The water in the swimming pool is warm, the wine is cool. Let's enjoy them. Life is brief and beautiful!" Claudia smiled doubtfully, and after the host went away, she turned to me, with careless words, "In fact, it is a perilous adventure, wouldn't you say?" I froze. So she did know something? "I mean," Claudia continued, her smile tinged with melancholy, "life seems to be handing us more terror than satisfaction."

I reached out to turn the lamp back on, but it seemed everything was far away, hard to reach. My arm felt like lead. I opened my eyes and my body fell back onto the sheet, all of this in a perfectly real manner, as I heard the thud. I groped in the dark and stumbled upon the lamp's switch. That night I slept with the light on.

The next day we had a date at our restaurant on Second Avenue. I was determined to tell him everything. I had run out of time. And I decided to throw everything into the game, to play it out. He presented me with a diamond-studded bracelet for my birthday. I thanked him. Then I set the box next to the bread basket and ordered as usual chowder and endive salad with Roquefort sauce. I placed my elbows on the table and looked him in the eye.

"I have no more time."

He did not understand and looked at his watch.

"It's only one. We planned to spend the entire afternoon together, didn't we? That's why I got some time off from work. After all, it's your birthday!"

"Yes, I'm thirty-eight."

He raised his wine-filled glass and said to me tenderly, "Happy birthday!"

"I have reached this age with no family of my own, with no children, waiting out the weekends and the holidays you spent with Claudia, so that we could be together for a few brief hours a week. And even those were stolen, spent surreptitiously. I can't take it any longer. I've run out of time. I want a husband, a home of my own, and a child."

He did not seem to be taken aback by my speech, which I had uttered breathlessly, lest it should sound pathetic.

"I know, you're right." And he took my hand, kissing it over the chowder plates.

"And I mean to get these."

Only now did he start, with a nervous twitch.

"Dana, you know there's no more I can do. I love you, I'll go on loving you all my life...."

I had a lump in my throat. We continued to tell each other what each already knew. We had reached a deadlock.

"Then we'll have to part ways," I told him, my voice choked with sorrow.

He was silent. Suddenly everything began to bother me. The way he slurped the chowder, his nervous swallowing, the jangle of the silverware he was carelessly touching, the soup dripping onto his chin from the corners of his mouth. I found him graceless, aged, alienated. And I did not know what I despised more – his cowardice or his selfishness. I felt the urge to humiliate him in return.

"Maybe I have another lover. Has it occurred to you? Perhaps I want to marry *him*."

"Is it true?"

I did not reply, but it was quite clear we had nothing more to say to each other. I knew everything was over between us and yet I could not help provoking him.

"You've got one week to think it over. Either you leave Claudia or we separate forever. You've got one more chance to choose. We'll meet Friday at Grand Central Station, at six p.m., by the departures area." I left, forgetting on the table, next to the bread basket, the bracelet he had given me as a present. I never saw him again after that.

All week I was on the verge of having a depression, and very early that Friday I left home to see some friends in upstate New York. At six fifteen in the evening I called Claudia from their house. He was supposed to be at Grand Central Station, seeking me out in the crowd, and hoping I wouldn't show up. I never disappointed him. And I could do no less.

I stayed overnight at my friends' house. In the past few days I had slept very little. I was exhausted physically and mentally, not to mention the miserable feeling left by my call to Claudia. I asked my friends for some sleeping aid. They gave me a vial of sleeping pills, cautioning me to take no more than half a pill, since it was a powerful new drug, which would put me to sleep right away. I heeded them, but an hour later I continued to toss in bed, awake, having reached the end of my tether, with tired blood-shot eyes. I swallowed another pill, to no avail. Then I can't remember exactly, I might have taken another one, perhaps two – I don't know how many – despairing of ever being able to fall to sleep.

I woke up in a tall-ceilinged room, painted white, and very chilly. At the head of the narrow bed two uniformed men were standing. With rigid movements, they help me get up. Actually they drag me out of bed. One of them tells me they've come to pick me up, since I am a suspect in the death of my lover, while the other informs me I have the right to remain silent. Each holds me by one arm, as we step out into a very long brightly-lit hallway. I am barely dragging me feet. The two men fall in step with me. We walk on like this for some time.

The light is brighter and brighter, so that I have to cover my eyes with my hand, to be able to bear it. Then we stop in front of an elevator with metal doors, which open and we step in. Inside is Claudia. She, too, is held by the arm by a uniformed man. The glint in her eyes freezes me. The elevator we are riding in starts to descend. There's very little room inside. An overpowering aroma of moussaka mingled with the fragrance of Magie Noir assaults my nostrils. We study each other, but neither utters a word. And neither of us is surprised by the other's presence in the elevator. The elevator continues to descend, with us in it, and somehow I have the feeling it will never stop, that we will plunge into Inferno.

*Translation by Dorin Motz*

## Somewhere in the East

All things were unfolding naturally and for the life of me I could not have guessed the madness I would soon step into, totally unprepared, surprised and defenseless, unfit emotionally for the stormy events that would ensue, after so many years in which I had practiced resignation, had become so accustomed to the usual, to the familiar. I had learned to take things as they came, to marvel at nothing, to aspire only to what was permitted and possible.

I had come to an understanding of sorts with life. All things seemed settled for the foreseeable future. I had even come to terms with the business of surviving. I had my own alliances, having found a way to communicate in a crooked, topsy-turvy world, in which little was being communicated and even that was in code. I had determined to put up with the conspiracies and the conflicts, and was by now even amenable to certain compromises, as long as I could enjoy certain liberties in exchange. I thought I had a good handle on any states of exultation. There wasn't much I could expect from outside, since events were so predictable, while on the inside I was putting on a front of calmness and indifference, for what should have been a real poise and equilibrium. In short, things were neither here, nor there.

Time had become sort of neutral to me. The children were now college students, my wife had stopped tormenting me with her fits of jealousy. I was working as an editor with one of the capital's dailies and prided myself on having deftly avoided landing any management position, which would have required a much too heavy dose of involvement in politics, which, in turn, would have entailed all sorts of shameful, humiliating compromises. I was more and more resigned to just age nicely, putting off as long as I could, as best I could any serious attempt to answer life's hard-nosed questions. I opposed nothing and no one. I made sure I never stepped out of line. I was a dutiful aspirant to the commonplace, a nostalgic seeker of normality. And at that very moment, just when I thought I had it all down pat, madness broke out.

I was living in one of those relatively "good" districts of the capital, neither too central, nor too peripheral. An area with prevailing tall, gray buildings, with ugly rundown balconies that were far too narrow, which had been built during the years of socialism with the express purpose of herding as many similar people as possible, in standard, one-size-fits-all tiny apartments appropriately nicknamed "matchboxes." The ground floor of these buildings invariably housed all sorts of stores, mostly of a useless variety. In fact, in those days many of them were almost always empty or stocked with unappealing, shoddy products nobody ever wanted. Their grimy, dingy windows displayed spinach jars and tomato cans, but even these were avoided by the customers after the Chernobyl nuclear plant accident, which everybody felt had contaminated all vegetation in the region with radiation.

Be that as it may, my own apartment, on the fourth floor of one of these buildings, was quite comfortable, well above average. There was no reason why I shouldn't have considered myself fortunate, content. Everyone in the family had his or her own room. I slept in the library, where I had managed to squeeze my desk, a bed and two armchairs. My wife had the exclusive use of our formerly joint bedroom. She enjoyed sleeping in our old king-size bed, which we were now sharing only on rare occasions. I snored, and she could not stand the bedside lamp by whose light I would read well into the night. Besides, each of us was tired, bored and preferred our own privacy to any conjugal bliss.

Again it was the system we lived under that had led to this arrangement. For two years we had had no lights after ten p.m. due to the authorities' supposed need to conserve energy. Naturally we had found a way to cope even with this inconvenience, by acquiring tons of candles, which came in very handy in those days, when our eyes could hardly penetrate the thick darkness on the streets, on the staircase and practically everywhere else. Kerosene lamps, formerly discarded by the stores, now made a triumphant comeback and if one had the right connections in an electrical appliance store, one could get, for a price and almost always under the table, Russian-made flashlights and electric rings from Czechoslovakia. Needless to say when the lights went out, the water and heat supplies were also cut, as well as the natural gas.

We were experimenting with a glorious "back to nature" movement! During the summer nights I could do a bit of reading by candlelight, but in winter this was almost always impossible. We would all go to bed very early, quite fed up with everything. Water was heated on the electric ring. Then we washed ourselves as best we could in a washbowl, put on warm socks, a track suit, donned a ski cap and slid under the covers, numb with cold. All these things were going on in the waning years of the eighties, when the world outside was abuzz with all kinds of wonderful high tech gadgets, with news of great breakthroughs in outer space exploration and with so many other out-of-this-world wonders, which nevertheless left us – in our sad, cold, forlorn corner of the earth – quite indifferent.

Bundled up like this, needless to say there were few, if any, romantic stirrings in us. Whatever passionate desires might have reared up in us would have been quickly stifled under these harsh circumstances. And so, was it any wonder that the birth rate in our country was steadily declining, in sharp contrast to mortality, which peaked among young women who were trying the abort their fetuses in their own homes, either by themselves or aided by some old woman, skilled in such matters, through the use of knitting needles, corkscrews, clothes hangers and other such unconventional instruments? The woman would consent to go to the hospital only at the very last minute, after desperation had overcome her fear of the authorities. Once there, next to the doctor, waiting for her would be the stern-faced secret police officer and the unmerciful prosecutor. An emergency curettage would ensue, followed by prosecution or rapid death.

Our daughter had her own room. Our son had taken over what in those standard apartment buildings was called the dining room, but was really the place where the family watched television.

We took turns eating our meals in the tiny kitchen, sparsely equipped like most kitchens in the disadvantaged countries of Eastern Europe. Only on Sundays would we eat lunch together, when all of us happened to be at home for the occasion. At such times the dining room resumed its original intended use. My wife hated having to carry all the dishes, pots and pans, and the cutlery for our meal, while our son was understandably upset to see all his playing records piled up in a corner, along with his cassettes, ash trays and an assortment of other personal objects: all sorts of devices, sports accessories, books, university courses and what not. We would each bring our own chair into this room, leaving behind, after the meal, odors of food and perspiration. The only one watching television was my wife, and even she wasn't doing it very often. We simply lived like everyone else and had no inkling of the madness that would soon follow.

My job at this daily had its well-set routines, running, as it were, on automatic pilot. Mostly I was in charge of the miscellaneous news page. I would dig up some "true stories," that would pass muster with the government censors, in an attempt to give the unhappy, sensation-hungry readers at least the illusion they were being informed about what was really going on in the country. The least I could do was to spice these stories up a little, employing as lively and attractive a style as I could, while at other times resorting to a dry, ironical tone, to describe what were really quite ordinary affairs – petty crimes that brought disproportionately heavy sentences on their perpetrators, traffic accidents, maybe an avalanche or two in winter, insignificant losses and ideologically-sweetened dramas. Nothing of the real social traumas ever made it into print. None of the on-the-job accidents, resulting in the death of scores of workers, were reported; not a word was written about the murders that occurred or the abysmal conditions under which children in orphanages, in hospitals, or in schools lived. And certainly not even a passing comment was allowed about the corruption permeating the leading political and economic circles. Not a word was breathed about these things, for, after all, such horrible things "only happened in the West," right?

Here's what a typical item in the miscellaneous news section would have sounded like: "A woman employed by the 'Spicul Rosu' company (i.e. 'Red Ear of Grain') was caught, upon getting out of her shift, with three loaves of bread, concealed under her padded parka. The illegally acquired goods were thereupon immediately seized and the company's party committee decided to issue a stern reprimand against her, after which she was duly prosecuted. She was sentenced today to three months imprisonment. Angela Balaci is the mother of three children, this being her first offense of the kind."

Meanwhile the communist oligarchy and the heads of the dreaded secret police, called *Securitate*, had bled the country dry, stealing whatever could be stolen, in order to pad their large Swiss accounts.

Everything was highly centralized, run by a handful of incapable political apparatchiks, who tailored the laws to their own taste, changing them at will or, as the case might be, breaking them if it suited their purposes.

The days wore on, long and boring. The sensational, the unusual, the out-of-the-ordinary always happened somewhere else, never here. What never happened was exactly the kind of events we desired fervently and knew in our hearts we badly needed for any good change to occur in our country. After a while we even ran out of conflicts. As for failures, for depressions, we had no time for such sentimental nonsense! Both radio and television were triumphantly spouting stories about our supposed victories, achievements, quotas met and exceeded, bumper crops in agriculture, incredibly high industrial outputs, in our exports and, above all, in our birth rate.

Happiness and triumph were rolling out in waves over the heads of the country's inhabitants, over the happy-go-lucky, grateful beneficiaries of tons and tons of pig iron, coal and other natural assets. All graphs showed unusually high values, shooting up vertically, while we went on living our miserable lives, half buried underground! And yet, when it came to sports championships and artistic events, we always came out on top.

Our children were the best. They crammed all day – what else could they do? They invariably won the highest places in the science competitions. And, of course, if by some miracle they were allowed to go abroad to attend international competitions, they always fetched first- or second-place prizes.

Our old folks were dying decent deaths, many of them still in their prime, having had but a few years in which to enjoy the ridiculously low pensions allotted to them, with which there wasn't much to buy anyway. They spent most of their time waiting in lines, grim, silent and determined, dragging their feet through the dusty parks or playing rummy on the benches in front of the dilapidated apartment buildings.

Our women would get up very early in the morning and throughout the day kept cooking, and washing – by hand – the household's dishes and laundry. Their natural beauty rapidly faded, as they didn't have time to look after themselves, soured as they were by life's hardships, with unkempt, disheveled appearances, embittered by hard labor and the absence of any basic comforts. Wherever they went, they carried with them their ubiquitous plastic bags, humiliating us when they got home with the display of their meager contents, acquired after much effort and at ridiculously high prices. Because abortion was illegal and contraceptives almost impossible to come by, they hated their husbands and had sullenly consented to include sex among those unavoidable, risky sacrifices that simply had to be put up with, in which all pleasure had long since given way to revulsion.

No one committed suicide. Officially there were no murders, no robberies, no sabotage, and no strikes. Come to think of it, in every town there was but one basic newspaper, coming out in two or three slightly modified variations, but all written in the same hollow and artificially pumped up style – just like the paper I was working for. People bought these papers mainly for the classified ads or for the obituaries page, which they watched feverishly every morning, in the vain hope that one day they would wake up and discover, with delirious joy, right there on Page One, framed in a heavy black border, the official announcement about the death of "the most beloved son of the nation."

Lest I should reach a plateau and remain forever buried in the miscellaneous news division, occasionally I collaborated with several cultural magazines, contributing now and then a literary review or an essay. Sometimes I would translate a book. The only gesture that might have conceivably been construed as heroic on my part was listening to the broadcasts of the foreign radio stations late into the night, after first taking every precaution lest I should disturb my neighbors.

Like everybody else, I would sometimes mumble some incoherent, barely audible criticism against the regime, but only within the confines of my close-knit circle of friends.

All along I read voraciously, saw countless movies on videotape, and generally did my best to stay well informed, and connected, as much as possible, to the outside world, aware of what was going on, but always on guard, lest my name should transcend the boundary of my immediate co-workers and the pursuits that were in keeping with my job and the properly approved actions I was supposed to be engaged in as such.

In spite of it all, I managed to keep my humor, quite convinced that we were not what we imagined ourselves to be. It was quite an exuberant, lively kind of humor. There was no shortage of jokes in those days, which acted as some sort of a safety valve, another survival mechanism. We seemed to be a surreal people who could not stop laughing, even while we were slowly dying!

The jokes covered a wide range, from the political to the social realm, many carrying an ethnic or regional flavor, evidencing that unique characteristic of our *wise* people: the ability "to laugh troubles away," or the more intellectual variety, based on the onomatopoeic similarity of the words "laughter" and "weeping" in the native language, all of these, no doubt, being attempts to cope with the ruthless rigors of the system. Some wag came up with the idea that even these jokes were being concocted and deliberately spread by the dreaded *Securitate* in their clever attempt to inculcate a certain illusion of freedom in us, to allow us the cheap privilege of a few harmless liberties. It should not come as a surprise then that this led to the development of a unique genre of science-fiction-like, surrealist, absurd literature so prevalent at the time.

Naturally, political jokes topped the list, being told with gusto, in a wide variety of situations. Example: "On Page One of the main daily there appeared, framed in black, the following obituary: 'The family of the head of state is deeply saddened to announce the passing, after a prolonged illness, of the entire nation'."

We repressed our feelings as best we could, while they were fine-tuning their experiment on us, the hapless guinea pigs, cynically resorting to psychology and to the so-called "national specificity" concept. I once had the privilege of getting hold of a copy of a report written by a foreign observer at the end of his two-month stay in our country, which he criss-crossed, studying people from almost every walk of life, looking, probing, taking notes and then summing up his impressions for the organization that had commissioned his research, in this terse paragraph:

> A talented but lazy people, wavering between the ridiculous and the hyperbole. Suspicious when prosperous, resigned when in trouble. Easy to manipulate, prone to going with the crowd, forever practicing the art of survival at the crossroads of empires, systems and religions. Oscillating between excessive praise and self-deprecation, between lamentation and victimization, now living 'under the times,' now beside them. Conjuring up fake heroes and ignoring their own values. Overestimating their adversaries, and downplaying the contribution of potential allies. Patient, resigned, passive, fatalistic. Displaying a great propensity for catastrophes. Always inclined to blame others for their mistakes, rather than their own selves. Incessantly coming up with dark, sinister plots, taking perverse pleasure in all sorts of inside but more often outside conspiracies, overcome with self-pity for their lot in life, which turns out never to be what they think it should have been. An interesting culture, and a lively artistic life, but with intellectuals who are yet to produce a decent *samizdat* literature. A divided, nationalistic, and opportunistic people. And permeating all walks of life, at every step, is the perennial mocking, the

> cowardly outlook, the predisposition to parody everything, to make fun of all things, to turn everything into an incessant music *lautari* played by those fiddlers whose bands are known as *tarafs*.

At first I got quite mad at this no-holds-barred, unvarnished description of us, but later had to admit the reporter was right. After all, things are much clearer when viewed from afar, through cool, detached eyes.

I held my vanity and pride in check. I was doing my best not to sink into despondency and arrogance. I had found my place in society, had sized myself up existentially, and generally avoided any unnecessary self-delusion. But, try as I might, I could not rid myself of momentary piques of rebellion, of disgust, of feeling that I'd just about had all I could take. At such times I felt quite fed up with the way things were going, gripped by revolutionary fervor, which however never translated into any meaningful, practical outworking, always ending up in resignation, as I was starting over and over again from square one, continuing my humdrum existence.

As for infidelities, I had not cheated on my wife for I didn't know how long. Years ago I had had a flaming love affair – enough to put a nice round cap on my memoirs if I ever get down to writing them. I hated the political system in a passive but unrelenting manner. I was totally convinced nothing would ever change in my lifetime, not a thing would stir in the political arena. I foresaw no reversal of the status quo, in spite of the constant message I was getting from the foreign broadcasts, that communism's days were numbered.

Eastern Europe was going through unprecedented turmoil. However to me these convulsions seemed quite laborious and somewhat contrived. Still, whatever they did in the rest of the region, I said to myself, for us there was no hope. For we were, in my opinion, an enclave, a cage deeply entrenched in totalitarianism, with no one capable or willing to pull apart its heavy bars.

True, the East was beginning to groan and shake, but I could have sworn the wave would lose its momentum by the time it reached us, that is, if they hadn't first nipped in the bud even the passing thought of a revolt. We had become quite good at being stuck in our isolationism. Terror reigned supreme in our country. The infernal oppression machine

– finely-tuned and driven daily by the contribution each of us, pliable puppets, were making, whether we realized it or not, to the triumph of the seemingly never-ending nightmare – was running on quite nicely, thank you.

However I did not make the mistake of attributing all failures to our all-pervasive cowardice. I knew there were people who thought deeply, who conspired albeit at a purely intellectual level, but all these forms of personal resistance were unable to trigger any meaningful, lasting change. It was a silent resistance, relevant only to the cultural space, extended as a compensation for the official political obscurantism.

We were like some individual oases in a vast desert, our only solidarity manifesting itself through our obstinacy to be different from what we looked like as a nation. As if viewed from an imaging space satellite, hovering over a dark area of the earth, we must have appeared as isolated pinpoints of light, in the blackness of the vast surrounding night, thereby intensifying our sad plight.

We were living a paradoxical existence. While barely above the poverty or should I say subsistence line, our artistic and cultural lives more than made up for our material destitution. On Saturdays we would stand in line for hours to buy tickets for all the shows that would be played in the city's playhouses during the following week. We had our own talented actors, our own skilled directors – at least the ones that hadn't yet emigrated. The censorship was again laying down its weapons before such texts as those composed by Pirandello, Shakespeare, Bulgakov or Chekhov and turned a blind eye to references to the underground, to political allusions and to directorial ironies. To be sure, we were permitted certain liberties. But these could not provide the heat we needed to keep from freezing in our apartments, nor did they satisfy our hunger. They could not cause the communist bloc to crack, but they did vindicate us to a certain extent.

In the concert hall where the symphony orchestra played it was so cold that the players had to perform with gloved hands, while the conductor had a heavy sheepskin hat pulled over his head.

While national writers had to do battle with the censorship apparatus, translations from world literature were curiously enough permitted. The top communist rulers simply did not care one way or another about this kind of literature. What the decadent imperialists were writing was not their business. Theirs was to watch over the national values. And so there were plenty of court poets, committed writers, slavish servants of the regime who, year after year, published, especially on the supreme leader's birthday, thick volumes of sickeningly obsequious poetry, paeans filled with incredibly low-taste high praise addressed to him. Everybody was happy. Thus our leader, the *Conducator*, as he was generally known, had a seemingly inexhaustible supply of willing pawns to build on his megalomania, and these, along with the other government-serving, "dime-a-dozen" writers were quite handsomely rewarded for their loyalty, either with government-allocated housing, with a trip abroad or with appointment to some plum job, such as the artistic director of a theater. After all, everybody had to live, one way or another, and every one coped the best they could. For the system did not appear to us in a hurry to expire. In fact, I was convinced it would survive me.

In those years a friend of mine, a journalist with a daily in the south of France, came to visit me. He had been sent to write a sensational piece about the Dracula castle, the only real attraction we could offer the West. So he took advantage of this trip to spend a few days at the Black Sea and then, on his way home, he stopped by and saw me in the capital.

I took him home, assuming not a few risks, given the government's strict laws against any contacts with foreigners. And should the latter just happen to drop by unannounced, we were under orders to immediately notify the authorities and report to the militia all pertinent information about them. My French friend was quite impressed with my large library. Like the rest of my family, I read whatever copy I could get my hands on of the latest books and magazines published in the West that made their way to us. We always seemed able to somehow watch the latest films produced in the West and seemed unaccountably well informed in all matters of culture. All this in spite of our precarious material conditions, which did not take my distinguished friend long to notice.

On that particular Sunday I was not allowed to drive my car. Again, because of the alleged need to save energy, the authorities had instituted a system of gasoline distribution, based on the alternating odd/even number of the vehicle's registration plate. To insure plentiful supplies for those Sundays I did have permission to drive, in our bathroom I kept two spare cans always filled to the brim with fuel. Naturally gasoline was another rationed product, so I had to save it up for trips we would take to the mountains, perhaps once a month, or for our annual family vacation.

So we hopped in a cab and I was thus able to show him the city. The old, beautifully ornate housing districts alternated with areas filled with horrible, ugly apartment buildings, which although new, looked already old and falling apart.

At that time, acting on the orders of the *Conducator*, they began bulldozing quite a few churches, and other historic buildings included on the National Trust list, all of this with a vigorous socialistic élan which filled my friend with disgust and dread. He could not understand anything from all that aberrant architecture and I had nothing to offer by way of an explanation. Filled with patriotic zeal, they were building an absurd universe. My friend was shocked to see on the streets the same make of car, multiplied ad infinitum. Then, too, he was bewildered by the empty stores and intrigued by the interminable lines in front of bookstores and theaters!

"You have nothing to eat, yet there you are, standing in line to buy books?!"

I explained to him that we lived in a world of "dependencies." Books were our hard currency. One could exchange them for milk for one's children, or with them one could get special, personalized treatment from a doctor who was going to operate on one's wife. No one would look at you unless you had something to give him. Whiskey, cigarettes, books, cheese, or chickens sent over by one's relatives in the provinces. You could find nothing in the stores. It was quite an adventure to raise a child. I would sometimes buy a ticket for the Orient Express, which ran through our capital, simply because I wanted to buy various goods from the traveling foreign tourists – maybe a little chocolate, a box of cookies and candy for our children. I would then get off at the nearest station and return by way of a dirty, cold, slow train, whose doors were sometimes off their hinges and the cushions on the seats all torn up.

Like everybody else, in addition to the refrigerator, I had a freezer box, which I had bought with lots of money through special connections, out of a batch destined for export. In this freezer we would place for long-term storage whatever food we had been able to garner through strenuous efforts, whenever we could.

Every fall my wife would spend a considerable amount of time canning vegetables, making *zakuska*, various juices, fruit preserves, syrups and tomato juice. She would place in the freezer plastic bags filled with green peppers, and ripe eggplant, with all kinds of vegetables and semi-preserved fruit, to provide us with sustenance during the winter. Then the freezer had special compartments for cheeses and meats. These were the most prized, usually reserved for our children. Adults were banned from using these delicacies.

The meat, obtained through all kinds of complicated, ingenious rituals, after waiting in line for hours, was carefully portioned for steaks, for soups, for minced meat, or for schnitzel. My wife would label each plastic bag, writing with an imported, felt-tipped pen called *Carioca* its intended use. In addition, we had a ration card, but, alas, it was so low in value! We could only buy ten eggs a month with it, one packet of butter, a kilo of sugar and one liter of cooking oil. Card or no card, some months these food items could not be found in any store.

In certain cities one could still use one's ration card to buy flour, cornmeal and two scrawny chickens, so tiny they could fit quite nicely into one small plastic bag. No wonder they had been nicknamed "sneakers," for they were nothing but legs! No one used the phrase "they are selling" this and that, but only "they are giving" or "they are introducing" these items. I was 48 when I saw my first banana.

One evening my wife and the children were out, leaving me alone in the apartment. Suddenly I felt an irresistible urge to eat a steak and drink a glass of red wine. I paced around the freezer, until I could take it no longer. Guiltily I pulled out a little bag on which my wife had clearly written "for grilled meat." I lit the grill and when the steak was done, I wolfed it down greedily, only to be later tormented by guilt not unlike that of a criminal. Guilt my wife exacerbated when she got home. Smelling the sweet of aroma of grilled meat, she quickly opened the freezer, pulling out the now empty incriminating meat drawer and voicing the forbidding, dreaded words:

"I simply can't believe it! You have taken food from the children's mouths!"

I saw my friend fidgeting uncomfortably, while I helplessly looked on, deeply embarrassed. Only when I began to explain to him the rules of our complicated, survival game, did I realize what an absurd world we lived in, what grinding poverty we were sinking into!

Whatever exciting sensations the Dracula myth might have aroused in him, what he saw in our family's living conditions that evening must have produced a far greater impression than anything he had seen on the rest of his trip. The next day they called me in to the *Securitate* office, where they interrogated me for six hours straight. They wanted to know who he was, how I got to know him, why he had come and what we had discussed.

In a sense we felt quite comfortable to live like this, secure in our knowledge that the *Securitate* was diligently watching over us, keeping us under surveillance, lest we should say something forbidden, which could bring all sorts of troubles on us. So after a while we began to control ourselves, to suspect each other and to even willingly inform on each other. Self-censorship was in full swing. We were looking after each other and after those around us, convinced that someone was peeping through our keyholes, through the windows, listening at the door, on the phone, in the offices, in the car, in the chalets we rented during our vacations – so much so that we strove to be correct, serious-minded, morally upright, disciplined, true living models for a model society!

But then again, we also had a few minor liberties. We would mutter complaints, make timid ironic remarks and generally keep up our inner silent revolt. We had our crises of conscience, we stayed alert and understood perfectly what was happening to us, but realized we were powerless to openly resist. We were patients in a militarized hospital, subjected to a utopian treatment for an imaginary disease, feeling both guilt and absolution. Guilt because of the cowardice each was prone to, and absolution because of the collective farce so perfectly played on us, allowing us no privacy, no real individual expression.

Once in a while our consciences would be pricked by a feeling of self-loathing and shame, but we would quickly rationalize these, finding all sorts of excuses for them. Many alibis were invoked in our defense, from the geo-political conditions to the curse which had supposedly been put on this part of the world long ago. Barbarian invasions, foreign-born monarchs imposed on us, Orthodoxy, our former dependence on Constantinople, and later on Moscow, the cruelty of fate itself and the cunning plotting of our neighbors, the games of the superpowers and so on and so forth – all of these we perceived to be stacked up against us. And over and above all these was history, always history, an abstraction which no one had the courage to get to the bottom of.

Everyone was living at least two parallel lives and, without putting up any opposition, we were more resistant than history itself – ultimately the universally accepted cause of our misery. History, the protagonist, was neither known, nor read, but constantly put forth as the enigmatic character to whom we could quietly attribute our false glory, guilt, and dramas, as if history could give birth to destinies, rather than being itself the sum total of our destinies.

For us history evidently had different, unorthodox meanings. By dint of history dictatorships could be excused, primitiveness and violence could be explained away. In short, it was a vehicle or an instrument apt to justify any aberration, no matter how horrific. So on and on they went, embellishing things, inventing events, characters, gilding eras, distorting the true nature of various well-known facts. Another sin the high and mighty of the day committed was to present history in a truncated, optional manner, conveniently leaving out anything they deemed detrimental to their long or short-term political interests.

Some areas of history were inexcusably expanded upon, while others were glibly glossed over. The same history that can only be one and the same was undergoing subtle changes from year to year, with whimsical erasures and additions, with heroes and events disappearing or appearing as the rulers dictated, victories or defeats being reversed at will. We were all running rings around history, juggling with time, hurtling from era to era, either condemning or forgiving it. History was being subjected to all sorts of manipulations by both the mighty and the weak. It seemed such an easy-to-manipulate, readily available commodity because so few people actually knew history – the real history – or knew only as much as they cared to or were allowed to know.

History was, by turns, our pride and our stigma, meeting every need, concealing warts and all, glossing over failures, perfectly capable of highlighting or obscuring almost anything. It was the being, the phenomenon, the concept or the science to govern. It stood for policy. It was converted into the ingenious instrument of governing, into the source of so much bragging and pompous flaunting of tasteless heroism. We were living with history at the table, at our bedside, in front of the TV, in the refrigerator, at work, on the street. I dare say we were about to be swallowed up by history, fed up with it and yet outside it, our eternal insecurity and our sole certainty.

I for one had no opinion on history. All it did for me was help me understand dictatorships and farces. As for the rest, I was afraid. By nature I am fearful and timid, hence dangerous. Clumsiness is blunder-prone. My familiarization with history was the result of intuition, rather than conscious study or cramming for exams, and anyway all I was really interested in was the history of the world. As for our much vaunted about national pride – it all seemed so childish to me. We were so hung-up on traditions, when in fact these should have been the easiest to overcome.

My conviction that we were in a time warp, dropped in a Europe traveling at full speed, was badly shaken with the fall of the Berlin Wall. My wife, having a far more sensitive nature, stayed glued to the TV, watching, with tears in her eyes, all these unprecedented events unfold, while I, for several days, had been under a strange kind of enthusiasm that was beginning to feel more like an anxiety. The possibility of some kind of change was gnawing at the fringes of my consciousness. Still, not quite free from my usual skepticism, I kept telling myself there was no way this temblor would leave communism as we knew it unchanged, but would definitely shake it from its foundations.

At night, the foreign radio stations I listened to assured me I was right, that it wouldn't be much longer until this irreversible process would roll over us too, that the whole decrepit system would blow up in the faces of the communist rulers and, with a mighty, roaring crush, would free us from the bondage of communism, from this howling oddity of history. From the West dissidents and exiles were bombarding us daily with promises, and encouragements, and with calls for resistance, and for specific bold actions, which only managed to increase our sense of foreboding.

In a few weeks my vigilance decreased, my enthusiasm waned. Even though things continued to heat up, I was no longer watching them. I even got used to the tension passed on to us every night by the foreign radio stations. In our country things continued to be calm, undisturbed, the days filled with dull, ordinary occurrences. People were minding their own business, carrying on as they had always done. We would make occasional careful comments among those we considered friends, with undisguised hopes that what was happening in the countries around us would somehow happen to us too, but I no longer believed it possible. Still, in all other ways, life went on unperturbed. I had returned to normality, indeed to a strangely abnormal normality.

My wife, several years younger than I, stronger and more conscientious, had a terrific sense of duty and responsibility which I had at first envied, but later found irritating. In the end I began to make fun of it, convinced that everything I was doing was useless anyway. No one needs our ideas, our gushy earnestness, I thought. Apathy wasn't going to make our survival any more difficult.

That mid-December 1989 my wife told me she would be going on a one-week business trip to a town not far from the capital where there was a huge construction project going on. Everything was huge in our country, so I marveled not. As head of the project, her turn had come to supervise the operation. Her enthusiasm was somewhat tempered by the realization that Christmas was just around the corner. Christmas was not an official holiday, due to the unbelieving attitude of the godless Communist rulers, who thought *they* were the all powerful and above "such nonsense." Yet among the population the tradition never died and this period of time from Christmas to the end of the year coincided with a general slowdown of things, a period used for looking back over the past year and taking stock, summing things up, drawing a line and planning ahead. It had snowed heavily and this further contributed to the slowdown. No one felt like doing any hard work, not under the privations and hardships we had to put up with. "They pretend to pay us, we pretend to work" was the pervasive work ethic. No incentive, no motivation. So I put up no resistance, made no comment whatsoever. There was no reason for me to do it and it never crossed my mind anyway to get involved in such things. These were the rules, that was the hand we had been dealt and nothing else mattered. We were merely living – nothing more, nothing less. And living as we were meant to live.

So she left.

Things did not change too much. The children were no longer children, but busy adults, taking care of their own business. We mostly ate out, whenever and wherever we could. Our son preferred the student cafes or the campus cafeteria. In addition he now had a girlfriend, who had brought him to her home and often her family would invite him to lunch or dine with them. As for me I would generally have dinner at home with Sonia, to whom I was not only a father, but also a son, a friend. She showered me with a tenderness meant for the yet unmet young man whose every quality I was apparently exemplifying. Sensitive and vulnerable, she was oscillating between exaltation and disappointment, in a horizonless world, whose meanings were never very clear. And I had neither the time, nor the strength to untangle them for her. I loved her enormously, although mostly in secret, and I reciprocated her feelings for me, holding her up as the model of my ideal woman.

There hovered over us a sort of contrived family peace. Each pulled in his or her own direction, now estranged, now bonded, now indifferent, now passionately interested in each other's wellbeing – an all too familiar tableau, so much so that its distinguishing marks were beginning to fade.

Laura, whom both I and the children called Lary, had left serenely, without an inkling of what was going to happen to us. Each of us had his or her own life, home being merely the place we would come to for a good night's sleep. Not that we did much while we were away from it! As far as I could tell, Lary had never had an affair, except, perhaps, a few brief flings in her youth. I was pretty bored, without any interest in any worthwhile pursuit, marked by a sportsman-like honesty. Indifferent to the point of seeming prudent. Cowardly when it came to surprises. The children were well-behaved and independent. Monotony was dragging us all along.

That morning I woke earlier than usual. Lary had already left. We had agreed she would remain there for the entire duration of the assignment, rather than commute each day, in view of the high snow and the snarling traffic. She had taken only a few things with her, just what she could fit into a duffel bag. Two books, tea, sugar and two cans of the local equivalent of *pâtés de foie gras*. I told her to take all the cash we had at home, since any trip away from the capital was bound to be costly. The money would make her feel more secure, although there wasn't much food she could buy in those unappealing provincial restaurants other than the usual vegetable stew and the perennial tough and chewy steak with fries on the side.

Having lit a cigarette, I sat on the edge of my narrow bed, looking at my bare feet. At the far end of the apartment I could hear doors banged shut, dull thumps, brief curt exchanges, a clattering of cups on their saucers – clear evidence the children were late as usual in going about their business. There had never been any harmony to speak of between those two. Of course they loved each other, but that didn't prevent them from having frequent bouts of mutual teasing and bantering.

Petru was absent minded, while Sonia possessed a special ability to make sound judgments about people and things. Sonia accused her brother of being shallow, incapable of staying focused, scatter-brained and immature. And, slightly jealous of his girlfriend, she never missed a chance to tease him about "that cross-eyed girl, who's so thin her clothes are falling off her; who's so clumsy she drops everything; who's so bowlegged, she'll scuff any decent pair of shoes." Petru gave as good as he got, telling his sister she was acting like an overly concerned mother, constantly nagging him; or that she was already displaying the typical characteristics of an old maid, with an obsessive insistence on tidiness and symmetry – traits he obviously disdained. And, he said, she was oscillating between two opposite states: languor and belligerence.

No one took their daily squabbles seriously. We always thought the best education was to ignore them. So we left them alone, to fend for themselves, while still watching them discretely from a distance, without neglecting our duties, freed as we were from the complexes many other parents labored under of always expecting gratitude from their children. I wasn't concerned about our children. They would do just fine, if left to their own devices, I thought at the time. I did not expect very much from them – certainly nothing in the way of any showy display of heroic sacrifice. My only real concern was that living in this country of ours, with all its limitations and privations, they did not stand too good a chance to make their lives count, to secure for themselves a decent future. I worried a lot about all the struggling I was sure they would have to go through, as their parents had done, in order to build for themselves as comfortable an existence as they could under the system. And what really scared me most was that I saw no way out of this predicament.

Neither of them took after me. They had inherited from Laura both defects and qualities, in quantities that neither caused alarm in people, nor made them notice them. While they didn't give us any headaches to speak of, neither did they make us terribly proud of them. We certainly did not glory in vain, fancy imaginings of parents watching their children with undiluted admiration as they climbed the podium of the very best and brightest being bestowed lofty awards for some unprecedented achievements. We were a just typical, ordinary Romanian family, that would fit quite nicely in any boring TV soap opera, with vague moralizing tones and little acts of daring, but alas, incapable of keeping the viewers awake for any extended period of time!

I was smoking quite a lot, and had become rather stiff, having got well past fifty. I was not a fatalist, but still I decided I should be take precautions and be ready for anything, just in case. After all, at this age, in spite of the glowing statistics pointing to a "second youth" for men, in reality they easily pick up one kind of disease or another. Or they simply get frozen in a form of highly suspect "good health."

I shaved, resting my cigarette on the ceramic tray over the sink, congratulating myself again for the fortune of having an apartment with two bathrooms – an essential feature that ensured I would not become a nuisance to any member of the family in the morning. I put on the water for the coffee and, without knowing why, I just ambled into Laura's room. I opened the massive wardrobe, where both of us kept our clothes, and hesitated, unable to decide whether I should wear a tie or not.

I was supposed to attend a wrap-up meeting at work. I was not a conformist but at the same time I didn't fancy being looked at with disapproval by my female colleagues, some of whom were well past their prime, biased, and paying homage to the distorted images put forward daily by the fake principles of socialist morals and ethics, as crooked as anything associated with the system.

The phone rang. It was Nicky, the paper's sports writer. Although we were not exactly friends, we would sometimes go out for a beer at the restaurant next door. Nicky was always well informed about everything that was going on – familiar with the goings-on of the soccer world, with the various transactions involving the transfer of players, and, of course, with the inner life and well-camouflaged scandals of the *nomenklatura*. They said he was enjoying close relations with the dictator's son, while some suspected him of being an informer for the *Securitate*. He enjoyed the rare privilege of being allowed to travel to the West, accompanying the soccer teams on their overseas tournaments. He did regular live reporting of sports events for the broadcast media – something that always made the authorities nervous. They went to great lengths in their attempt to make sure only those people could go on the air who had been thoroughly vetted and had proven themselves to be reliable, obedient citizens, highly unlikely to suddenly take off on a tangent and begin broadcasting remarks critical of the communist leadership.

"Hi there! How are you? Aren't you coming to the office?"

I looked at the clock. It was still early, both for the wrap-up meeting and for this inopportune telephone call.

"Hi. Has anything special happened?"

"You mean you haven't heard?"

"Heard what?"

"About the match in the border town."

"What match?" I asked, bored.

"The whites were clobbering them, but the reds put up a fierce resistance. Violence broke out. The teams had been dead even, until the whites got the upper hand and finally scored.... The whole stadium is now up in arms. Get it?"

Frankly I didn't get it. Now I knew him to be quite fond of jokes and of somewhat enigmatic stories, but this time I couldn't figure him out.

"The police stepped in," he told me breathlessly. "The spectators are enraged. They are throwing, as we speak, anything they can find into the field. A lot of players got hurt, many of them quite badly. The whites are pressing their advantage. Boy, there's such mess on the stadium! I have no idea how it will end, but it sure doesn't look good! Anything might happen."

"What exactly are you trying to tell me? What match?"

Nicky's voice was tremulous. It didn't sound as if he was cracking another of his vintage jokes. It was more like he was talking in code, trying to communicate to me something very important.

"The match of the century.... I thought you knew. Why don't you come here right away?"

And he hung up on me. I stood there, speechless. It was way too early for him to have become drunk. Perhaps it was just one big prank he was playing on me. I tried to figure out what he wanted from me, why he had telephoned me, but I could make neither heads nor tails of it.

In the end I did manage to pick out a tie to wear around my neck. I wasn't too concerned about Nicky's telephone call, which might have been merely a whim on his part. I even succeeded, after a few minutes, in putting it out of my mind altogether.

Laura was an unexceptional, ordinary person. However, in her youth she had been quite pretty. Intelligent, but also endowed with strikingly beautiful features. She had loved me with deliberation, obstinacy and tenacity. For my part, I had given her too many occasions to suffer, to doubt my honesty, such as it was. Yet in the beginning our marriage was not shaken by her bouts of jealousy – which often lacked a precise object, being directed in a wide sweep at everything I had, at whatever I was interested in or liked. Equally jealous of my friends, of our children. She constantly felt like a second-class citizen, forever wronged, betrayed and hurt by my indifference, by my few professional successes, which she felt I had won far too easily. She watched my every move, even the most insignificant gesture I made, pondering every word I said, interpreting every mood, always suspicious and quite convinced she was being deliberately kept out of my own private world which I was supposedly so keen on building without her. Sometimes we would fight even for the thoughts she imagined I had.

She submitted, with that characteristic masochism peculiar to women, to all sorts of highly charged, dramatic states. She ran the gamut of extreme forms of despair, from biting taunts to suicide threats. I had gotten quite used to it all, and was no longer impressed by her, which added insult to injury, threatening to push her over the edge, into a nervous breakdown.

Of all these, the hardest to bear were her occasional attacks of loneliness. A paradoxical kind of loneliness, given the fact that she did have her children around her, not to mention her husband, if only she would care to take any notice of him. These storms would brew up suddenly, out of the blue, but would blow over just as quickly. Naturally, afterwards we made love. I could never tell how much she suffered during those states of delirium, but for me it was quite unpleasant. I felt ridiculous and helpless, wishing I were anywhere but next to her. A bit of hypocrisy always comes in here; this is what a woman's histrionics are all about. She throws tantrums in her husband's presence, lest he should spoil the show, eager as he is to patch things up, and thus lead her to give up her state of belligerence. Or on the contrary she would try to soften him up, determined to extract regrets, promises, vows, pleas and pity from him.

I would just keep silent, waiting for the whole awkward episode to pass. Then she would become her natural, tender, and considerate self again, as if unable to remember the nightmare she had just put me through. She would behave serenely, as though nothing untoward had happened. She resumed loving me passionately, yet already hoarding new suspicions and fresh negative energies for the next opportune moment another show like this could be put on.

I consoled myself with the thought that all marriages are more or less like this. If anything, ours had been quite resilient, due, in no small measure, to my inexhaustible store of long-suffering patience and to other assorted defects, which on the contrary later turned out to be highly useful virtues. To be sure, I was far from being the ideal husband, though as a father I did slightly better. All the same, I was the kind of man a woman could safely live next to her entire life, without fearing a brutal separation. Hadn't I chosen her? Well, now I had to keep her, didn't I? Besides, I had given her children, so I was duty-bound to raise them. I had taken this path in life of my own accord. And since I am not a quitter, as far as I'm concerned, I'll never give up – I said to myself.

Things were quite simple and, for the life of me, I could not understand why she preferred all those complications, most of them of her own making. She had not come to understand me so well as to stop being afraid of me. For a while she had dreaded I would leave her. It is true that at the time I was caught up in a serious extramarital liaison, but not for one moment had I considered divorcing her. For Laura had her well-established place in my life, she was for keeps! The passage of time had done nothing to shake that conviction, although, for all intents and purposes, it had been relegated largely to the past. But then, weren't we all living in the past? The present was but an unfortunate consequence of the past, while the future held no hope whatsoever for us.

The water for the coffee was already boiling. In the meantime, I changed my mind about the tie I had just picked out, dropping it on the bed, among Laura's things, while she had gone away on an assignment to finish another project for the victory of socialism, in a little town that meant nothing to no one, in a forgotten country, outside of the real world, where even the migratory birds no longer showed any desire to return.

I sipped my coffee at leisure, looking at the wall across the room, smoking and thinking of all sorts of trivial things, which probably meant I was bereft of any serious thoughts. In the meantime I had almost forgotten about Nicky's weird call. I'm not a morning person. At this early hour I am usually morose and uneasy, my entire body flabby; unusually taciturn, overcome with a raw solemn air which makes my facial features appear rigid, as if I were deep in thought, bound to manifest a scorching disapproval to anyone who would happen to be around. The truth is that at such moments I am actually unable to concentrate, being totally incapable of intelligent talk or decent behavior.

Next I went through my ritualistic bout of tobacco-induced coughing, barely audible under the onslaught of the slew of patriotic songs blaring, as usual at this matinal hour, from the national radio station, alternating with a good dose of triumphal brass band fare. The latter was a bit easier to bear. From time to time the anchor would break in, bringing the listeners loud breathless reports about miraculous bumper crops, about an industrial output whose extraordinary increase no one seemed able to control any longer, about an unprecedented growth in all areas, in all shapes and forms, so as to spite all those Coca-Cola drinking Westerners, condemned to live under ruthless, putrefying capitalism.

The dictator's name was evoked piously at the rate of twenty or thirty times a minute. People of all walks of life, from the youngest to the oldest, paid homage to him for the "wonderful" life they had the good fortune of living. Soft, tender children's voices were also enlisted to sing the praises of communism, reverently thanking the dictator's wife for being "the mother of the nation," for providing such a sheltered existence for their childhood. They were employing the same words, never veering from tried and true formulas and slogans, repeating them over and over again, so much so that a dictionary of the language might easily have been published with only a few pages, and it would have been enough for us to understand one another perfectly.

Among the slew of mandatory things we were subjected to, words played a predominant role, since they were always chosen carefully by someone other than ourselves, with the intention of sparing us the unnecessary effort of thinking for ourselves. So we ended up having someone else decide what was right and wrong, what we liked and disliked, what we did and did not do, what we were and where we were. Our lives had been mapped out in precise detail, our destiny predetermined. But they had chosen without any input from us, perhaps even before we were born. We merely stepped into our preordained roles, dutifully taking our places like cogs within the infernal machine, eagerly taking our crosses and marching out in perfect discipline.

It seemed as though God was nowhere. All we had around us were these midgets, these self-styled taskmasters, driven by their demented aberrations, watching us as we wearily plodded through the darkness toward a glorious nowhere.

Absent-mindedly humming a patriotic tune they had implanted in my mind through countless hours of listening to the national radio and TV, I began to walk towards the bus station. Getting to work was another ordeal we had to endure. There were only a few buses, running at 30 or 40-minute intervals, dirty, overcrowded, with doors forced open by the overflowing mass of packed-like-sardines bodies, precariously hanging outside the bus, clinging desperately to whatever they could, lest they should fall under the wheels. I was hoping to squeeze into the first bus that came along, even if that meant riding on the steps, half-way in, halfway out. Actually this wasn't too bad, for I would be able to enjoy the invigorating air outside, not to mention that I would be able to quickly get off the bus, once I reached my destination, with all my buttons intact and without toes stepped on by my fellow passengers.

During those mornings when we held this special meeting at the office they would check our ID badges at the outside gate even more rigorously than usual. Should any of us come in late, even as little as two or three minutes past eight o'clock, the guard would inform the institution's director about this infraction, which would in turn lead to a loss of pay for the entire day, to say nothing of the humiliation and mortification we would suffer at this ignominious treatment. The otherwise decent gatekeeper would suddenly turn officious, rude, authoritarian and even abusive. He would treat us with undisguised disdain, with an air of barely suppressed superiority. Naturally he was not merely a gatekeeper and his salary did not come solely from the publishing house. He had what was called in those days "special duties," i.e. he was charged with watching over us at the direction of a unit within the secret police.

I was not late. In front of the building – a huge Stalin-era complex, hosting under its cavernous roof a hodge-podge of newspaper and magazine offices, publishing houses and assorted institutions – an unusually large crowd of people had gathered. I quickened my pace. Some of them were quiet, milling about or talking in small clusters, exchanging apprehensive looks. Others, more agitated, paced back and forth across the lawn, at times huddling together, as if to whisper into one another's ears the news about whatever somber or mysterious event had transpired, only to quickly break up in bewilderment, afraid they might have already learned secrets that were not supposed to have been partakers of.

I elbowed my way through this crowd, greeting acquaintances left and right. No one made any attempt to stop me. I could not figure out what was happening, nor was I eager to find out. Eventually I made it into the big entrance hall and without bothering to wait for the elevator; I climbed the stairs to my office, feeling short of breath, almost choking after such a prolonged use of cigarettes. My colleagues eyed me with questioning, frightened, disapproving looks. I couldn't understand a thing and no one was in a hurry to explain to me what was going on.

After this rather noisy entrance of mine, my colleagues lowered their eyes, staring at their desks with guilty silent looks. I felt as if I had broken some highly suspect meditation spell they had fallen into and once I had got through to this space, they no longer paid any attention to me, being preoccupied with who knows what. And so they sat there, at this unearthly hour of the morning, looking lugubriously somber and conscientious, with long faces as if all their ships had sunk at once.

I pulled out my pens, my sheets of writing paper and rose from my seat to collect the latest news from the teletype machine. Again they cast admonishing looks at me. They were highly sensitive to movement and noise. I felt as if they expected something of me. Perhaps an excuse or a confession. I felt ill at ease, and even a bit guilty. Evidently I was inconveniencing them. Or perhaps our editor-in-chief had another one of his notorious bad days.

We were led by a political apparatchik, with false pretensions of intellectualism, a character with a split psyche, a failed journalist with a sole occupation: boss! He had not written one line in his entire life, had not published anything worthy of being read other than a string of stupid little articles oozing with high praise towards the dictator and the Communist Party who had appointed him head of the publication solely on political considerations. He had taken a correspondence course in philosophy, but even this he had done at the Party's prompting. He kept us all on tenterhooks, practicing his authoritarian traits on us, without any professional background to back it up with. We had nicknamed him "The Madman," although he was not mad, merely a scoundrel. An impostor, like so many others who filled the director's chairs of so many other institutions.

"What's up? The Madman's having a bad day?" I diffidently tried to defuse the tension they seemed determined to keep up.

I felt kind of humiliated that nobody bothered to answer me.

"So what is it? Someone sick? Or the union is no longer giving us any butter this month? What's with you? Has someone died?"

A bug was droning incessantly around the room, batting its wings against the window pane, and the filing cabinet, as everyone's eyes followed it, irritatingly, apparently without any will to do anything about it. Had this been an ordinary day, like the rest, Victor would have cursed it, while Madam Simon, plump and graceful, would have risen up from her seat to guide the miserable creature to the nearest exit through the open window, waving a folder at it or saying with puckered lips, "Shoo, shoo!" – as she though she had been put in charge of protecting the office's little critters and insects. Which would have been just as good an opportunity for her to parade her lively figure again before the eyes of Mr. Carp, her constant admirer, a man nearing the end of his career.

But Madam Simon prolonged that silence, that immobility until I dropped a stapler – a very thoughtless gesture, followed by a loud thump, which pushed my high-strung colleagues to the verge of hysteria. They lowered their eyes, looking at the incriminating stapler, which, had it but been able to, would have bored itself into the floor, such was the intensity of their collective ire. I could not ascertain what had come over them. At long last, the occupant of the desk next to mine finally had pity on my ignorance. With pious concern, she gravely addressed me:

"A flying saucer dropped on Russian soil!"

I looked at her as if she was raving mad.

"It happened yesterday at lunch. In a bus-stop in the middle of Moscow. Hundreds of people saw it."

I did not know whether I should burst out laughing or feign surprise. But the woman was dead serious.

"It's official, public knowledge."

The rest were also looking at her as if she was out of her mind – our Nadia who was working for the International section. She was a translator from the Russian and regularly read the *Pravda*.

"Just think of it! A genuine flying saucer smack in the middle of Moscow! This could change everything."

For a moment I was grateful to Nadia, except that the others began to buzz and mumble amongst themselves, deeply displeased about this diversion which was messing things up for them, dissolving the air of mystery and weakening their dramatic resolve.

"This is a godsend for my column in tomorrow's Miscellaneous News!" I said with relief.

To which Mr. Carp advised me paternally: "That's not what it's about…."

"What do you mean?" jumped Nadia. "A flying saucer drops out of the sky, in plain view of everybody, and you say that's nothing? Are you really that blind? Can't you see how it all fits in? Nothing is at random."

By now the tension had dissipated. They started to bicker about flying saucers.

"It's all a farce," insisted Mr. Carp. "Finally our turn has come!"

"Why don't you just shut up!" snapped Victor. "Do you want them to come and arrest us?"

And then, to me, in an angry, vexed tone, "What planet have you dropped out of ?"

The hallways of the publishing house echoed with shouts, angry exchanges and catcalls. Pandemonium broke out. We rushed out of the office. The long corridors were teeming with journalists, directors, technical personnel, and blue-collar workers. Everybody was talking at the same time. Someone cried out, "Go to the windows, go to the windows!"

We dashed back inside. In front of the building there were by now huge crowds of demonstrators, with flags, and banners, with the words, "Freedom!" and "Down with Communism!" written on them. Many carried the dictator's portrait, badly vandalized or mutilated. They were heading in the direction of the city's main square. On their way there, they stopped under our windows, shouting, "Come join us!" "Victory or death!" They all seemed quite determined, full of enthusiasm, and energy, at last happy and strong. The whole city had poured out into the streets. Most had come out in a hurry, before they had time to dress properly, some of them just grabbing their winter overcoats, in their haste to join the demonstrators' swelling numbers.

I had been left behind in the office, where I was trying to find Laura. She had left me her telephone number at the construction site, but it was ringing busy all the time. One thing was clear: I had to bring her back. I called home, thinking I might speak with the children, but no one answered. I tried to keep my reactions under control, but eventually my mind was being invaded by emotions, too – especially since these events had taken me completely by surprise. So, the wave had finally reached us, too. Yes, we could! Finally, when I least expected it to succeed! I kept trying to contact Laura, when Nicky stepped into the office. He was soaked in perspiration.

"What *are* you doing here? You know, I wouldn't have thought you would have such a hard time putting two and two together.... You really annoyed me this morning. At the border, the rebellion started two days ago. There are casualties and many wounded. The Army opened fire against the demonstrators. They kept things under wraps, hoping they could stem the revolt. It's quite bad, really nasty. Why don't you come with me right now?"

"Where? To the Square?"

"No, silly, not to the Square. First we've got things to do here. Then we go to the television. Our forces took over everything. The Central

Committee headquarters, the Radio, the Television. The dictator and his wife have fled in a helicopter. The Army has already switched sides, being now with the people."

I found it hard to understand the barrage of information Nicky was communicating to me, in rapid-fire succession, as if he were reporting live on a soccer game. And who exactly were "ours"? At times he had been both theirs and ours. I felt grabbed by the sleeve and dragged out. Nicky had mapped things out in his mind.

"We go to the editor-in-chief and demand his resignation. The Madman is a coward. He won't have the balls to resist. He'll cave in right away. Then you take over the running of the paper. Next we print a special edition, such as they've never seen before. On the front page, in huge bold letters, there'll be just one word, 'Victory!' followed by 'Communism has fallen!' in smaller letters. And you'll write a magnificent, penetrating historic editorial to cap it all with."

"Why me?"

"Because you're the only one I found," laughed Nicky, as he continued to drag me by the sleeve down the stairs towards the boss's office.

We found the door wide open, slammed against the wall. The Madman was nowhere to be seen. His office had been ransacked. He had left it in a hurry, barely managing to take with him a few documents, and folders, whatever he could under pressure. The safe was also open, allowing us to see inside three bottles of whiskey, several cartons of American cigarettes, a cassette recorder, several video tapes, with what later proved to be pornographic material; a book of poetry, with a humble dedication from the great national poet, otherwise also known as a dissident in the West; a copy of *Playboy* magazine, condoms, a pair of handcuffs and a bunch of keys.

"The swine!" exclaimed Nicky. Then he pocketed the keys and kicked the safe's door angrily. "There! Now we know who has ruled us with an iron fist all these years! A sexually-obsessed, impotent fiend! No wonder he took off when he did – before anyone had a chance to catch up with him!"

He continued to hold my arm in his vise-like grip. He kept pushing at me until he got me behind the desk where the Madman had sat only a few minutes earlier. Finally he got me to sit in his chair.

"There! From now on you are our editor-in-chief. Get cracking. There's work to do. I'll run over to the printers to give them some money, so they can put out for us a special edition of our paper."

Then he placed in my hand the gold nib fountain pen the Madman had left behind in his hasty retreat.

"Get your thoughts together and write a historic editorial, along the line 'Communism has fallen!' I have no doubt you can do it. You're good. But now being good is not enough. You've got to be great! This is your moment of glory! I'm gonna be assistant editor-in-chief. I hope you've got nothing against this."

And with these words he trotted out of the office, making his way to the basement printing shop.

So there I was, all by myself, a bit ridiculous in that huge leather chair at the enormous oak desk. I set the pen down. What was I doing there? I had always hated myself for one of my biggest weaknesses: allowing just about anybody to push me around. My heart was still pounding hard in my chest. And now what was I going to do? I could never write a revolutionary article on cue. I saw on the desk towards the left side a multi-line wide telephone which probably connected the Madman through a hot line to the Censorship office, to the Party and to who knows what. Still trembling, I picked up the receiver, feeling like a law-breaker, with no right to be there. I fished in my pocket for the piece of paper on which Laura had scribbled her work phone number. She answered on the first ring.

"Lary? Is that you? Are you OK? Hello!"

"Yes, of course I'm OK. Why, what's the matter with you?"

"Nothing!"

"Something happened?"

"No, nothing. Well…haven't you guys heard anything?"

"Heard what?"

"Lary, come home immediately."

"What's got into you? Are the children all right?"

"Yes, they're all right. But you've got to return. Today, now!"

"What's all this nonsense? I've just got here. The project is well underway. Everybody's out on the platform. I can't just pick up and leave. I've got a job, you know? I have my responsibilities. What exactly are you trying to tell me?"

"Listen, are you all living on the moon out there? Haven't you turned on the radio or the TV? The madness has started. The dictator and his wife have fled away. The whole city is out in the streets."

"Where are you calling from?"

"From the newspaper. Take the first commuter train and come back at once."

The trouble was I myself was not too sure things had really happened as I had described them to her. Was it really true? I had had no tangible proof, other than the big to-do outside the office and Nicky's word, which I wasn't too sure I could trust. My conversation with Laura was rudely interrupted and a coarse voice, mumbling something in Russian, suddenly came on the line. Then the connection was lost completely and the phone went dead. No tone, no buzz. Just then Nicky burst into the office, perspiration dripping from his face.

"Leave the article for now. You'll get a chance to write it tonight. Anyway, the printing shop is deserted. All the printers have gone out. We've got to go too. Things are heating up."

"I head a voice in Russian when I used the phone. What the heck is this?"

He saw the bewilderment in my eyes and again grabbed my arm.

"Get this: we've got to move fast. Miracles don't last long. I've got my car outside. We are heading straight to the TV station."

"Nicky, calm down, won't you? Stop being so impatient. Tell my why I should go to the television station. What's going on there?"

"Look, there's no time. I can't explain it to you now. Anyway, you wouldn't understand. But, believe me, I do know what's going on. And I also know we can't afford to lose a single moment. What's required at this moment is unity. Come to think of it, this nation of ours, so fractured in the past, has only been united in times of crisis, when hit with disaster. The only things uniting them are earthquakes, floods and revolutions.... We've got to act intelligently and quickly, and get organized."

"Who's 'we'?"

"Us, you and me, our own, all the good and decent folk."

"And who are our own? Who are 'the good and decent folk' you're talking about?"

"Come on, stop playing the fool. Those of us who suffered, who are entitled to this revolution. You do admit it's a revolution, don't you? Ours, for us. Haven't you waited so long for this moment, have you not hoped like everybody else that one day we would all be free, victorious at last? And now what are you doing about it? Dropping out? Shirking your responsibility? Our time has finally come, but we've got to do something, we have to get involved...."

His rambling speech was shot through with inconsistencies, but he wouldn't let me get a word in edgewise. Brooked no questions, no defense. He just prated breathlessly, as he led me towards the exit, and then to the wide marble steps, continuing to hold my arm. For the first time I felt like a prisoner in the much vaunted freedom Nicky talked about with increasing excitement.

"At such a time, we need highly-intelligent, capable people, with a clear vision, outstanding morals and unimpeachable characters, who can take over the reins of government, do you understand? There is such a chaos all around us and a big power vacuum. What matters is who steps in first."

"I don't want to be in front, thank you. Besides, I wouldn't even know how to help you...."

"Listen, don't you worry about these little things. You're a good journalist, uncompromised, that's what matters. We can't afford to let the uncalled-for have free rein of the country. In such times of upheaval, all kinds of amateurs, waverers, and self-styled revolutionaries will show up."

As he prattled on, we finally got to his car, which was parked at the curb in front of the building – a superb red Volkswagen, the likes of which few people ever saw, let alone own in our country then. He pushed me inside and locked the doors, so he could feel more secure.

The trip to the television center, which would have under normal circumstances, taken about ten minutes, now lasted for an hour and a half. Sure enough, there was plenty of madness to go around. The city was roaring as if caught in the midst of a powerful earthquake. It was a warm December day, with plenty of sunshine, so people came out into the streets in even greater numbers. Some were walking leisurely, some were singing, while others danced. Men carried their children on their shoulders, women were laughing hysterically, old people were crying for joy. Almost everyone flashed the two-finger, V-shaped sign for victory. They hugged, photographed, and filmed one another. They threw flowers from balconies, rushed into the unattended stores, climbed the tall walls of the special residential districts reserved heretofore to the privileged, who had all disappeared right after the flight of the dictator.

The crowds broke into the headquarters of the Party and the government, devastated the offices and reception rooms, driven by hatred and vengefulness. Each took whatever their fancy struck them – fountain pens, typewriters, drapes, towels, coffee cups, glasses, cutlery, bottles filled with alcoholic drinks, without any compunction whatever, fully convinced they were entitled to these long-denied luxury goods.

The streets presented the viewers with quite an impressive view – a topsy-turvy world of sights and sounds. Excitement, enthusiasm, deafening noise, thrilling disorder. Drivers leaned on their horns, flying the national flag through the open windows. It all looked like one great city-wide, open-air party. "Just like the euphoria we felt after some great victory of our national soccer team," commented Nicky, brimming with excitement, his eyes searching mine, for a read on my emotions.

Eventually this euphoria reached me too. It was absolutely fantastic. It appeared we had finally ridden ourselves of the nightmare that had maimed our souls for so many decades. Oh, and how easy it all looked now! The dictator's flight, the former institutions of oppression now crumbled, having come over to the people' side, without the slightest resistance – so much so that one was bound to ask why we hadn't done this much earlier, why did we have to live for so long under the wicked totalitarian regime, when it was clear things could have been solved apparently in a jiffy!

Although I did not know what to expect next, I too joined this overwhelming, intoxicating euphoria.

When we got to the television center, a hitherto forbidding institution, with maximum security around it, to my surprise we were ushered right in as if we were stepping into a hotel lobby. All doors were now wide open. The hallways were filled with revolutionaries, soldiers or merely curious citizens, who had dropped by to see what was going on. Nicky knew the place quite well, so we went straight to the broadcasting studio, where we met with the by-now usual devastation. I quickly recognized actors, writers, directors, dissidents, anti-communists, public figures. They were all crowding in front of the cameras, snatching the microphone from one another and shouting at the top of their voices:

"Let's stay calm. We have won! We're free at last."

Like the people in the streets, they too raised two fingers, in a V-sign for victory. Some, overcome with emotion, were merely content to shout out one slogan, and then pass the mike to others who were waiting in line. There were some with a propensity for speechifying, who would launch into little patriotic discourses. The already founded National Salvation Front was getting underway, busy with the creation of a platform, necessary for the takeover of the government.

Nicky stepped up to the microphone, shouting at the top of his voice, "The Army is with us," after which he withdrew, exhausted, behind the group of self-styled leaders. I, for one, stood aside, avoiding as best I could any exposure. I was finding it incredulous that the national television was broadcasting these proceedings live and the entire nation was seeing what I was seeing there and then.

"It's the first revolution broadcast live to a watching world," piped in Nicky, somewhat disappointed that he had put so much hope in me, and I had not come through, proving so awkward about things revolutionary.

I took advantage of the crowded atmosphere in the studio and, when Nicky lost sight of me for one moment, took off discreetly, risking complete alienation from my friend. As I walked home, I ran through several hot spots in the heart of the city. People continued to pour into the streets. All the major institutions were by now in the hands of the revolutionaries.

By the time I stepped into my apartment, darkness had already descended over the capital. It kind of sneaked up on us unawares, as it often does in winter. The children had not arrived yet. I lit up the gas stove – our only source of heat at the time – and ate a slice of bread with butter, washing it down with coffee. Then I turned on the TV. The studio continued to be the stage of this grand dialogue some of the most odd characters as well as perfect strangers, all talking in a highly dramatic excited tones, were having with the nation, all confirming that an irreversible victory had indeed been won.

Three anchors, who had until yesterday been singing the praises of communism, were now broadcasting, choking with emotion, the victory of our revolution against the dictatorship and totalitarianism. They were using more and more frequently and insistently words such as "we," "ours," and "for us," so no one should be in doubt as to what had really happened.

I lit up a cigarette and returned to the kitchen, to pour myself a glass of wine. It was then that I heard the first gunshots. At first few and far between. Later more intensified, mingled with reports of machine-gun fire or even the sound of cannon. As I opened the window, the boom increased in volume. By now it was pitch dark outside, while far away towards the center of the city the sky was orange-red, with the heavy barrage of firearms.

I ran back inside, to watch television and was terrified by what I saw. They were broadcasting scenes from the Main Square engulfed in flames, with bullets whizzing by, in what appeared to be a stampede, as people desperately scrambled for cover, to avoid the unrelenting machine-gun fire. They had set fire to the National Library and were shooting non-stop from all directions. The walls of the buildings in the square were riddled with bullets. In the balcony of the former "Communist Party Central Committee" building, undaunted revolutionaries defied the gunfire peril, shouting into microphones, "No violence! Hold you fire! Stop shooting!"

The terrifying images from the central plaza alternated with cuts from the main studio where I had been just a short while ago and which was now occupied by a different set of characters, issuing contradictory orders to the Army, to the *Securitate* and to the population at large. Old generals, until recently mothballed, had been hastily brought out, officers and former collaborators of the old regime who had suddenly switched sides and were enthusiastically supporting the revolution, some of them dauntlessly joining the street fighters.

A reporter came on, announcing that the dictator and his wife had been apprehended and were now securely in the hands of the revolutionaries, in a place not far from the capital. There was talk of a possible riposte from the elite guerillas, still faithful to the dictator, who had presumably tried to snuff the revolution, to set him free and restore him to power.

I watched in awe, unable to make head or tails of what I saw. Another reporter told us we were being surrounded by terrorists who were shooting from the roofs of buildings, having barged into hospitals, schools, and apartment complexes, their paths littered with slaughtered bodies. Alarming news continued to pour in from various sources about an impending onslaught on the capital by gunship helicopters, machine-gunning the population or public buildings, and chemical plants being blown up, in the context of nearly depleted blood banks and hospitals overflowing with the severely wounded, the dead and the dying.

As I sat glued to the TV, panic gripped me. Thank God the terrorists had not thought of pulling the plug on the live TV broadcast! I grabbed the phone, to warn Laura to stay put, to find some place to hide, and forget about returning home, given the news I heard from the anchors about every major city being under attack by counterrevolutionary forces who wreaking havoc everywhere in the provinces, about airports and train stations being shut down and major roads being blocked by troops and tanks.

I was desperate because I had no idea where the children were. They hadn't been home all day. What should I do? Should I keep calling, trying to reach Laura at the construction site, or should I leave the phone alone, so the children wouldn't get a busy signal if they tried to call me? I searched the apartment for phone numbers of Sonia's or Petru's friends. Then I would run back to watch the latest news on television or look out the window or check the front door – in a word, I was getting more and more agitated and afraid, my knees knocking together.

The TV was praising the valor of the young people who had put up barricades in front of the University and defied the evil repressive forces with their bare chests. Scores of students had lost their lives, the anchor said. I was crushed, sick with worry, overcome with my helplessness and panic.

The telephone rang and I rushed to pick it up, almost snapping the cord from the wall outlet in my anxiety. It was Nadia, calling from the office, the one with the story about the flying saucer.

"Hello? Don't drink the water! It's poisoned! Pass this message on. Call as many as you can."

"Hello, Nadia."

"I can't talk right now. It's very urgent. We are racing against the clock. The water's poisoned!" she repeated cryptically and disconnected.

I went over to the kitchen and turned on the tap, watching the water flow as if I could actually see the poison in it. I got a lump in my throat. Then I looked inside the refrigerator. We were out of mineral water. As if on cue, I suddenly felt very thirsty, my eyes and my head seemingly on fire. And how long were we supposed to put up with this?

I heard raps on the front door and hurried to open it, hoping it was one or, God willing, both of the children. But it was only the building's superintendent, leaning on a rifle. I was stunned.

"We've got to get organized," he said to me without any preamble. "They have distributed weapons to the people. Already they organized themselves into law-and-order pickets, with lots of volunteer groups joining in. You'll recognize them by the tri-color bands around their arms."

It was only then I noticed Mr. George was wearing himself such a band with the national colors on his sleeve.

"Every building must be secure. We will take turns standing watch. Starting with the second floor, for the ground floor is occupied exclusively by widows. The main entrance into the building will be barricaded. You are to allow access into the building only to the people who actually live here and only after they have produced proper identification. If attacked, you are to shoot on sight. The watchers have to sign out their weapons."

"What's going on, Mr. George?" I asked imploringly. "Who's doing the shooting, who are the terrorists, where have they come from?"

"I...I don't know. Maybe *Securitate* or KGB people, or the dictator's snipers. Who knows? They say he had taken them under his wings as orphans and raised them underground, giving them special training to offer him the best protection ever. They had no mother, no father, no God. He and his wife were mother, father and God to them, the whole fanatic lot. Arabs of Sadam Hussein's, special troops, how should I know?"

I realized he was just as uninformed as I was.

"You are scheduled to go on duty tomorrow night, between 12 midnight and 6 in the morning."

"I don't know what I am going to do. I have to find my children, my wife. None of them are at home. I might go myself. I'm waiting and waiting for any one of them to call. I have no idea what I am going to do. Please don't count on me. Why don't you find someone else to replace me?"

"We've thought of everything," nodded Mr. George and I thought he looked at me rather reproachfully.

"Don't open the door to anyone. They say terrorists barge in on people's homes, killing them, and them shooting from their windows into the crowds outside."

Just then the phone rang, so I almost shut the door in Mr. George's face, in my hurry to pick up the receiver. It was Sonia. She had spent all day in the main plaza, she said. Then when the shooting started, she found refuge at a schoolmate's house. Thank God everything was OK. She was also worried about Lary, and about Petru, whom she had left around noon with a group of students in front of the University. I told her not to drink the water because it was poisoned. She already knew. She and her friend had been warned by a woman in the neighborhood.

"Shall I come and take you home?" I asked her, by now a little calmer.

"No, I'll stay here overnight. It would be too dangerous to travel. Don't worry. It's a solid house, and we won't go out anyway. Give me a call when Petru shows up and try to find mom. Are you watching any television?"

"Yes. Why? What's new?"

"A truck with fifty soldiers who had been summoned to come to the airport as reinforcements…well, all of them were shot dead."

"By whom?"

"By the Army. By mistake. A false alarm or friendly fire as they call it – they thought the soldiers were terrorists."

"Don't open to anyone. Take care."

"You too."

I poured myself another glass of wine and sat in front of the TV screen, on tenterhooks. Where could Petru be? Finally I managed to get a hold of Laura. She said there was no shooting over there. Soon they were going to move into the local doctor's house, who lived near the construction site. She burst into tears when she learned from me Petru was nowhere to be found. They had also seen on TV the havoc wreaked in the capital. I tried to soothe her, although I felt as if a knife was tearing my up insides.

I sat down on the sofa, with the wine bottle and the telephone next to me. On TV they announced that the dictator and his wife were going to be tried in an emergency criminal proceeding. Citizens of different ages, with hatred in their bloodshot eyes, were demanding the immediate death of the dictator and his hated wife. They wanted revenge for all the bloodshed going on around them. The anchors called the people into the streets, urging them to resist the counterrevolutionary forces. They said there were already tens of thousands of victims all over the country.

I couldn't understand a thing. Who were the shooters? Why did everything start like a carnival, only to degenerate into violence and bloodshed and madness? How did those glorious events – the flight of the dictator, the Army and the *Securitate* switching sides – turn into the current mess? Who was behind this change of scenery, this sudden turn of events, just when we thought we had won? And what about me? What should I or could I do? Should I go out into the streets? Or stay put at home, waiting for my family to return? What was being expected of me? And when and how was it all going to end? Maybe the terrorists would continue to harass us for a long time, making us hide and turning our lives into another nightmare. Who knows, I said to myself, perhaps we will stay indefinitely in this state of limbo, in a quasi permanent state of emergency, in a continuous civil war.

I felt helpless and ridiculous, ensconced on the sofa, watching on TV the madness that had spread throughout the land. Just as helpless and ridiculous as I had felt all those years of obedience to dictatorship. Again things happened independently of me, outside of myself, while I remained a mere passive witness to this extraordinary turn of events. After midnight the show went off the air, signing off with the newly-minted national anthem, which unlike the old one no longer sounded sickeningly triumphal, though it had an unmistakably funeral undertone. Even its beginning words, so mobilizing, so arousing – "Arise from your slumber…from your death-like sleep…" – were quite repugnant to me. I fell asleep, with my clothes on, hugging the phone, my brain racked by questions, guilty, firmly in the grip of terror.

Towards morning, I heard a loud banging on the door and agitated voices on the landing. I jumped up, as if burned, looked through the peephole and could not recognize the lens-distorted faces, which elongated and curved them into grotesque images.

"Who's there?" I asked, quite terrified.

"Open up!"

The banging continued.

"Aren't you ever going to open? It's Nicky. I've got your son with me."

I opened the door and stood there petrified. Petru was held up by two young men. His head was bandaged and his coat was torn around his right arm, which was in a cast. I stepped aside and let them in. I scooped up my son in my arms. He was completely exhausted. Not a word came from his lips.

"Oh, my God!"

"Calm down," Nicky told me, "it's not so bad."

"Let's go to the hospital…," I said weakly.

"We've just come from there. It's nothing to worry about. We've brought him home, because the hospital is filled with badly wounded people. They ran out of beds. But he's all right. He's going to be well soon. There would have been no point in leaving him in the hospital, not with his relatively minor injuries. His arm is broken, true, but it's going heal. Besides, he's young!" said Nicky, smiling, and I felt a shade better.

Petru's two colleagues helped into a makeshift bed on the sofa in the dining room. He was feeling lightheaded.

"How're you feeling? Can I get you something?"

"I'm OK. I really am. My friend Sebastian was shot dead."

I looked at him stunned, realizing for the first time what he must have gone through, and what a close escape he had had. I saw tears in his eyes, as he turned his face towards the wall.

Recovering from my momentary weakness, I thanked his two colleagues who had practically carried him home. I offered them a cup of coffee, but they said they were in hurry. It was only then I noticed Nicky had come with another man, a young fellow with a reddish beard, who had already sat down on a chair in front of the sofa.

"He is Alexei," said Nicky, simply, by way of an introduction. "A good friend of mine from Chisinau. We were together in the University Square when Petru was injured. We realized he was your son and took him to the hospital. We knew one of the doctors, so everything went very smoothly, and fast too. He assured me there was no reason to worry."

"Thank you very much," I said to them, but looking mainly towards Alexei, who nodded modestly, as if to say, "You're welcome."

"You got quite a son, there. He was the piercing end of the spear," added Nicky. "These young people are irresponsibly brave. Personally, I don't think the revolution would have succeeded without them."

I cast him an unfriendly glance. His speeches about the "victory of the Revolution" annoyed me no end, especially since the victory seemed to have been paid for with innocent lives.

"Can you get us some coffee?" asked Nicky, as he took off his leather jacket. It was then I noticed the handgun in his pocket.

"What is that?"

"They gave us weapons, didn't you know? How else can we be expected to defend ourselves from the fierce reaction of these fanatics? By the way, you took off yesterday. I wanted to get you into your position, but couldn't find you anywhere."

"I am not a good speaker," I answered morosely.

I brought out their coffees, lit up a cigarette and took a worried look at Petru, who had quietly fallen asleep on the sofa.

"I want to ask you something. Alexei has nowhere to sleep tonight. I'm caught up with all kinds of things to do. They assigned me to the television center – the main target of the terrorists. I wonder, could he stay here overnight?"

I regarded Alexei, who looked so gentle, so harmless, sipping his coffee, his eyes never leaving Petru. I didn't know what to answer Nicky. Then, all of a sudden, I jumped up as if burned, and grabbed the cup out of Alexei's hand, screaming with terror, "Don't drink it! It's poisoned!"

Nicky looked at me as if I was raving mad. He had not yet got to sip from his coffee.

"The water! You see, the water is poisoned! I completely forgot about it."

Nicky's face broadened into a relaxed smile. "I can't believe you've fallen for all these false rumors. There's no poisoned water! Just a diversion, meant to sow panic among the populace."

I looked at him doubtfully, determined not to touch my own coffee. Petru let out a moan. And inside my head was roaring something fierce.

"Let me talk to you in the kitchen for a moment," said Nicky to me.

We closed the door after us.

"Listen, you've got to calm down. The water is not poisoned. Your son will get back on his feet, the injuries are not serious. Don't let your nerves kill you."

"I can't understand anything," I confessed to him, vanquished.

"There's nothing to understand. These are the death throes of the hydra. This too shall pass. The devil is not as black as he looks."

"When? And who are the shooters, who are the terrorists?"

"The special services are settling scores with each other. The Army is battling the *Securitate* forces. But they'll settle in the end and the fighting will die down. At least I think so.... Now, listen carefully! Alexei is a very special man. He's a healer. He can interpret auras. He's a genius about establishing a patient's diagnosis. He can treat people; he is a thinker, a Zen practitioner. He is endowed with...what shall I call them? Paranormal powers? I hope you have nothing against these things. I'm not expecting you to believe in them, just admit they might be true.... By the way, he was there when the incident happened, in fact one might say he was the one who saved your son."

Nicky's clarification only served to increase my confusion.

When we returned to the dining room, we found Alexei with his eyes closed holding his hands with the palms turned upwards above Petru's head, while he was mumbling something. I looked at Nicky, who winked at me encouragingly, to signify the procedure effected by Alexei was beneficial to Petru. Then he donned his leather jacket, checked his gun in the rear pocket and tapped me on the shoulder:

"Go ahead, write the article, for this thing can't go on much longer and then we'll have to get down to some hard work."

How did Nicky know when and what was going to end, what lay behind his calm and lucid appraisals? I, for one, was increasingly confused and unsure of what was to follow. Naturally, I was glad that the proverbial *mamaliga*, that cornmeal porridge, with which our nation was sometimes associated, did at last blow up, but what frightened me was the chaos and the violence, which looked as if they were to stay for a while.

But to hear Nicky say it, everything was unfolding in a predictable fashion, within "normal" parameters as he put it, that is in accordance with an imaginary script of their own making, known only by some. For the life of me, I just couldn't see any "encouraging" signs about this revolution which Nicky kept touting as "so evident." My outlook was somewhat darker. The only sensation that really struck me in those moments was fear.

I went into the bedroom and turned on the radio. It had been left tuned to Radio Free Europe, the station I had been listening to, surreptitiously, for years and years. The station broadcast messages of encouragement for the revolutionaries, interviews with political dissidents who had emigrated abroad. Among them was David Cosma, my former high school mate and good friend, until he had been forced to ask for political asylum in Germany.

He was a great economist, having incurred the wrath of the communist regime through his theories, which lashed out at the maddening industrial policies of the late dictator, which he never missed a chance to criticize. They considered it too big a risk to do away with him, because of his notoriety. He had become a well-known world personality, having been awarded numerous international commendations. So they encouraged him to emigrate. Now he was living in Frankfurt, where he became the head of an economics/bankruptcy-prevention research institute.

I was very moved to hear his voice. He sounded as level-headed and smooth as I had always known him, speaking in measured tones, avoiding euphoria and exaltation. I had not seen him since the day he had left the country, eight years before. I kept in touch with him sporadically, through people who traveled to Germany. Whenever he could he sent me various books and once in a while a bottle of whiskey. He too was thrilled with what was going on in our country, but a bit skeptical about the future.

I returned to the dining room and turned on the TV. They had switched back to live broadcasting of the revolution. Things had taken a turn for the worse. The same anchors, now looking quite bedraggled, their faces lined with fatigue, were telling the viewers about the rising toll, now well over sixty thousand victims, mass graves, bodies hacked by bayonets, unique national treasures set on fire, and many other incalculable losses. They talked about an alleged call that had reportedly been made to the Russians to come to our aid and try to put an end to the violence, about a possible military rule or the danger of a civil war outbreak.

They had brought into the TV studio a terrorist who had fallen into the hands of the revolutionaries. He was wounded. The blood had soaked his thick black undershirt, strange attire such as I had only seen in movies with special shock troops. The anchors, the civilians and the other people still found there madly set upon him, overcoming him with questions, each more final than the other: "Tell us who you really are, scum of the earth?" "Who do you work for?" "In whose pay?" "Why are you, despicable thugs, killing our people?" And all along they viciously hit him with their fists, and feet, peppering him with questions in a chaotic, haphazard manner.

The terrorist did not breathe one word, but was merely trying to parry the attacks, with sad, unfocused eyes.

"He's mute," someone said. "They raise them from a very early age, then cut their tongues and turn them into killing machines."

"He is an Arab," opined someone else. Naturally all of this was going on live on national television, for everyone to see. Then he was taken out by two soldiers, who resumed striking him.

Next they brought in a little old lady, whom the volunteer fighters apparently had caught in a street car with two automatic pistols hidden in a wicker basket under food which she claimed she was taking to the soldiers who were guarding the Radio building.

"In fact she was feeding the terrorists with weapons," the anchor informed us, looking at her scornfully, with hatred in his bloodshot eyes. The old woman just wept, mumbling something incomprehensively.

The whole thing sounded and looked very melodramatic. The population was urgently requested to come out into the streets and resist until total victory was achieved. A trial panel was to travel that day to the place where the dictator and his wife were held prisoners to begin emergency criminal proceedings against the two.

I was smoking with desperation, having finished my coffee and forgetting the water might have been poisoned. Outside I heard steady machine-gun fire. We were told about the threat of other terrorist commando units aboard helicopters, who were, presumably, mounting an assault on the city. Petru was sleeping, while Alexei continued to watch over him, his eyes closed, so I could not tell whether he was meditating or just napping.

I called Sonia's friend to see how the girls were doing. The girl's mother answered. She too was in a panic. The girls had left more than an hour ago to deliver food to the soldiers guarding the metro station in their residential district. I felt I was going mad.

"Well, madam, how could you ever let them out of your sight?"

"What did you expect me to do, sir, wrestle them? Can't you see what a mess we're in? Aren't you watching any television? I couldn't make myself understood. All these young people are filled with the urge to do something; they want to help…they're fed up too."

"Do you know how many have been shot?" I asked her, feeling I was going under.

"So what can I do?"

I disconnected and plunked down on a chair. I heard a key turn in the front door lock and ran out into the hallway. It was Lary.

"Oh, am I glad to see you!"

She threw her handbag down and made to enter the dining room. I stopped her gently, taking her into my arms, to allay any suspicions on her part. I simply had to prepare her a little.

"How are you all? What are you doing? Where are the children?"

"Everybody's fine. How did you get here?"

And, very discreetly, I led her towards the kitchen. She took off her overcoat and sat down. There were bags under her eyes, and her hair was disheveled.

"The local doctor let us use the ambulance. He said it would be more secure, as they would be very unlikely to shoot at a clearly-marked medical vehicle. As we entered Bucharest, three volunteer patrols stopped us, demanding to see our ID's. They were looking for weapons. Apparently terrorists enter hospitals aboard emergency vehicles, and then shoot the wounded in the head. There's no way the doctor could have foreseen this. What do you think of all this that's happening?"

"I don't know what to say…."

She put her head between her hands and looked at me in silence. I stroked her hair.

"Please don't be frightened. Sonia is with that girl, a friend of hers. She's all right, I was the one who told her not to come home, because of the danger she would face on the streets, with all this shooting. Petru is in the dining room, sleeping. Last night he was with his colleagues, in the University Square…. He was slightly injured in the head. And his right arm is in a cast. But he's not badly hurt."

I saw her face go white.

"What…? What are you telling me?"

And she dashed into the dining room. I followed her. Petru was still asleep, under the influence of the powerful sedatives he had received in the hospital. Alexei was now seated in the middle of the room, with his legs drawn under him, perhaps in a yoga position, meditating with his eyes closed. She stayed for a while in the doorway, taking everything in, with maternal instinct and female intuition. She took a long look at Petru and I saw the worries drain from her. She looked once more at Alexei, who continued his meditation, completely ignoring us, and then closed the door gently behind her.

"Who's that?" she asked me calmly.

"A friend of Nicky's, Alexei. He's the one who pulled Petru out of that stampede at the University. Then both of them took Petru to the hospital, and later home. Nicky asked me to put him up for one night. He's from Chisinau, and has no place to sleep. How could I say no...."

"Naturally," said Lary. "My dear child, mommy's sweet one. Is his head badly hurt?"

"They assured me it is just a superficial wound."

"Please dial the number where Sonia is staying. I want to talk to her."

"Why don't we let her call...? They must be tired with all the calls I've been making all morning."

Lary trusted me and relaxed a bit. Then she turned on the tap, to check whether we had hot water. We had. So she stepped into the bathroom to take a shower. I made a surreptitious phone call, to find out if Sonia and her friend had arrived home. This time I found the girl's mother in a state of hysteria. The girls had not returned and she was considering going out to try and find them, as she couldn't take it any more. In their district the gunfire was heavy. Her neighbors had told her the terrorists had climbed the roofs of buildings, let themselves down on ropes, then broke the windows and entered apartments, killing their occupants and hunkering down in some of these makeshift command centers, from which they could launch new street attacks.

"Do you know Professor Andrei? Have you heard of him? He was the head of the mental hospital. Well, he was shot in the head, after he had gone over to close a window. Just then a bullet pierced his forehead. Isn't this stupid? Dear Lord, what is happening to us?"

It was my turn to calm her. I asked her to call us as soon as she had some news. On TV they were talking more and more about the unusual trial of the dictator's family. Everybody was waiting for the verdict, which was due in a matter of hours.

"Do you realize that tomorrow's Christmas?" inquired Lary, who had stepped out of the bathroom, with her hair wet, and had turned on the oven, our multi-use source of heat.

"There are rumors flying about the water being poisoned...."

"I heard it too. But I don't believe it. I think it's just an outgrowth of the people's fear. And anyway, I've got to do some cooking, haven't I? It's Christmas, so, no matter what, at least *sarmale* I am going to cook, poisoned water or no," she said, proudly, referring to the famous national dish of stuffed cabbage.

I smiled to myself and loved her for it. I was so glad to see she hadn't lost her humor, that she knew how to defuse a crisis. I loved her too for keeping her cool when she saw Petru wounded, when she found out Sonia was not in, when she discovered a stranger meditating in a yoga-position right in the middle of our dining room. Women possess this paradoxical ability to maintain their poise at the height of some of the most dramatic moments, while at times breaking down for some of the most ridiculously unimportant reasons. Danger seems to stimulate them. The sudden rush of adrenaline makes them stronger, keeps their blood cool, and may even make rescuers out of them.

I don't how, but with Laura safely home, I regained some of my confidence and was able to overcome my fears. Somehow it seemed to me nothing evil could happen to us anymore.

My hopes were confirmed. Later that evening Sonia came home, safe and sound. Petru had already awakened and, after being fed by his mother lots of soup and grilled meat, he felt his strength returning. A wonderful aroma of *sarmale* and apple pie wafted from the kitchen. Outside the sound of gunfire continued to reverberate, the television went on with its live broadcast of the most brutal and bloody of Eastern Europe's 1989 revolutions.

Sonia and Petru would have liked to go back to the Square, where all their colleagues stood up for the Revolution, ready to pay with their lives for its success. We were lucky to have Alexei with us, who seemed to hold greater sway over them. I don't know how he managed to persuade them, what arguments he resorted to, but the young ones did give up the idea and now all three were huddled in the dining room, holding hands and mouthing something which Alexei said was a joint prayer of deliverance.

Neither Lary nor I objected, content that at least they were out of harm's way. Then Alexei put Petru through a healing treatment for his head wound, by running his hands in circles around Petru's eyes and forehead.

He quickly won Lary over too. He merely looked at her, as she was, with her clothes on, doing her work in the kitchen and came up with the perfect diagnosis: biliary diskinesia and cervical spondylosis. She made her lie down on the sofa in the dining room, pressed some vertebrae in the neck area, kept his hot hand on her abdomen, pushing gently, the way he only knew how. And Laura, impressed that someone gave her so much attention and took care of her in such a special way, declared that she already felt better, that Alexei was absolutely great and from that moment she showered him with her utmost affection.

He advised me to give up smoking and to be careful, because I had a very sensitive duodenum, and to watch what I ate, to avoid stress and forgo some of the spicier foods, raw fruit and drink less coffee or even to eliminate all spices from my diet.

Soon all of us ended up being friends with Alexei and, what was even more important, he inspired in us a sense of trust and security. The feeling was apparently mutual. Sonia read his palm. He was calm, gentle, spoke little and every day we were drinking in his words with undisguised admiration.

We brought up the subject of our revolution, eager to hear what he thought of it.

Here he waxed metaphoric. In addition to it, he didn't speak well our language and we didn't know Russian. We tried very hard to decode his strange messages: "…the wager of great powers, the treachery of those close to the dictator, the provocation and manipulation of the populace, simulated shooting, amplified by speakers in order to spread panic, special troops, the need to authenticate the revolution by having a lot of dead people…." We were not very sure we understood very much of all this. For us, at that time, Alexei's opinions made no sense, so we just dropped the subject. As a matter of fact, we were convinced Alexei had no way of knowing what was going on, in spite of his paranormal skills. He was just a young healer from Chisinau and no matter how endowed and talented he seemed, he was out of his depth about the revolution.

"You know this is the first year we don't have a Christmas tree?" Lary said to me, while she was setting the table for five in the dining room.

Although it was a holiday, we didn't want to miss anything of the revolution's horrors. In addition, the trial of the two dictators was underway, which was going to be broadcast soon. So we took our seats around the table in such a way as to make sure everyone could see the TV set. Again we were living out a surreal experience, this time adhering to traditions, against the backdrop of the tragedy that had enveloped the country.

For a few minutes, Alexei kept his eyes closed, in deep concentration, then he opened them, saying the two dictators would be shot dead. That very night. And that following this, the violence would stop. Apparently he had had a vision. Come to think of it, Nicky had told me about his fortune-telling abilities. We made no comment, although none of us believed him at the time. We just nodded skeptically and began to eat.

Shortly after Alexei's prediction, just as we had finished the *sarmale* and were about to eat the meat, there was a special breaking news announcement on TV. A national message to say the two dictators had been tried in an emergency procedure, had been found guilty and sentenced to death for sabotage of the national economy and genocide. A hastily-constituted death squad had already executed him. Everything had been recorded on videotape, which the whole world would soon be able to view on TV.

We shuddered. All eyes turned on Alexei, who had again closed his eyes.

"What can you see?" Lary asked him, giving in to curiosity and open admiration for his seer's powers.

We didn't get to hear the answer because they were now showing the trial on TV. The formerly fierce dictators, now two scared old people, so vulnerable, so pitiable, defending themselves as best they could against the avalanche of charges leveled at them by the very person who was supposed to be their public defender. The dictator was trying to temper his wife, who was more garrulous and more rebellious, by laying his hand discretely on her arm, in an attempt to stop the torrent of explanations. He constantly referred to foreign agencies who were intent on destabilizing the country and to the coup staged by those closest to him, in whom he had trusted completely and to whom he had entrusted himself. Two words recurred: "traitors" and "treason."

"Apparently Alexei said something similar," Laura whispered into my ear.

I laid my hand on her arm, signifying she should keep silent. The dictator kept looking at his watch, then would gaze at the bars in the window, to the ceiling and to the floor.

"Why does he keep looking at his watch?" asked Laura impatiently.

"It is a transmitter-watch, so his supporters might easily locate him. He's waiting for the terrorists to rescue him," explained Alexei. "What he doesn't know though is that the terrorists are now serving the new rulers. He *is* right: they have all betrayed him, down to the last one."

"And what's he rambling on about a coup? What about the hundreds of thousands of people who came out into the Square of their own accord? Has anyone called them? And what about all those kids who were shot dead?"

"He knows the truth only too well...and he's the only one who could have really told what had happened, had they not killed him first," foretold Alexei calmly.

We were living in a fairy-tale like atmosphere, much like in an absurd story. Alexei's commentary really amused me: "All one needs is a Latin country and a dictator for surrealism to be born."

It all happened very quickly, in less than half an hour. At the end of the trial two soldiers stood them up, and the sentence – punishment by death – was read. Their hands were tied behind their backs, after which they were led into the courtyard of the military barracks where they had been held and placed against a wall. "I have been like a mother to you," was all she still managed to say. As for him, he began to sing *The Internationale*. Both of them refused to be blindfolded.

The squad commander requested three volunteers out of the twenty who were lined up in the courtyard eager to carry out the execution order. All twenty military men responded, by stepping forward as one man, enthusiastically offering to fire on the two dictators, such was the level of their hatred. Barely had the commander managed to order "Fire," than tens of bullets riddled the dictators' bodies. They fell in a heap onto the concrete, in grotesquely twisted positions, with blood gushing from their heads.

It was over. Finally the people could breathe a collective sigh of relief. Everybody had waited eagerly for that moment. All had dreamed of this sweet moment of revenge, having intensely and passionately wished to see them dead. I looked on, with horror in my heart. I simply could muster no reaction whatsoever. Alexei's eyes were closed again. For the first time his gesture grated on my nerves. Actually, in those moments I wished I had been alone. I think everybody did. I was overtaken by a feeling of shame, pity and disgust, while I was both obscenely glad and frightened by the horrific nature of the images I was seeing. I couldn't believe all of this was actually happening, in the real world.

In just one hour after this the representatives of the National Salvation Front announced a ceasefire throughout the country, declaring the revolution a complete victory, the opening of the borders, and the recognition of the newly installed government by the world powers. They issued a few democratic decrees, legalized abortions and required the urgent return of all the weapons that had been distributed to the citizenry. The terrorists had vanished into thin air. Soon we were to learn also that the total number of casualties was not over sixty thousand, as we had been led to believe by radio and television reports, but only about a thousand.

Alexei dressed, thanked us and hugged each of us. He promised Petru and Sonia to stay in touch by telephone and to look us up, should he come again to the capital. We had grown fond of him. Laura gave him a large package with broiled meat, *cozonac* (that traditional cake usually made for religious holidays), and oranges.

He did not know exactly whether he would stay with Nicky or return to Chisinau right away, where people apparently lived under even harsher conditions than we did. Before he got out the door, he parted with these words, "Things have not been wrapped up. There will be more violence on the street, but only in pockets here and there, and only related to the consolidation of the new power. Hard times are ahead. The society is sick, the economy in shambles, and the order of things corrupted. Only now will a true measure of the abject poverty be revealed. It will take at least twenty years to return to normality and build the much-vaunted democracy. New generations will have to be sacrificed…."

His words had a foreboding ring and did not sit well with us. The last thing we were thinking of then was the future, when the present filled our minds with so many unpredictable, exciting things. Then he cast one last friendly look towards Sonia and Petru, picked up his rucksack and disappeared.

His presence in our home for Christmas, especially during those dramatic events, had a good impact on us. He had emanated wisdom, confidence and protection. He was a well-educated young man, obviously well-read and informed about a host of subjects, although he would not discuss in detail any subject. Now he was writing a book of teachings and Zen meditations. He had worked in a parapsychology institute in

Moscow. He had a great capacity to synthesize and analyze phenomena and implied that he knew far more than he said, but did not flaunt his knowledge, nor did he try to persuade people or to force his ideas on them. After spending a while in his presence, it was impossible to deny his special insights. The palms of his hands were always hot. As if by miraculous powers, he could cause a migraine to disappear, a toothache, a renal colic to vanish, to mention but a few of the ones that could be readily verified.

Between Christmas and the New Year nothing noteworthy happened. Some were mourning their dead, while others, who had held important political posts, were in hiding, fearful of the outcome of an anti-communist revolution.

The city was cleaned up a bit. Suddenly, people were surprised to see on television scantily-clad women dancers – something they would never seen before – and in the food stores there were now plentiful supplies of hitherto hard-to-find food items, exotic fruits, such as bananas, quickly imported to allay the long-pent up frustrations of the people. The apartments were now well heated, the water supply plentiful, and the electricity was never cut again. All the food in the national reserves was put on the market.

A little calmer now, we began to ask ourselves all kinds of questions, almost all of them without answers, such as: "Who opened fire on us?" and "Where are the arrested terrorists?" "How was it possible to have only one thousand dead, after days of uninterrupted shooting?" and "How could the radio and TV broadcasts put the total number of casualties at 60,000?" "Why did they kill the dictators in such a hurry?" "How was it possible for the television to continue to broadcast unimpeded throughout the traumatic events," "Who spread that rumor about the water being poisoned?" "What about the fleet of terrorist-laden helicopters attacking the towns and cities, about hospitals blown up and all those incredible scenarios which we had gullibly bought into, while constantly called into the streets to defend who knows what, from a never-specified enemy?" There was an obstinate call for the truth about the revolution rising from many sectors of the population.

To hear Nicky put it, "What's the use of all these questions, when we got what we had dreamed of for so many decades – the elimination of the dictator, the fall of communism, freedom itself? It's like a soccer match: what counts in the end is the final score. What does it matter how the teams played, how many misses they had, or how many were faulted, or expelled from the game? All that matters is the outcome. We've got our freedom, haven't we? You want the truth? Which truth? There are so many.... Besides, in every lie there is a grain of truth. Some risked their lives, others were killed and most of them stayed at home, in their pajamas, safely watching the events unfold on television and now here they come, demanding the truth." I felt I belonged to this category, so I always avoided any further discussion on the subject.

The new rulers had a new kind of answer to the haunting questions posed especially by the intellectuals and the timid so-called emerging civil society: "The truth? Well, they don't yet know the truth about Kennedy's assassination, even after more than forty years. So what can *you* expect?"

All kinds of phrases were bandied around, from "stealing the revolution" to "coup d'état." Finally the most decent formula, used primarily by the feeble opposition and the democratic press, was "the events of December 89," on which they continued to embroider all kinds of fanciful exaggerations, suppositions, scenarios and dilemmas.

Right after the New Year Nicky insisted that I should come to the publishing house.

"Well, old pal, what're you up to? Looks like you dropped out of the picture. I thought you'd be over the shock by now. The country is perishing and you loaf around? Come over quickly and let's get to work. I hope you haven't forgotten you are our new editor-in-chief?"

"I thought it was a joke...this business about making me the boss.... I told you I'm not cut out for this."

"Leave your modesty aside, for now. It's nice, but something else is required. The whole team is waiting for you. We're shaping a new world, old chap; we are laying the foundation for democracy and mapping out the country's future for a long time. And you are an essential piece in this!"

I don't know how, but all of Nicky's speeches reminded me of the mentality permeating the old system, with its cheap, stentorian, cynical rhetoric. And Nicky's optimism these days knew no bounds, determined as he was to get ahead, even further than he had done under the previous regime.

So I decided to take him up on the offer. There I was in the office of the former editor-in-chief, of whom no one had heard anything, where everybody was gathered together, the whole team, from the journalists to the graphic designers to the proofreaders. Nicky lorded it over all, with his air of authority which befitted him as newly-minted deputy chief, a position he had rewarded himself with. To my surprise, I stepped into my new role quite naturally. My colleagues liked me and were glad they could finally work with someone who was calm and normal, after the trying times they had lived under the old boss, an obsequious and paranoiac tool of the old communist regime.

Nobody raised any objection. No "Why him?", "who appointed him?" or "by whose authority?" None of that. They just took my appointment in stride, as a natural, welcome change. I was qualified, wasn't I? So why not me? – they seemed to think. I began right away to build a completely new paper from the ground up. First I changed its name, I designed new section headings, put together a list with the current contributors, established an editorial policy and laid out rule number one: "From now on everything we write will be in the spirit of truth, liberty and democracy."

I finally wrote the editorial for the front page which Nicky had been dreaming of and suddenly I found myself entrusted with new responsibilities, putting a firm shoulder to the task of laying a solid foundation for our new society. Being by nature thorough and conscientious, humorless when it comes to the business at hand, I dedicated myself wholeheartedly to my new duties. Ready to take on whatever difficulties lay in my path and deal with the novelty of my new position as top journalist in a world whose rules I did not know.

All my life I had exercised myself in the art of adapting and resisting within the communist system, convinced that it would never end – at least, not in my lifetime. I had found my own equilibrium, the coping mechanisms whereby I could survive, I had come to terms with fate, and now here I was turned upside down! Thrown into the arena, where I had to start everything from scratch, relying mostly on my instinct, intuition and imagination.

A month after the December revolution, begun as a revolt against the dictator and concluded as a smashing blow to the communist system as a whole, our paper found its niche in the market. We had a large circulation and enjoyed a certain moral authority. Then we had an unexpected visitor at our office. It was around noon, just as we had finished the daily wrap-up meeting. The reporters had left the meeting room, rushing to the wires, to get their stories for the day and the authors of the main sections had retreated to write their articles.

I ended up alone with just my secretary to whom I was dictating the editorial. There were a few light taps on the door. I did not turn to look who it was and the secretary rose in an attempt to protect me from the intrusion, meaning to ask the visitor to wait in the hallway.

"I'd like to speak with the editor-in-chief," I heard through the cracked door.

I started, recognizing the voice that had haunted me for so many years.

"It's all right," I told the secretary, a young woman I had just hired. "Let's go into my office, so we can have some privacy."

I avoided his gaze and did not reply to his "Hello" which he addressed to me rather timidly. I sat down at the massive oak desk and invited him to take a seat. I was feeling awkward and did not know what tone to adopt. From behind that same desk the person standing now before me had terrorized us year after year.

It was our *ex*-editor-in-chief, in an entirely new pose. I scanned him up and down rapidly. There was nothing left in him of the old terror. The upper button on his shirt was undone, the tie he wore out of fashion, the shirt sleeves dirty, the hair disheveled. He had bags under his eyes and looked very messy. In the few minutes it took us to try to get used to the change of roles, all kinds of scenes from the old power play flooded my mind. I experienced all kinds of contradictory feelings and was unable to break the ice first, so I just waited for him to open the discussion. I felt uncomfortable, not knowing what to expect.

"So far I have hesitated to come…."

So the tone had changed! No longer condescending, superior, but fawning and humble.

"I can't take it anymore…living like this. You have got to help me, sir…. I'll take any job, proofreader, courier, anything. Please help me! I helped many in my time…. I badly need a job now, or I'll go insane. I'm already taking medication. In fact, I've just been hospitalized…."

It was only then I noticed his bandaged hand.

"What happened?" I inquired, looking at his hand which he was ineffectually trying to hide under the chair.

"Oh, nothing, just a scratch, really.... It's my nerves I've got a problem with. I don't want to retire. I'll lose my mind if I stay at home...."

"I am sorry, sir, but I'm afraid there is no way I can help you. Though, humanly speaking, I'd like to. Except that I simply can't. We are talking about a new world, a new paper and a new outlook. You wouldn't be able to fit in, to cope with all the changes that have intervened. And anyway no one in the board of directors would vouch for you. You've got to understand this, sir, and I regret I have to put it to you so bluntly: Your time is up. The days of people like you are over! Please try to live with this...."

It was perhaps the most embarrassing little speech I had ever had to make. But the real embarrassment would come a little later.

My former boss confided in me that during the days of the Revolution he had had a terrible fright, having fled to his brother, where he stayed in hiding for three weeks. He was convinced the revolutionaries would punish the entire *nomenklatura*, would hunt down all the *Securitate* people who had served the old regime from the height of their many perks. He felt they were zeroing in on him, were threatening him and since he was very fearful and cowardly by nature, he decided his best chance to escape the consequences was to run away. Hence the slight wound he staged on his left hand, as if he had been shot, which he put forth as a genuine proof of his siding with the Revolution and in the remaining moments doing some fighting against communism, which he claimed he had abhorred all his life. But how could he have opposed it? Would there have been a real chance? You know, these were the times... and all that!

When the heat subsided somewhat and it appeared as if there would be no punishment meted out to them, all these sinister characters crawled out of their hiding places and tested the waters. No big changes had occurred, after all, especially when he considered that some of his former colleagues had found cushy places within the new order, in hastily-cobbled democratic parties, in parliament, in government. So why wouldn't – shouldn't – he make a stab at it? He felt nostalgic for the old perks, missed his secretary, the limo waiting for him at the curb, his minions, and the power he wielded over them. Oh, for the sheer, intoxicating elixir that power bestowed on him! Although his age would have entitled him to retirement, he wouldn't hear of it. There was no way he could imagine rotting away in the park, looking after his grandchildren.

He wasn't too surprised I refused to hire him. Several months after his visit to the publishing house to ask me for an ordinary job, however menial, I saw him on television. He had made it big time! He joined the main ruling party, where he actually held an important position. Based on his bandaged hand, he obtained the requisite revolutionary certificate which entitled him to numerous advantages. He was exempt from paying taxes, received substantial social aid, traveled free on all public transportation vehicles, and was given priority in any private enterprise initiative. Soon he was to become the owner of a prosperous supermarket and a paper mill in the provinces. Once more he was feared and obeyed as secretary general of the most powerful social-democratic party in the country.

Later that summer I would meet him at a party given by the President in honor of a visiting head of state. He had a young female assistant in tow, who was never far from him. Also a Mercedes limo waiting for him outside, a cell phone, and a very satisfied, happy countenance. He seemed to have grown young and regained his self-confidence and arrogance. He greeted me jovially. So once again I was to be the one who felt awkward. I remembered the naive speech I had made on the occasion he had groveled to my office, begging for a job, however menial, and felt terribly uneasy about myself, about the whole, stinking farce.

Troubled days followed. Alexei's predictions proved correct once more. The revolution's euphoria had long since evaporated. People were again discontent. They wanted changes, but were unwilling to make the necessary sacrifices. They wanted changes, but these were proposed by the same influential goons of the old regime who converted overnight from tyrants to professing democrats. And if possible, they wanted all the changes to occur outside, so they would not be touched in any way and would not have to modify their attitudes and mentality.

What proved to be the hardest was living in freedom. Suddenly they found themselves in the spotlight. Alone. With only their limitations, inabilities, and failures which were now starkly showing in the unforgiving, glaring light of public scrutiny. Freedom highlights a person's individuality, stripping the crust of collective protection through which a dictatorship levels out a society, bringing it to the lowest denominator, the better to manipulate and conquer it.

Freedom scared a lot of people out of their wits, who for years and years had been used to act in the spirit of the crowd, always bent on blaming others, hiding behind the excuse that one cannot assert oneself in a closed society, hostile to personal initiative, values and competence. Now suddenly thrust into freedom, they felt terribly frightened and insecure. The old values system had been reversed, forcing them to come up with new motivations, with new underpinnings. Under these circumstances, it became quite fashionable for people to reexamine their past in a "new" light, to reevaluate history and culture from "different" points of view, acting most often at the prompting of the lackeys of the old regime, who had so quickly changed their spots, but not their wills as well.

A veritable witch-hunt started, exposing a host of hitherto carefully camouflaged evils, such as primitiveness, worthlessness, imposture, vengefulness, all under the guise of post-revolutionary justice. And another syndrome that became evident was the desire to camouflage their cowardice, lack of professionalism, provincial spirit. In a country where the overwhelming majority had humbly accepted all the aberrations of totalitarianism, which some of them even improved upon, there appeared overnight hundreds of dissidents, revolutionaries with diplomas, and fighters for democracy.

They created fake biographies and fashioned ideal destinies out of whole cloth. Some suddenly lost their memory, conveniently forgetting what they had been, and pretending to be completely clean, uncompromised, hoping the world would thus forget their past and forgive their sins. In short order, there was an overabundance of engineers, upholders of the law, profligates who suddenly became monks, noisily declaring their love of justice, wholesome and pure characters, superfine intellectuals preaching about the truth, about the need of a moral cleansing, about regaining the "national identity," about putting communism on trial and restoring the dignity of the nation on the international arena.

Essentially everyone tried to save himself, to secure for himself a place as close to the top as possible, be that a seat in parliament, or a profitable business, an apartment or a house from the government or a scholarship to study abroad, now that freedom caused another reversal of values, based on new but equally deficient criteria.

The same old poverty, but with the added ingredient of insecurity, the first signs of the transition to the market economy and the consequences of the attempts to reform the economy, resulting in unemployment, a dramatic rise in prices, housing shortages, and a lack of a social net. The political scene was occupied by the same old apparatchiks or dilettantes in search of a retouched biography.

Tens of parties and mediocre leaders were spending their energies in useless infighting. The members of parliament were quite pathetic, the members of the government hesitant, incompetent, influenced by the old mentalities, quickly adopting the new slogan: "We are not selling our country." So they divided it among themselves instead. They constantly invoked the costly legacy of communism, and again and again blamed the cruel and ruthless history which they used as an excuse for the mismanagement of the governments that came and went, helpless to create an alternative to the old system, unable to offer a decent standard of living to the masses of people dumbed by ideologies, utopias and fantasies.

Little by little disappointment, pessimism, and hopelessness set in. People were bewildered in a world whose rules only a few select ones knew. As it happened the easiest to adapt to the new regime were the old *Securitate* people, the *nomenklatura*, those who had money and had already been well-connected before the Revolution. Apathy gave way to despair. "We were hiding from the terrorists, while they were already busy putting together businesses" was the refrain heard everywhere. "The Revolution was made especially for them, to benefit them. In vain was all the blood shed."

People were living hard, miserable lives. Within a short time a parallel underground economy was created, a banking mafia, against the backdrop of the sudden devaluation of the national currency. Corruption was spreading like an octopus, all the way to the top, drying up the meager resources left by the centralized communist economy and the megalomaniac tendencies of its rulers.

Mr. George, my neighbor, watched every night to see when I came home from the office.

"What is happening, sir? How much longer before this damned transition is finally implemented? You, as an informed person, ought to have an answer. I've had it with these people. My pension is ridiculously low, my wife is sick, my son is unemployed. I feel like ending my life. It's sickening to see how all those people are fighting for a bone on TV, while we barely make it, from one day to another. The devil take them all, with all their politics! I'm itching for a new revolution."

The capital had turned into a surrealist place, typical of all underdeveloped countries. It was filled with the new flashy buildings, built overnight by steel and glass, where banks had their headquarters. At every turn one could see the latest models of famous luxury cars, pricey restaurants open only to their own members, and outside of Las Vegas, the largest number of casinos. Cellular telephones, stray dogs, prostitutes at every corner, abandoned children living in the city's sewers and along the underground corridors of the subway.

From time to time the miners rebelled, occupying the city and randomly beating up whomever they came across, always attempting to overthrow the government. There was an increase in the number of con artists. Now the time had come for impostors, for all the crass moral and social contradictions, this time under the benign protection of emerging capitalism. There was an unending stream of strikes. Foreign investors were cautious, reluctant to come and even if they somehow managed to overcome their misgivings, they would quickly be routed and forced to retreat, because of the precariousness of the legislative and fiscal system, because of the cheating they were subjected to, the large commissions they were forced to pay under the table to public servants in high places who held sway over the industry and agriculture.

More than half the population already lived below the poverty line. And, as an irony of fate, more and more people, although living in the long-awaited freedom, of their own accord requested to have their heating and hot water services cut, since they could no longer pay the bills for them. Increasingly retirees could be seen begging in front of drugstores or supermarkets.

The great expectations that had so exhilarated people back in '89 were now forever gone. The young people's sole goal was to emigrate, while the middle-aged people resigned themselves to living with endless privations. Only a fraction of the population, who held the economic and political power, played on unperturbed their enrichment games, feigning from time to time, just to please the West, a supposed desire to be integrated into Europe and to join the North Atlantic security organizations. This they did it more out of pride, since the financial aid from the West was pitifully small.

The political discourse was sadly inefficient, with many attacks below the belt. There were no ideologies to speak of, only interests. The government and the opposition traded accusations and blackmailed each other. But when it came to personal financial gain, they fraternized serenely. Perhaps it was Nicky again who best described the power play between the opposition and the ruling sector in our country: "You see, old chap, this too is very much like a soccer match. For all intents and purposes, we are dealing with the same old team. Only the shirts are different. Friendly game, ending in a tie, with no one scoring."

The real grinding struggle was nevertheless experienced by the masses – divided, disoriented, lacking role-models and moral leaders who might have shown them where they were going, how long it would last before they get back to normal, what were the steps they need to take for the next ten years, where and what this country aimed to get. The act of governance was carried out haphazardly, from day to day, with the rulers making up their rules on the fly, without any vision or planning.

From time to time, in order to avoid the outbreak of social conflicts, they resorted to noisy jingoistic and nationalistic declarations, citing the dangers of a splitting up of the country and the ethnic tensions, stepping into the fray being joined by extremist publications, run by populist characters, who promised justice, military dictatorships, the punishing of the corrupt and an abundant living for everyone. No wonder so many began to look back wistfully to the "good ole days" of the former regime, melancholically claiming, "Things were better before, under the communists." Even the dictator, who had been put to a rushed, violent death, suddenly began to be mourned by some.

A host of political analysts, essayists, and other assorted experts competed with each other, in the mad rush to criticize, to indiscriminately tear down whatever came their way, good or bad, without any of them offering any alternative. There was a voluptuous obstinacy to negate, to destroy everything, but where were the builders? Did anyone think to put something else in place of whatever was destroyed? The truly ethical ones, those minds with unquestionable credentials, prudently stayed aside, frightened by the empty noise of the impostors, who had hogged the stage – discouraged by their inability to impose true professional standards in a world run by political calculations and percentage formulas. Some of them chose emigration, while others preferred to remain anonymous.

We were slowly crawling towards the capitalist mirage, most of us paying a hard price for a freedom that up to that point had not brought many advantages. Although I was aware of the farce they had played on us so impeccably in that December of 1989, I had to agree with Nicky that what counts is the effect. I was glad we had gotten rid of the communist prison and was working hard to overcome my apathy and bitterness, which beset me too, at times. It didn't do to give up fighting at that moment, even though the struggle against the inertia of the old structures was quite fierce. I tried to see further afield than we had been taught to look.

I liked working for the newspaper, as there was no shortage of subject matters. The press enjoyed total freedom and displayed a certain authority. We would launch investigations, in which we would employ a very biting style. We would get to the bottom of corruption cases, and influenced decisions that were made in the political structures. We were courted by both the government and the opposition. Everyone wanted to get on the good side of the independent press.

In my capacity as editor-in-chief of a large-circulation national daily, I was constantly invited to take part in radio and television talk shows, in debates and round-table discussions at various conferences. I had unwittingly become a public persona. As such I was granted access any time to any party leader, member of the parliament or the government. I was invited to all sorts of receptions, parties or cultural events. It was exciting to possess information most ordinary people never had access to, to try to make heads or tails of the intricate maze of conspiracies being hatched behind closed doors.

At the office I had a safe in which, in addition to the money for the employees' salaries and for sponsorships, I kept a wide array of stunning documents, with amazing revelations about various compromised leaders, about dishonest, underhanded business deals involving the country's high and mighty, dossiers on well-known current dissidents, former collaborators with the secret police. All of them have been obtained – who knows how and from whom – by Nicky. I never used them and the very fact that I knew they were there made me feel uncomfortable. Nor did Nicky ever ask me to make them public.

The paper prospered. The number of pages increased and we added several weekly supplements. We were a privately-owned corporation, with state capital, each of us having bought shares. Hence our interest in seeing a larger and larger circulation and an increase in profits, without any diminution of our professional prestige. The board of directors had approved the funds for buying modern printing equipment. We were offered a good deal by a German firm and I was selected to travel to Germany for negotiations and for signing the contract.

My secretary made all the arrangements for the trip, getting hotel reservations, and securing the tickets for the flight to Frankfurt. For the first time in my life I held a passport in my hands, about to embark on my first trip to the West. From the office I placed a call to my old friend David Cosma, letting him know I was coming to Frankfurt. He was ecstatic and forced me to give up my hotel reservation, insisting I stay with him while in Germany. He was an extremely busy man, but he said he would try to cancel several meetings, to streamline his schedule, so we could talk…and there was such a lot to talk about, he added. He would pick me up at the airport.

On the night before my departure, Nicky called to invite me to dinner at a restaurant. I was not too enthusiastic about it, but could not resist under his typically strong arm-twisting.

"Old chap, I've got to see you before you leave. It's really important…. A really great restaurant just opened its doors. The owner is a friend of mine. He's got great food. You'll like it. And a bar, the whole works. He insisted I come for its opening. He is a fan of our paper, a potential sponsor, so you have to come."

I gave in and went. The food was indeed delicious, the place quite chic – what can I say? Just another example of the surrealism that surrounded us. As usual, Nicky was exited and mysterious.

"Listen, while in Frankfurt no doubt you'll be seeing your friend David Cosma, won't you?"

"How do you know we're friends?"

"Everybody knows."

"Yes, I believe I will. Why?"

"Be careful. I have just seen the president."

"Which president?"

"That of the country. He asked me to give you something…."

"How come you know him so well?"

"Everybody knows him," grinned Nicky. "What do you know, he is a soccer fan. He's got a favor to ask of you…. He wants you to pass on a message to David Cosma."

I looked at him uncomprehendingly. Nicky never ceased to surprise me. Although I was aware of his rather unconventional ways, of all kinds of odd alliances he struck with both the old and the new, with the right and the left of the political spectrum, somehow he continued to be on my good side.

"Do you see the mess we're in? The country has become almost ungovernable. These weaklings are good for nothing. The president is desperate. He has had an irretrievable break in his relations with the prime minister. So he had an idea to bring someone in from the outside to fill the position, a professional that nobody could find fault with. A person of uncompromising moral rectitude *and* an expert, to boot. David Cosma perfectly fits the bill. And – let's not forget – he's a first-rate, world-class economist! A genius. Should he accept the offer to be the new prime minister, he would really rescue us, I'm sure you'll agree. The president is going to call him too, but first you'll have to size him up, sound him out. You two are friends, so you can pave the way for the president's own meeting with him, so that the offer will not take him by surprise. For it would be quite a pity if he should turn us down. What can I say, that would really sink us."

"Are you sure of all this?"

"Absolutely! You are doing us a great favor."

"Doing a favor to whom?"

"To us, to the country. The president is grateful to you. Needless to say, everything must be held in strict confidentiality."

On my way home, the full impact of this request finally began to hit me. Here I was about to act as a high-level go-between in matters of state. If up until that time I had looked forward to seeing David again, now I dreaded the reunion.

He met me at the airport. We agreed that neither of us had changed too much. He had divorced Mara, a former colleague of ours. He had no children and lived in a sprawling villa in the suburbs, built by an Italian architect. He had a woman who took care of the housework and cooked for him. In addition to her he had a gardener, two Labrador retrievers, and racing horses. He was an art collector, world traveler and much sought-after consultant for large private corporations and governments on economic issues. Probably one of the most successful compatriots living abroad. In addition he was well-educated, with subtle elevated tastes, known for his generosity. Loved music and philosophy, possessed a great sense of humor and was a very charming person, capable of winning over any audience. While we had caused him to flee, the Germans had quickly seen his exceptional qualities and treated him with the deference and respect he deserved.

I set aside one day for visiting the institute he was head of. I was deeply impressed with the aura of command and authority he exuded, by the way a first-rate research institute looked and operated, but especially by the huge gap between the Germans' pinnacle of success and the pit we were in. In the evening we attended an informal meeting of the business club he belonged to, where he introduced me to all sorts of company managers, research specialists and government ministers. Evidently he had access to the highest and most rarefied strata of German society.

Later we repaired to one of the rooms where we could be alone. He remembered I had told him I had never eaten caviar, oysters and lobster, so he ordered some of these delicacies. I had already signed the contract for the purchase of the printing equipment, and was due to return home the next day, so he wanted to spoil me just a bit. I noticed he was not motivated in this by any snobbish or capricious desires. The food was really very good and from that moment I became an enthusiastic lover of seafood in general and oysters in particular.

This was also the best opportunity for me to deliver the message I had been entrusted with by the president, through Nicky. In fact it was David who broached the subject. He asked me how things were in our country, what was going on, and what the true situation was like, since the international press presented dark images of a country devastated by corruption and poverty, with one of the lowest standards of living in Europe. I described to him the political atmosphere. As I was speaking, I became acutely aware of the enormity of our isolation, by the slow pace of reforms, by the inertia, by our backwardness, by the confusion caused by the transition and the overall surreal quality of our lives.

To my surprise, the idea of leaving everything he had going for him in Germany, and just picking up and returning to his country of birth, in order to accept the position of prime minister did not shock him too much. In fact, he took it quite seriously. Neither did he ask me how I ended up being the bearer of such a sensational message.

"We economists are like doctors. If the patient requires it, we have the duty to render assistance. It is an interesting experiment. It's not every day one has the opportunity to treat special cases. I might be tempted to give it a try. Let me think about it. There are quite a few loose ends I would need to tie up here, in connection with the institute, with my professional duties. But I am not ruling it out. You see, I have no children, I have been living quite happily for a long time, I can't complain, but loneliness is really getting to me...the idea that I have done nothing for my country. And now suddenly I *can* do something. And I happen to know what needs to be done."

In the four days I stayed in Frankfurt my friend overwhelmed me with his graciousness. He took me to the offices of "Frankfurter Algemeine Zeitung," introduced me to the editor-in-chief, to the editorial team and to several journalists specialized in Eastern European affairs. At the end of my visit there he gave me several gifts: a laptop computer, an expensive watch, and several other things for my children and my wife.

"I do not know what it has been for you like, but for me, in my first trip to the West, more than the abundance of products, what impressed me was the packaging. In our country they would have handed you the salami or the bread just like that, without any wrapping. There we would wash, time and again, for months, the same old plastic bag, recycling it," David told me at the airport, laughing. He embraced me and promised he would think about it.

When I got home, I found my family in deep meditation. Alexei had returned. In the four corners of the living room there were lit candles and sticks of sandalwood. Sonia and Petru were seated in yoga positions, holding hands with Alexei, who was muttering something no doubt magical. Laura motioned for me to leave them alone, gave me a hurried kiss, pulled me to the kitchen and explained to me,

"Alexei called. He came back for a longer stay in the city. The children brought him to our home and insisted we let him stay with us."

"For how long?"

"Not too long. Maybe a week or two. He is going to open an office in town. I don't think he is going to be in our way and the children are very happy. He is doing us all good. Take me, for instance: he's healed me of my backache."

The kitchen smelled good. I was tired and hungry.

"What are you cooking?"

"Spaghetti. Alexei's favorite dish. Made with his own recipe, with garlic and marjoram."

Then she showed me then some tubes of medication.

"Look what he brought us. Multivitamins with antioxidants and all kinds of miracle herbs. They are made somewhere in America based on some ancient Chinese formulas. You can't buy them on the open market. Alexei says they strengthen the immune system and can heal any illness. Isn't it sweet of him to give us these gifts?"

"It sure is."

In fact I was glad Alexei was staying with us. All of us were going through a crisis. Mine was a time crisis. Basically I slaved at the office, working on the paper from morning till night, and on weekends. The evenings were filled with talk show television appearances or with attending various parties.

The children were going through an identity crisis. They saw no future here and were desperately seeking an opportunity to go to America. They sent countless applications to colleges and scoured the Internet for scholarships. They were deeply disappointed by what was happening in our country, stressed out, bewildered and unhappy.

My communication with Laura was harder and harder. She was going through her own crisis, related to her age. She complained that she was lonely, misunderstood, used and unimportant. The institute where she worked was on the verge of bankruptcy. On top of everything else, she discovered feminism and terrorized me with all kinds of weird theories. She had just joined the *Association of Free Women with a University Degree*, whose meetings she started attending regularly. She began a series of lectures and every time she came back from such events she was all the more antagonistic towards me.

She read a lot of books which taught her how she could be a successful woman, how she could be happy, how she could love, and save her relationship with her partner. That was me. I had become her main adversary and a convenient guinea pig on whom she could practice her emancipation, her nerves, and readings from Chopra, plus a whole lot of other strange stuff those women crammed down her throat. She adored John Gray and kept on her nightstand the bestseller *Men Are from Mars, Women from Venus*, in lieu of the Bible, right next to the children's photograph. She had changed a lot, displaying a stubbornness and fierce determination I had not known her to possess, of a continually alert activist, under the pretext of seeking equilibrium.

She was constantly listening to relaxation music on cassettes, peppered with calls for universal harmony, love of one's neighbor, the victory of good over evil and spiritual exaltation. What was worst was that she lost her sense of humor and no longer realized the embarrassingly low depths to which she sank each day, with her loose personality, easy to manipulate through her inability to resist all kinds of collective farces, staged by experts in the theory of the couple and straight-faced prophets, who swayed the international arena, reaping millions of dollars from the poor saps who were desperately seeking their own selves, the child in them, the astral half.

Little by little we had become divided, estranged, each of us seeking our own refuge in other areas, and hiding our feelings, anxieties and concerns from the other. Under these circumstances I too saw in Alexei a temporary savior of our relationship, and therefore treated him with consideration and friendship.

I spent many hours with him in the kitchen, till late into the night, drinking the tea he would prepare for us from roots and leaves, discussing this and that. He told us about the book he was writing, about the project he had come to accomplish this time, namely opening a string of *Valeology* clinics. He treated each of us for our various illnesses. He read the future in palms, in tea leaves, in cards, to Laura's and the children's delight. He held meditation and concentration sessions with them, through which he claimed he strengthened their psyche, released them from their fears and complexes, educated their will and programmed their subconscious for success and achievements.

Most of the day Alexei was out. He had become famous in the capital for his healing powers and was called by various suffering people to come to their aid. He was paid very well for his services and highly recommended. His visions and premonitions had become front-page news. Merely by holding a photograph in his hand he could tell just about everything about that person, guessing even his or her relations with the closest friends and family, about their future and, interestingly enough, the date of their death.

Our world was a genuine paradise for Alexei. Everyone was ready to believe anything. There was no limit to their gullibility. We were not a people lacking in faith, but overly given to superstitions, and therefore easy to manipulate. We were constantly oscillating between the magical and the farcical, between the fantastic and the surreal.

A lot of paranormal literature was being published. All kinds of healers had appeared. On television many gypsy fortune-tellers advertised their services, purporting to solve any problems, from marriage to winning the lottery, from healing sexual impotency to helping people become members of parliament, to exorcising evil spirits and protecting people from bad luck.

There weren't too many differences between religion, superstition and magic. We were living at the end of a century marked by the re-emergence of religious wars. Murderers wearing a cross around their necks, sectarian fanatics and false messiahs converted their psychic collapse into divine grace. And many of these crisscrossed the country, in which poverty increasingly led to superstitions and the need for miracles.

In their turn, the politicians worshiped with two hands, and never missed a chance to appear on television while attending a church service, with two or three Orthodox priests around them. They developed the cliché, "So may God help us!" despite the fact that not too long ago they had been atheists.

Through Nicky's help, Alexei wheedled his way into the highest political, artistic and business circles. He heard confessions from people, on some of the most intimate details about their health, job, ambitions, failures, and future plans. To all of these Alexei discreetly and honestly offered his advice. I believe he had come to know many secrets from the lives of influential people, but he never talked about them. I never heard him make any comment about anybody. We felt privileged to have him stay with us, enjoying his friendship and the special treatment he offered us and hoping some of his aura and inner strength might to rub off on us.

He ended up amassing fabulous sums of money, which he saved for the string of *Valeology* institutes he intended to open in large cities, naturally with the support of experts from abroad. He never offered us too many details and we never bored him with our questions about these.

Apparently it was Nicky again who took him to the speaker of the house of parliament whose mother he had healed. Also to several ministers' houses, who within a very short time became dependent upon his treatment and advice. I don't know if Nicky was exaggerating, but he told me Alexei was a consultant for people in the highest echelons, in decision-making bodies, in matters of state, in secret missions. All his predictions proved true.

He had become the most spectacular presence, liked by all, assiduously courted and respected. No one could imagine life without Alexei. But he preferred to remain in the shadows, refusing to grant any interviews to members of the press or to appear on television. Modest and temperate, he did not allow the astounding success he enjoyed to go to his head.

Everything would have been confined to a small area, and therefore oblivious to the great masses of people, had not a truly sensational event occurred. It was a beautiful April day, right before Easter. The trade union confederations had reached a consensus and agreed to stage a big strike which would disrupt practically all essential services, such as transportation, industry, and professional associations. The law-enforcement people were on alert. The ruling government was afraid they might be forced to resign under pressure from the masses.

In the city's Central Square, scene of the 1989 Revolution, tens of thousands of people had gathered early in the morning. Stands had been erected, an audio system was installed with microphones and bullhorns, and barricades set up. The area was surrounded by trucks, taxis, and buses belonging to the teamsters union, its members on strike. The streets were crowded with people who were headed toward the Square, some holding children's hands, others with dogs on leash.

As the fall of communism coincided with the cancellation of the May Day celebration, this general strike somehow superseded it, being a convenient excuse for people to leave their homes and get some fresh air, catching some exercise and getting things off their chests, while nostalgically looking back on the old days when they had attended all those public rallies under communism, with the military brass bands, the parades, the waving of flags, the hula-hoops, the placards, the slogans; with the portraits of Marx, Engels, and Lenin, and those of the family of the national dictators. After which they would eat hot dogs and drink beer at the numerous booths erected everywhere to boost their sense of holiday.

This time the parading crowds carried placards with the words, "Down with the government," and an assortment of trade union demands, as well as the new slogans characteristic of the transition society was engaged in, with all sorts of ironical remarks making fun of the emerging democracy and of the various government leaders. At noon hundreds of thousands of people had gathered around the marble pedestal in the Square, which used to support a gargantuan statue of Lenin, with his finger pointed threateningly towards the East. Right after the Revolution the statue was lifted from its moorings by a large crane and unceremoniously dumped in some hole outside the city. The only use it was still being put to, from time to time, was in occasional movies or advertisements. The giant bronze statue of Lenin was lying on its back near a fence, overgrown with weeds, urinated on by dogs and climbed on by children, while parents used it as a background for family pictures, as they did with the statues of stone lions and bears. On the cover of a large-circulation pornographic magazine a famous model appeared naked, standing on Lenin's head and declaring, "I'm doing it on Lenin."

However the pedestal had been left behind in the Square, well anchored to the ground, the statue having been replaced with a cross in memory of the revolutionaries who had lost their lives in December 1989.

I showed up with two photo-journalists for our paper, and found a spot near the big stand where law-enforcement personnel had reserved space for the media. The meeting started off with three priests saying along with the demonstrators the Lord's Prayer. At this, those standing in front knelt. It was the only moment of some solidarity and order. However right after the blessing of the priests, and the obligatory "So may God help us!", people immediately began to vociferate impatiently.

It was hot and the crowds were agitated, emitting a resounding rumble. Some had come with the entire family, others accompanied by neighbors or friends, talking animatedly, laughing, smoking or eating their packed lunches and from time to time remembering to shout whatever slogans were being urged upon them. Various union leaders, public figures and representatives of the students' associations, as well as oratorically-inclined intellectuals took turns speaking in the microphone. Some read their speeches, others shouted slogans, to which the crowds responded with jeers or whistles, depending on the contents, at times clapping their hands, or expressing their noisy approval. Right next to the stand I spotted Sonia, Petru and Alexei. I sneaked in under the rope setting off the press area from the rest of the crowd and joined them.

"We brought Alexei so he can see what our meetings are like," explained Sonia to me.

"And what are they like?" I asked Alexei.

He merely smiled.

"We won't hang around here too long," added Petru bored. "We'll head home."

I winked at Alexei and he smiled again.

"Dad doesn't understand a thing," chimed in Sonia. "Can you let him in on it?"

Alexei nodded, amused.

"Let me in on what?"

"Alexei can make things disappear."

"Or appear," added Petru. "This morning he put on an astounding demonstration for our benefit. Zap, zap, off went glasses, books, the television!

"You've got to see this, dad! How they vanish without a trace for a few seconds. Or at least to us they appear to vanish. It's absolutely fantastic!" gushed Sonia.

"We're going back to practice. I'm fascinated."

I smiled benignly, without paying too much attention to the children's exultation. In the Square chaos was slowly taking over. The speakers raised their voices higher and higher, while the tired crowds showed signs of impatience. Bored children were crying or running through the legs of the union members, agitated because of the heat and the shouting around them. In one corner there was a bit of a stampede. Someone had been caught in the act while trying to steal a wallet. Several men tore into him, wrestled him to the ground and were viciously kicking him with their feet, unleashing their blind fury as though they were thus hitting the government. The law-enforcement people stepped in immediately. At that moment a real fight erupted, with people hitting each other, very few of them knowing why or whom they were attacking. Reporters and cameramen rushed to the scene of the incident. Calls were made from the stand for violence to cease, for people to calm down or for the government to resign. The three priests made the sign of the cross, urging the people to renounce violence, to get along with each other, to love and to be humble. Like other young people in the crowd, Sonia and Petru were having a great time. Suddenly Sonia had an idea: she pounced on Alexei's head, hopping on one leg.

"Can't you make a miracle right here? Pleeease, pleeease, do it now, and here!"

"Sure enough, that would be great," chuckled Petru.

Alexei looked suspiciously at them, although he seemed well-disposed.

"Please, don't disappoint us," insisted Sonia with abandon. "So dad can see it too."

Alexei closed his eyes. In the Square the most incendiary of the speeches was being uttered at this time. Behind the mike was a well-known dissident from the old regime, an important personality, widely known among the people, with great mass-appeal, who had been very active during the Revolution. He was offering a scathing denunciation of the ruling party and an unflattering analysis of the nation. He told us about the ghosts of communism which were still plaguing our society. He exuded charisma and authority, electrifying the crowds, which had suddenly grown quiet, drinking is his every word.

I heard Alexei emit low, guttural sounds. While his eyes were still closed, he concentrated his thoughts, setting himself off from the reality around him. And all of a sudden the hundreds of thousands in the Square let out an infernal roar. A desperate, panic-filled awesome shriek. At first I did not understand what was happening. I looked around with bewilderment, as though something sinister had happened. Sonia circled her arms around my neck. On the marble pedestal Lenin's statue had reappeared. With the finger threateningly pointing towards the East. For a few split seconds, a sepulchral silence fell over the crowd. Everyone could see it, with eyes bulging from the shock and surprise of it all, with bated breath. We had lost our tongues. Lenin was back on the pedestal, with the cross commemorating the Revolution's victims stuck between its legs. Then just as quickly he disappeared. We continued to stare at the pedestal, which was now empty as before. At that moment pandemonium broke out. Some were running away scared, others fell to their knees, saying the Lord's Prayer. The three priests, their hands clinging desperately the crucifixes around their necks, had climbed down from the platform in a hurry. The crowd passed from consternation to panic. Everyone offered his or her opinion, seeking a plausible explanation.

"It's a miracle!"

"A wonder!"

"An illusion!"

"Mass hypnosis! The Americans have David Copperfield. Didn't he make the Statue of Liberty disappear for a few seconds?"

"It's a divine sign!"

"Another trick from the government, in an attempt to fool us!"

"The end of the world is upon us!" cried a woman next to us.

"Dear God, what sin have we committed? What shall befall us?"

"It's a farce!"

"A vision!"

"We are the chosen people," preached a fanatic. "The New Jerusalem shall rise on this land. The second coming of Christ will be here, in the very blessed Square."

"Make that *cursed* square," barked someone, about to punch him. "Can't you tell we're dealing with a diversion? The blasted communists! When are you going to be cured of your fantasies? See where all your satanic ideologies have brought us!"

The photojournalists, cameramen and reporters were milling around the pedestal, taking pictures, broadcasting live from the Square for their television stations and media outlets.

Sonia and Petru cast a satisfied, vindicated glance at me. I did not know what to tell them. Alexei avoided my eyes, convinced that this time he had gone too far, allowing the children to push him into an error. He wanted to leave that place as quickly as possible. Suddenly a man rushed towards us. He went straight to Alexei and hugged him, with tears of joy in his eyes.

"You've done all this, haven't you? I know you have!"

Then he regained his composure, squeezed his arm conspiratorially and went away, thrilled.

"Do you know him?" asked Sonia.

"Yes, I healed his daughter of a bone degenerative disease. He thinks I'm a magician."

I urged them to go home, then I collected my two colleagues from the newspaper, who continued to photograph the pedestal from all angels, and sent them back to the office. Everybody was excited, writing article after article. For several days on end, the television stations continued to broadcast scenes from the meeting, with the crowd before and after the miracle. But no one had managed to capture a single snapshot of the miracle. There was no photograph or image of Lenin back on the pedestal. The dailies had their own special editions, carrying interviews with seers, illusionists, scientists, paranormal experts, and specialists in mass hypnosis, wizards, tricksters, psychologists, sociologists, historians and prophets. Alexei had also been contacted by several reporters, but he refused to grant any interview to the print or broadcast media, declining knowledge of the phenomenon or any involvement in the alleged miracle. The whole thing was so much part of the fantasy world that I didn't need to feel guilty for the secret I was harboring. Anyway no one would have believed that the miracle could have been produced by the young Alexei.

Rather, suspicion fell on occult forces, working hand in hand, plotting in high spheres.

As a matter of fact the impact in the rest of the country was minimal. People were used to all sorts of strange things going on in the capital, from the illusory terrorists of the Revolution to recurring strikes. So the reemergence of the Lenin statue on the pedestal for a few split seconds impressed no one. Some didn't even know he had been brought down to begin with. But even the ones who had been in the Square at that moment found it hard to believe they had actually seen Lenin back on the marble slab. It might have been a visual trick, an illusion – who knows what? And who cares, anyway?! They had their own problems to worry about, such as inflation, and unemployment. So they concluded the famous adage, "No miracle lasts for more than three days" had been proven true once more. Likewise, we at home avoided any further discussion of that fantastic incident on that April day. In fact we too had begun to doubt it had actually taken place, that Alexei had really caused it to happen, on a whim, casually giving in to Sonia's insistent pleas.

Alexei went on unperturbed, seeing to his healing sessions, predictions and premonitions. Always in the shadows, but constantly called upon by the high and mighty, solving difficult cases, winning over the admiration and trust of everyone, his fame spreading daily.

The justice minister, after Alexei had saved his son from his drug addiction, even offered to make him an honorary citizen of our country, promising him the religion portfolio in the cabinet. Alexei politely declined, nevertheless taking care to let the minister know how grateful he was for the implicit trust manifested towards him. The only reward he was willing to accept was the officials' assistance in securing headquarters for his *Valeology* institutes.

One day, shortly after my return from Germany, Nicky told me the President had spoken personally with David on the telephone, had offered him the prime minister post and had invited him to meet with him for private talks, as soon as he could arrange to make the trip to his native country.

I called David in Frankfurt. He confirmed that he had made all the necessary arrangements, having convinced the Germans to let his deputy take over the directorship, while promising to continue to serve them in an advisory capacity, for a year or two, as he was ready to embark on a new mission, helping his native country in this critical moment for its economy. He rented his house, settled his affairs and made the announcement that he would arrive next week.

Nicky was thrilled with our success. In the country things were going from bad to worse, so I too became convinced that perhaps the only way out was to go with David's option. Still I was afraid for him, realizing he didn't know what he was getting himself into. He simply had no realistic idea of the true dimensions of our distorted little world, of our crazy originality. He was stepping into an environment with its arcane rules and I feared that he might be attacked, subjected to bashing and mud-slinging, only to be run out of his country once more.

One night, as we sat around the table drinking the tea Alexei had prepared for us as usual, out of the bark of some Latin American tree, I told him about my friend David Cosma. What a good man he was, how well trained in his field and how special he was. There were just the two of us there in the kitchen. Laura had gone to bed. The children were away skiing in a mountain resort. We felt very cozy together. I trusted Alexei. After warning him about the confidential nature of what I was about to reveal, I told him the president aimed to make David the prime minister. Alexei showed no surprise. I asked him what he thought. He looked me straight in the eye and said simply:

"I don't know."

I didn't show any surprise either at his candid reply. We dropped the subject and went on talking soul-to-soul (that dark chamber of all our terrors that lie buried in our subconscious) about life after death and the spiritual thresholds. I had read somewhere a French copy of "The Book of the Egyptian Dead" and Alexei now let me read "The Tibetan Book of the Dead."

It was such a pleasure to converse with him, especially if you broached a subject he was a master of. He proceeded to draw life on a napkin left behind on the kitchen table. An egg wrapped in a thread shirt, covering our material body. When the thread breaks off in one point, the whole shirt begins to unravel. That's where death comes in, Alexei informed me.

Abruptly he asked me if I had a picture of David Cosma. I looked inside the candy box where Laura kept our old photos and brought him a group picture, with my class on vacation at the seaside. We were young and emaciated. I pointed David out to him. Alexei looked at him closely, then covered the photo with the palm of his hand and closed his eyes. By now he had managed to communicate to me a state of tension. I was awaiting his verdict with bated breath. After a while, he laid the photograph down and looked fixedly at me:

"I don't know."

"He is coming tomorrow from Germany. I'd like you to meet him."

"Nicky told me about him, too," confessed Alexei. "He too thought I should see him."

"Sure," I said awkwardly, "we'll arrange it somehow."

I couldn't get over my surprise at finding Nicky had already told Alexei about David, but I did not pay to much attention to it. Since Nicky had told me it was a confidential matter, I was absolved of any blame for having told Alexei, who already knew from him about this matter.

The next day I went over to the airport to wait for David. Nicky was with me. He was agitated and couldn't wait to carry out his plan, point by point, as he constantly reminded me about it.

"We pick him up right from the plane's door. Then we put him aboard the minibus that's waiting for him on the tarmac. I got all the necessary approvals for that. Afterwards we all go to your place. I will go to the Palace and will call you from there, to let you know when he should go down to the street. The license plate is 003. A black Opel. The President will see him in the blue salon. Then the same car will take us to the hotel. I already made a reservation in my name, to avoid publicity. Careful with the press. We mustn't have any leaks. Anyway, if things work out, we'll have a scoop on the story. An exclusive. It's crucial that no one will know he is in the capital. And above all why. The entire success of the operation lies in its being kept secret."

Nicky's preoccupation with dark, sinister scenarios was sometimes tiresome. Except that I wasn't paying too much attention to it. Still I followed his carefully mapped out plan. Nicky dropped us in front of my apartment building and then sped off to the presidential palace. It was mid-morning and my family was out. The only one waiting for us was Alexei. In the elevator I told David that we were sharing the apartment with a friend of mine who was endowed with paranormal powers. He seemed amused by the idea and gave me a friendly slap on the shoulder, as one would to encourage him not to worry if he was a bit too naive.

"As long as you won't talk to me about flying saucers, I am open to just about anything."

The contact between David and Alexei was not what I had imagined it to be. Alexei avoided David's gaze and David ignored his presence. Any attempt on my part to bring them together into a meaning discussion or to bridge the gap between them failed miserably. Although he continued to be polite, David was only talking to me. I caught Alexei studying him surreptitiously. There seemed to be no compatibility between them.

David took off his winter coat, opened his leather bag and produced whiskey, champagne and chocolate, which he placed on the table. He then inquired after Laura and the children. He was elegantly dressed, had a lofty bearing, and could easily have impressed anyone. He went into the bathroom to wash his hands. I heard him cough violently, and was surprised, because he did not smoke. Then I remembered that he had had such coughing fits in Germany. I had heard him from my room. While David was out of the room, I raised my eyebrows to Alexei, as if to ask what was going on.

"I don't know," he said.

I was also out of sorts. David came back with the same calm demeanor, emanating poise and strength. We engaged then in some chit-chat, neither of us broaching the crucial meeting David was about to have. Finally Nicky called to say his car was downstairs. I showed David to the street and wished him success. He replied somewhat ambiguously and I couldn't tell whether he was sure of himself or just sad.

Then I ran back upstairs. Alexei was sitting with his feet drawn under him in the middle of the floor, feeling a glove David had left behind on an armchair. Or perhaps Alexei had deliberately held on to it. His eyes were closed and remained so even after he heard me come into the living room. I left him alone and sat down on the sofa. After a long while, he told me,

"I don't think your friend is going be become prime minister."

I looked at him unwilling to accept his verdict.

"How come? When the President himself has promised David the job and after he has put his affairs in order so he could be away from Germany for at least two years?"

"Maybe, but I just can't see him as prime minister."

"That would be terrible! Any chance you could be wrong?"

Alexei shook his head.

"No, but I could try to change things a bit. Are you sure you want to see him prime minister so badly?"

"You bet I do!"

The telephone rang, so I did not get to hear his reply. It was Nicky. Filled with panic, he was talking breathlessly, making it very hard for me to understand what he was saying.

"Damn! The whole thing fell through. There is a big conspiracy against him. The cabinet members, the parliament, the opposition – everybody. They had got wind of the president's plan and put up a stiff opposition. They don't want anyone from outside. They say they don't need specialists or technocrats who had stayed away safely in the West, and were now coming to give them advice. The President is being blackmailed. His hands are tied. They put out a rumor about David that he had collaborated with the secret police and that his dissident stuff was just a front, when, in reality, they claim, he had been sent to the West as a spy, on a mission to collect economic intelligence."

"Oh, my God!"

I was stunned and almost dropped the receiver. Alexei was looking at me intently, trying to figure out what it was all about. I tore into him, screaming,

"Do something! You said you could change things. Now is the time to do it!"

He remained calm. He asked me for a glass container, an egg, candles, two metal coins and requested that I leave him alone. Through the partly open living room door, to which I pressed my ear, I could hear that long, penetrating rumble. I had no idea what he was doing in there, but I was desperate and felt intense shame and embarrassment, first towards my friend, whom I had drawn into this ridiculous farce, and to myself, for having miserably clung to this ritual Alexei was performing, to his claim that he could improve on a situation that seemed all but impossible to be solved.

After about half an hour, Alexei opened the door and allowed me into the living room. He was drained of energy, perspiring profusely and in such a state of devastation as I had never seen him before. I was waiting for him to say something.

"I don't know. I tried...."

He went into the bathroom, washed his hands and face and returned a little calmer.

"What is worse is that your friend will die in less than two years. And I can't do a thing about it."

I thought I hadn't heard him right.

"Are you mad? Are you stark raving mad?"

My voice was tremulous and suddenly I felt intense rage and aversion towards Alexei. How dare he come up with such a wild, crazy scenario?!

"I saw this last night when you showed me a photograph with him in it. But I didn't know how to put it to you. I can understand how painful this must be for you."

"I don't believe one word of it," I cried out sharply. "And I don't give a damn about your visions. Only God knows when we will die. I know that much myself."

"I'm sorry," said Alexei, as he proceeded to gather his things.

He realized that he simply could not stay in our home any longer, and I was glad I didn't have spell it out for him. From that moment we never spoke to each again. He packed his rucksack in silence and gently closed the door after him. I never saw him after this.

I recovered, somewhat, and called my office, requesting that they send the car to pick me up and take me to the Intercontinental Hotel, where David was staying. The meeting with the president must have ended by now. Sure enough, I found David in his room at the Intercontinental. He opened the door to me in a jovial mood. Seeing his calm face, I regained my composure.

"How was it?" I asked him hopefully.

"Neither here, nor there. We lunched together. The President is and intelligent, charming man."

"And?"

"And nothing. We spoke about the globalization of information, about the glories of the Internet, about great China, about the irrigation systems in Israel. The thing is one can't get a decent meal at the Palace. The beef steak was tough and too dry."

"You mean to tell me he didn't offer you anything?"

"No, nothing even close to it," he said dryly. "I have to admit that for me it was a rather pricey lunch, more than it was worth. Next time I suggested the president to come to Frankfurt."

I collapsed on the sofa, defeated. I felt a sense of dread and shame.

"David, I am very sorry…."

"You've got nothing to blame yourself for. Rather I'm the one who learned the lesson once and for all to rid myself of this candor and naiveté. It's not the first time I have chosen the farce instead of the tragedy. Really, you mustn't feel guilty. Let's go out. Perhaps we'll be able to find a pub where they serve decent food."

He gave a stifled cough, pulled out his handkerchief and discreetly dabbed at his lips.

The next day, the lobby of the hotel was filled with members of the media. All the dailies ran on their front page a picture of David, with matching big, bold type, calling him "a collaborator," "a spy," "a turncoat" or "a traitor." I was able to get him out of the hotel through the service entrance, which let out into the garage. I took him straight to the airport. I felt miserable, humiliated, torn apart with pain and helplessness. Although David was trying to keep his sense of humor, I could see how much this outcome had affected him. He returned to Germany where his old job was given back to him. He got back his house, his professional contacts and would never visit his native country again.

I would have gladly gone with him. I would have gone anywhere, for I felt I could not go on here. This feeling of nausea and rage did not leave me for a long time. I was living in the desert, and hated it. I no longer expected anything. The universe was closing in on me, again, and the pinpoints of light at the end of the tunnel, promised by the previous governments, were barely visible, offering little hope.

"A bunch of morons," suggested Nicky, who was also disgusted with the national circus. "They're getting their comeuppance. This country cannot be helped, if they refuse to be helped. What a mess we're in! By the way, do you know anything about Alexei? He disappeared without leaving a note."

"No, I don't know," I shrugged. "He just picked up his things and left. He never gave me any warning he might do this."

"He'll turn up eventually," predicted Nicky.

"How did you meet him?"

"Well, to tell you the truth, I can't remember.... Someone must have sent him.... He wanted to open a *Valeology* institute or something like that. And he probably knew I am well-connected...."

Things were far more complicated at home. Laura wouldn't speak to me and the children regarded me with lugubrious disapproval, quite sure Alexei had left because of me. He had become like family to us and they could not conceive that he had left without seeing them. Blaming me for this, they isolated me, each of them going on with their business without ever sharing with me any of their plans or activities.

There seemed to be no end in sight for all these trying times. The following year our family broke apart for good. Petru had obtained a scholarship in America; Sonia married a young businessman and moved to a city in the north of the country; and Laura divorced me, giving herself over to feminism and to the Association of Free Women.

I continued to edit that independent paper, dragging myself through all my daily social and professional duties, without any enthusiasm or goal to pursue. I was smoking a lot, had put on weight and felt quite bored. Once Alexei had told me that the destiny of a place impacts on the destiny of the individuals living in that area. I could only conclude that I was living in an unfortunate space. I felt how I was growing old and for me it was too late to change, to leave for another place, to start off from the beginning. I had few expectations left.

Nicky opened a casino and gave up the newspaper business. He was also the owner of a model agency. As such he traveled a lot abroad, from where he would dutifully send me postcards with unimaginably beautiful images.

One morning my secretary told me I had a call from Frankfurt. I rejoiced. Finally, I said to myself, a sign from David whom I had not had the courage to look up, after that embarrassing farce I had unwittingly played on him. His secretary informed me about David's death, as well as the day, time and place where the funeral would be held. Cause of death: cancer of the larynx.

I didn't have the strength to go. Instead I just walked all day through the streets of the city. I entered a church, lit a candle for David and sat in the pew, looking at the altar. I was bereft of any thoughts. I wanted to pray, but did not know any prayers. I silently started to say the Lord's Prayer, but gave up half way through it. I reviewed all the madness of the past few years. At some point I had felt proud to see the day communism fell. I had lived the euphoria of freedom, had made plans, had had dreams, as well as illusions. I had dedicated myself completely to the paper, had placed myself totally at the disposal of the newly emerging democratic society. And I paid for my portion of freedom with the breakup of my marriage, loss of a good friend, and with a never-ending fatigue, with an overwhelming sense of cold and ashes.

I do not remember how long these reminiscences went on, but by the time I came out of the church, darkness had already descended. Across the street from the church there was a beautiful, tall, slender building, brightly lit. I walked across. The city was changing under our very eyes. Overnight new buildings popped up everywhere, hosting newly formed companies, banks and stores. I drew close so I could read the discreet sign with the name of the firm, hanging above the elegant glass door: "The Valeology Institute."

I pressed the buzzer and a bearded young man opened the door to me. He was holding a book in his hands. I had evidently interrupted his reading.

"Excuse me, I'd like to ask you what is the business of the institute."

"I don't know," replied the young man. I am a student and am working part-time as a night guard."

"Do you happen to know who the director of the institute is?"

"A gentleman by the name of Alexei."

"And when could I see him?"

"I think I heard he lives abroad."

"What exactly is *valeology*?"

"I don't know. Never heard the word before. In fact, I don't think there is such a word."

"I see. But look! Here it plainly says, *Institute of Valeology*."

"Yes, but there is no such thing as *valeology*."

"Are you sure?"

"I am not sure of anything," smiled the young man enigmatically.

He went inside and closed the door after him.

*Translation by Doru Motz*
*Edited by Bruce Benderson*